EUGENE H. VAUGHAN

Building Beyond Thyself

A Vaughanderful Life

CHAMPIONS PRESS

Every effort has been made to find and credit the photographers whose work
adds so much to this book. If the sources of other photographs come to light,
they will be acknowledged in any subsequent reprints of this work.

Design and production by BW&A Books, Inc.,
Oxford, North Carolina
Printed in the United States of America

ISBN: 978-0-692-07874-7
Library of Congress Control Number: 2018935352

To my beloved and loving family:
Susan, my wife, best friend, and consummate partner;
our treasured children, Margaret and Richard;
my cherished Mother and Dad; my remarkable grandparents,
Mama and Papa Vaughan and
Mam-maw and Granddaddy Woodard Musgrave.
With special love to my wonderful grandchildren
who are just beginning to write their own stories:
Corbin, Avery, Bo, and Lizzie.

Contents

CONTENTS

Foreword

This is the story of the life of a creator, a builder, a leader, and a nurturer, someone who focused his tremendous energies on his beloved family, his adopted hometown of Houston, and his favorite American institutions. Eugene Vaughan has been described as insightful and inspiring. Whether he speaks to a friend or to a large gathering with his soft Southern drawl, you admire his wisdom and vision, always balancing enthusiasm with intelligence. He seems driven by a restless energy to do good things and to fix whatever is broken in the world. When he picks up a cause that he believes in, things happen.

This was true from the start of his career. Within a decade of graduating from Harvard Business School, he founded his own investment management company in Houston and led it successfully for over thirty years. Gene, a native of Tennessee, went to college at Vanderbilt, which has benefited for four decades from his passionate participation on its board of trustees and his philanthropy. Once Gene cares about an institution or community, he is hooked.

Gene was hooked quickly by Houston. He brought his financial skills and strategic thinking to the benefit of this community through his long tenure of service on the board and executive committee of the Greater Houston Partnership. Feeling that the Partnership wasn't bold enough in envisioning the city's future, he founded Center for Houston's Future and served as its inaugural chairman and continues today as a devoutly caring director. I will never forget our dinner with Gene and his wife, Susan, when I was among the first to hear about his dream for an organization focused on a bold, long-range, strategic plan for America's fourth largest city. I immediately told him with great enthusiasm that this was exactly what Houston needed, and I became the first member of its board of directors. Gene's list of contributions to Houston is long and impactful. In every case, he has been a passionate and persuasive champion for progress and innovation.

Let me emphasize that under his gentlemanly Southern veneer there is a tough and tenacious man of steel. Not just in business. I have known Gene through a number of illnesses and marveled at his ability to tolerate discomfort and pain and keep up his hope, optimism, and positive attitude in the face of serious challenges. He is a giant among men, setting the highest standards of integrity, respect for others, and love of humanity. I am thrilled that he has created this story of his experiences.

Dr. John Mendelsohn in 1996 became the third president of The University of Texas MD Anderson Cancer Center since its founding in 1946. He served until 2011, during which span his leadership resulted in the institution being perennially ranked the #1 cancer center in America. He is currently director of the Institute for Personalized Cancer Therapy at MD Anderson.

G ene Vaughan is one of the most extraordinary people I've known. A fine investor and a loving family man, he has excelled in many fields locally and nationally. I have known Gene since our early days in the investment industry. Gene is a modest guy, so most people in other areas of his life have no idea that throughout his career he has been a foremost leader, inspiration, and unrelenting force for visionary improvement in the investment management profession.

At an unusually early age, he was elected chairman of the Financial Analysts Federation (FAF), and despite the market in 1973–74 undergoing its worst crash since the Depression and a powerful clique contriving to put the profession under New York State regulation, Gene was undaunted. He asked me to chair a committee to create a Self-Regulation Plan, and he personally traveled extensively to FAF societies to foster the plan. Passed overwhelmingly, this plan remains the core of the profession's strong ethics enforcement.

Gene and I worked together in leadership roles in the investment industry over many years. When he was elected to the Institute of Chartered Financial Analysts (ICFA) board in 1986, he was determined to bring about a merger between the FAF and ICFA to unite the goals and energies of the split profession. At first a lone voice on the ICFA board, Gene gradually won over other trustees until in late 1989 the ICFA board voted narrowly to recommend the merger. The vote by charterholders was overwhelmingly pro-merger. This unification of goals and effort has propelled the resulting CFA Institute to fivefold growth in the intervening quarter-century. Gene was the founding chairman and with his Southern graciousness soon brought the previously fractured profession into harmony. Gene always has stood for everything good and right about our industry—his values, character, and integrity continue to shape the profession.

Gene and I share thirty-plus years of membership in the "Group of Nine," heads of investment management firms who gather yearly to discuss the investment industry, our firms, and family matters. There is a special trust and connection among us and our wives.

When Gene was elected trustee of his beloved Vanderbilt University in 1972, he got to know my father-in-law, Dan May, a longtime Vanderbilt trustee, and they developed a special kinship through their devotion and hard work on behalf of the University. Gene served loyally on the board for thirty-six years, after which he became an emeritus trustee in 2008.

Most important, Gene and Susan have been friends of my wife, Betsy, and me for more than forty years—a friendship we cherish. Our close relationship qualifies me to make two definitive statements: first, Gene is proudest of his wife, Susan, his two children, and four grandchildren; and second, his has been a life well-lived.

Walter P. Stern, CFA, served as the head or as senior officer of various Capital Group companies, including Capital Guardian and Capital International. He is past chairman of the Financial Analysts Federation (FAF) and Institute of Chartered Financial Analysts (ICFA) and longtime chairman of the Hudson Institute.

Preface

And whether or not it is clear to you,
no doubt the universe is unfolding as it should.

—"Desiderata"

The idea for this book was triggered by a request from our son, Richard, to write down my history, followed by a request from our daughter, Margaret, a world-class raconteur, to tell "my story." I would do almost anything for them. Their requests gave impetus to an idea which germinated in 2003 when I realized I would turn seventy that year and my wife, Susan, and I would celebrate our fortieth anniversary. That same year also would be an inflection point in my career, if not my life. Three years earlier, on January 1, 2000, the first day of a New Year, New Century, and New Millennium, I had passed the CEO baton at the firm I founded in 1970. However, the loss of giving up my "third child," as Margaret and Richard call the firm, was diffused because I already was so deeply absorbed in the creation of Center for Houston's Future. But in 2003, while remaining founding chairman, I would step down as full-time chairman of the Center's board, an inflection point indeed.

Writing this personal history has been an undertaking that stopped and restarted several times over a number of years. A few serious shots over the bow regarding my health forced me to put down my pen temporarily, but I continued to pick it back up. I am forever grateful to Dad's longevity and good genes that I have been able to persevere!

Susan and I at approximately the time we met—a dashing U.S. Navy officer turned Harvard Business School student and a beautiful Pi Beta Phi senior at Randolph-Macon Woman's College.

I am pleased to honor my children's wishes and record some of the events and stories that shaped my life as well as provide them and their children with some "history shot-on-the-wing" record of their forebears. I always had longed to know more about my ancestors. I only knew my grandparents when they were "old," and I hardly knew anything about their own aspirations and challenges, much less the generation before them. In the process of weaving the pieces of my story together, I got to experience the pure joy, with occasional pain, of skipping back across those incredibly wonderful years.

While I am predisposed to plan everything meticulously, ironically, I do believe the miracle-like game changers in my life were happenstance; at least it feels that way. Perhaps it is more as the philosopher Seneca described, "Luck is what happens when preparation meets opportunity." In either case, I am very grateful. I have been Fortune's Child; good examples are the against-all-odds opportunities to attend Vanderbilt University and Harvard Business School. But far and above the greatest stroke of luck was when Fortune smiled upon me and introduced my future wife, Susan. If Vanderbilt and Harvard would have made a bright future probable, it is Susan who made everything possible.

One of my few regrets—one I ceaselessly encourage our children not to repeat—is that I did not keep a journal consistently. Ethereal moments of beauty or achievement must be captured because, like champagne as the bubbles effervesce, usually even overnight is too long to capture the essence of the moment. I did, however, keep a regular journal during my U.S. Navy years, and as much as I treasure it, I learned another important lesson about recording history: as with sharing photos from a trip, too little is far better than too much! So I have tried to capture the effervescence of my life, or what the friar Dom Perignon called his champagne—"the stars in a bottle"—without belaboring the fermentation process.

CHAPTER 1

"A Good Place to Live"

Almost anybody that ever amounted to anything grew up in a small town.

—Sam M. Fleming, CEO of Third National Bank, Nashville; chairman of the American Bankers Association; and "Mr. Vanderbilt" for decades as chairman of Vanderbilt's board. He grew up in Franklin, Tennessee, and was only half-kidding when, on many occasions, he said this.

The sign on the main highways welcoming people to my hometown of Brownsville, Tennessee, reads: "A Good Place to Live." That says a lot. Brownsville's population was around 7,000 while I was growing up. It was a town where money truly did not matter much, if at all. Being a "landed family," which did not indicate if you were rich or poor, did have meaning, and the families on both Mother's and Dad's sides were landowning and thoroughly respected.

I was born October 5, 1933, in the depth of the Great Depression. Few places in the country were more insulated from the Depression than this epitome of the agrarian society in West Tennessee about fifty miles from Memphis; however, the devastation of twenty-five percent unemployment throughout America had ramifications for my family and future.

My dad, Eugene H. Vaughan Sr., was of Welsh heritage. The Vaughan name is prominent in Wales, Ireland, and England. I would learn more about my heritage later in life. In 1981, just before departure on a family driving tour of England and Scotland with my wife, Susan, and our children, Margaret and Richard, Susan turned our calendar to the month of July, and depicted there, to our astonishment, was the ancestral home in Wales of Henry Vaughan, the celebrated seventeenth-century poet.

I made some rapid itinerary adjustments, and thus we had the thrill of standing on the land in Wales on which Vaughans have lived for centuries. We spent several hours at Tretower Court, which Vaughans occupied for over 200 years, and climbed about Sir Roger Vaughan's Tretower Castle, now inhabited by sheep and cows.

Interestingly, while our family name in the U.S. and Canada is often spelled Vaughn, in Britain it is invariably spelled as we spell it—Vaughan. This corruption, as Dad and I contended, was a source of much kidding between his brother, my Uncle Earl, and us for decades. Earl changed his name to Vaughn while in college. He and Dad even had a partnership entitled Vaughan and Vaughn. Earl arranged for the county road crew to put a sign reading Vaughn Road on the road leading from the major Jackson Highway through the family farm to the old home place, much to his delight and Dad's chagrin. Only after Dad's death and only after I presented evidence that Vaughan is the original ancestral spelling did Earl quietly tell me he "sort of" regretted changing the spelling of his name. Hear that, Dad!

My dad had a true love of the soil and, but for the financial exigencies of the Depression, would have never left farming. Upon graduating from Haywood High School, as the oldest son of three children, Dad moved from the family farm to town to work. In those dismal years of the national Depression, he was one of the few graduates able to get a plum of a steady job with the Post Office, where he eventually was promoted to supervisor. Thus he was looked upon with favor when he called on the "Musgrave girls."

Musgrave's General Store, located about three miles east of Brownsville on U.S. Highway 70—the spine of Tennessee linking Memphis, Jackson, Nashville, and Knoxville—was an economic and social center of the county. In the Haywood Historical Museum, there is a picture taken in 1903 of the original Musgrave's General Store. My grandfather is eight years old in that photo. My maternal grandfather, the prosperous and beloved Woodard Musgrave, died of pneumonia early in the Depression, leaving six children under age twenty and a small fortune of accounts receivable from good folks to whom he had been generous in hard times. I grew up with the knowledge that there were many Brownsvillians who never had paid their debts to my widowed maternal grandmother. Mam-maw, to her credit, never identified a single debtor. Mam-maw struggled with the store several years before selling it to Tom Mulligan. She did, however, retain the land. Mulligan's General Store, which stood next to the large Musgrave family home and farm, became a fascinating part of my boyhood, where I bartered hen eggs for the store's irresistible treasures.

The Musgraves are Scotch-Irish and were part of the great migration into the Carolinas. Mam-maw's brother, Dr. Guy Musgrave, was a prominent physician in Memphis, and on my birth as the first grandchild it was immediately projected that I was to be a doctor. That was considered a certainty by everyone, including myself, and caused a lot of consternation about twenty-five years later.

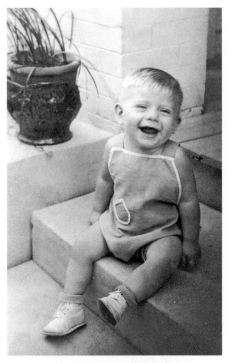

As the first grandchild in the Musgrave family and the first Vaughan grandchild, I had ample opportunity to be spoiled. Circa 1934, at one year old, I am doing my utmost to take advantage of the situation!

My mother, Margaret Musgrave Vaughan, was the fourth of six children and the third of four girls. Dad dated Mother's older sister, Elizabeth, for some time, and it apparently came as a large surprise to the family, especially Aunt Elizabeth, when he asked Margaret, five years his junior, to marry him.

Dad's older sister, Aunt Olga Bessie Jacocks, already had two children, Katheryn and Robert Gene, by the time I was born. I was the first baby Vaughan, however, and hence became the favorite focus of my paternal grandparents, Beulah Kirby Vaughan and Dan Richard Vaughan, "Mama" and "Papa." Because infantile paralysis was the terrifying disease of that era and it was associated with cities, I spent most of every summer until high school in the country with my grand-

Aerial view of Vaughan Home Place.

*My "Papa" and "Mama,"
Daniel "Dan" Richard
Vaughan and Beulah
Kirby Vaughan, in the
stern pose of the day.*

parents. If the values of a small town are good, the joys and lessons of the country are invaluable.

Papa would build me an enormous five-foot-high sand pile under the huge box elder tree in their backyard on the farm. I honeycombed roads, airplane hangars, and secret rooms throughout the sand pile, and I think whatever creativity I have was engendered by the imagination I poured into playing alone on the farms those summers. Papa would ask me to help him grind his axes and hoes. Like a fine sculpture, the grindstone used by three generations of Vaughans today has a cherished place in our garden in Houston. At our Texas farm is the bell that once called everyone in from the fields for dinner, the main meal of the day. Getting to ring that bell at noon was a privilege of my rural summers. What I adored most was following Papa in the fields, pulling my own handcrafted plow in emulation and adoration of him. He was a Randolph Scott look-alike, reserved, deeply informed internationally, and wise. My fondest memory in wintertime was when I got to sleep with Papa in his big featherbed and watch the embers glow in his enormous fireplace until I fell asleep.

Both my parents were industrious and creative. My dad's electing to become postal supervisor was strategic. Postmasters changed with political administrations, whereas the non-political supervisor remained constant. Dad was "the Post Office," which was prestigious in a small town in which the U.S. Post Office was a large building and the newest. In addition, he was vice president and part-owner of the major medical clinic in Brownsville. This opportunity grew out of his friendship with an entrepreneurial physician-owner who respected my dad greatly, as did all of Brownsville.

Still, times were tough, and I stand in awe of the fiscal management it must have taken during the Depression to be able to hold my fifth birthday party at our brand new home, built by Mother and Dad. It was wondrous. Built on a hill on three wooded acres located on East Main Street, it was a white clapboard house with a trellis of ramblin' red roses on my end of the house. I had my own bedroom with twin beds. Mother designed our new home herself. It sticks in my mind that Dad once said to me, "It is too bad I cannot afford more because Margaret has such exquisite taste." Still, it was a dream home for the three of us.

Dad and five-year-old me circa 1938, the year we moved into our wonderful new home.

I was so proud to have friends visit. Years later classmates told me they were "awed" by my home and the kindness of my parents. The house even had a central floor furnace, very advanced in those days, over which I warmed crackers while studying. Another feature was a disappearing staircase to the second floor where I eventually "home-built" a Ping-Pong table and created a polo field with Ball jars as boundaries.

Mother created a gorgeous rock garden in the backyard and a jewel of a flower garden with roses, gladiolas, marigolds, and more, just beyond

My beloved Mother, Margaret Musgrave Vaughan.
She believed in me, loved me unconditionally, and
inspired me for a lifetime.

the white fence. Dad produced a vegetable garden that seemed a veritable cornucopia of corn, potatoes, black-eyed peas, snap beans, okra (ugh), and turnip greens. Beyond that were the henhouse, field for calves and pigs, and a grove of tall maples—perfect for treehouses and Daisy "Red Ryder" BB gun target shooting.

I adored Mother, purely and simply. She was radiantly beautiful to look at and even more so inside. I basked in her love and pride in me.

At every family gathering in Papa and Mama's home, there was almost continuous laughter. The favorite theme was to tease Mama, here being done by Uncle Earl, Dad, and Aunt Olga Bessie Jacocks. Mama reveled in being the center of attention.

I spent eight kaleidoscopic years at Anderson Grammar School, starting as the youngest in first grade (October birthday) at age five in the class of the beloved Miss Annie Ree Harvey. In second grade, encouraged mightily by Miss Pauline Currie, I discovered books. That year I read more books than anyone—twenty-two! Miss Pauline fueled my love of reading, and it still roars today, tangibly visible on many shelves in many rooms. In third grade came the inexplicable enrichment which elevated my life. We had an Audubon Society Club because Arm & Hammer Baking Soda put a picture and facts about a bird in every package. Against all odds, I became president of our club; the marvelous Miss Annie Laura Williams, my teacher, had engineered a life-changing experience. I was the smallest boy in the class and the youngest, but suddenly everyone thought of me as a leader. More important, I began thinking of myself as a leader.

Fourth grade brought a huge setback for me. Miss Gladys Wetzel liked to cold-call students, and it terrified me. This fear carried all the way to Harvard Business School. In elementary school, I dealt with it by praying I would not be called on. That did not work in fourth grade—or at Harvard. Fifth grade, however, was stratospheric, filled with the fabulous Miss Ila Voltermann and building World War II model airplanes, which elicited my competitive side in high-profile school-sponsored races. My two entries placed first and third, which launched me school-wide.

Sixth grade turned painful. I was teacher's pet (again, Miss Ila) and still winning contests of all kinds. My friends responded as any twelve-year-olds would and turned on me. One who was older and much bigger challenged me to a fight. I can still feel his left fist plowing into my stomach. This incident, however, led to years of my training in our garage punching a heavy potato sack filled with sawdust and lifting weights borrowed from my Uncle Earl. The next time someone picked a fight would be the last time! By seventh grade the center of our after-school life was the amazing land around Silver Bridge. The little stream that flowed under the bridge coursed through a large primeval forest, a cow pasture, a cemetery, and near one of Brownsville's best baseball diamonds. It was heaven for the "East Main" bunch that played ball there regularly: Sonny Tyler, Beverly Watson and his brother Alma (that's right, Beverly and Alma—their mother never did get the girl she wanted), Railey Powell, Bill Massengill (who graduated from Harvard Business School a year after I did), me, and other regulars. What we boys shared was camaraderie and utter freedom in a town where no one locked their doors and in the summer we did not have to be home until the lightning bugs came out.

The cow pasture was God's gift to us. We started off throwing pieces of dry cow pies, known as cow chips, but we soon graduated to soaking the pies in the stream before throwing. I became so gifted at throwing cow chips that when the Financial Analysts Federation held its national conference in Houston in 1982, I won the cow pie–throwing contest in the Astrodome.

My closest friend during grammar school was Sonny Tyler. We were both only children, a pattern of friendship that would follow me through life—"onlys" seem to find each other! Sonny had a Shetland pony. At our first encounter, I pulled its tail and the pony kicked me in the stomach. I absorbed the Tennessee truth that you do not learn much getting kicked twice by the same pony! Sonny and I were at each other's homes almost daily.

Another big part of my life was Brownsville Baptist Church. Dad was superintendent of the Sunday school and Mother headed the primary department. Dad also was president of the men's Bible class and the youngest deacon when first asked to serve. Later, for many years, he was the oldest deacon. Usually our pastor, Brother Bob Orr (widely considered the smartest person in Brownsville), and his wife, Sally, would come to our home on Sundays for fried chicken, creamed potatoes, Le Sueur peas, and lemon icebox pie. Mother and Dad and Brother and Mrs. Orr were very dear friends and often took trips together, with me included. Brother Orr was a trustee of Union University in Jackson, Tennessee, and, but for God's intervention, it certainly would have become my alma mater.

In eighth grade we started playing organized sports. Our principal, Ed Thompson, had been an outstanding lineman at Memphis State (now University of Memphis). One night at supper Dad told me that Mr. Thompson had stopped by to tell him that I "had the makings of a good athlete." A person can be dramatically—and perhaps permanently—altered by the words of others. I was small and worked unusually hard, but I had no image of myself as an athlete. Ed Thompson's remark changed my self-image and led to some of my most satisfying endeavors in high school and college.

The first thing to know about Tennessee high schools is that as basketball is to Kentucky, football is to Tennessee. Even though I was small, it did not enter my mind *not* to try out for the varsity Tomcat football team. I did not care much for Coach Taylor initially. But what I did appreciate from the start, and still do, is that he took no pity on me. Whatever my size, I was out for football and that settled it. Coach Taylor had been a great tailback at the University of Tennessee in General Robert Neyland's famous single-wing formation in which the tailback did everything: called plays, ran, passed, and kicked. Coach Taylor assigned me to play tailback on offense and safety on defense. I played,

I never weighed more than 123 pounds, although on the programs I was listed at 142. When Coach Bill Taylor was asked why, his answer was "to scare our opponents." Nevertheless, I was offered a scholarship to the University of Tennessee at Martin, which was trumped by the NROTC!

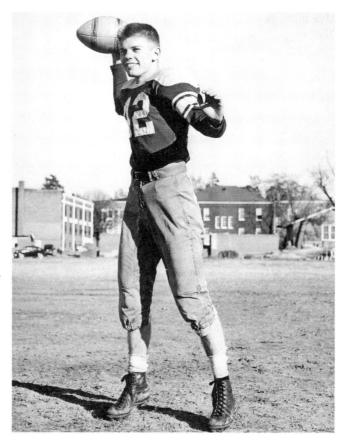

or rather practiced, my freshman year alongside behemoths like All-America high school tackle Charles Hudson, and our captain, Alex Moore, who at the end of the season threw his jock strap against the locker room wall, and it stuck there. Our team went to the championship playoff of the Big Ten Conference, one of the toughest conferences in Tennessee, for three of my four years at Haywood High.

In my junior year of high school, Mother developed breast cancer. Thus began a nightmare. Mother had a double mastectomy, which was the only known treatment, with follow-up by X-rays in the early stages of the learning curve of treating the disease. Concurrently, I also was treated by a pair of physician brothers in Memphis who believed they could cure severe acne (my curse through high school) with X-ray treatments. On many Saturdays throughout my junior and senior years, Mother and I would travel together to Memphis for our separate treatments. It was a dreadful time. Each time they performed surgery on Mother there would be a few months of hope and encouragement, but inevitably the doctors would inform Mother and Dad that the cancer had returned.

I was unaware of it at the time, a credit to my parents, but the heavy costs of Mother's medical treatments and mine ran through their savings. Mother took a job. She always had a beautiful smile on her face, as though everything was wonderful. Though I was aware of Mother's condition, I was not realistic about it whatsoever. Prayers so permeated our home and Mother's faith was so strong that I never even realized she might not get well.

To make some money between my junior and senior years, I, along with two fellow Tomcats, took the toughest job around: cutting right-of-way for the Tennessee Valley Authority (TVA). The TVA's enormous power lines crisscross the license-plate-shaped state and run through forests, swamps, and mountains. We swung bush-blades to cut down small trees and shrubs that had grown up. For bigger trees we used axes. As the lightest and most agile, I was the designated climber, a dangerous job. When limbs of very tall neighboring trees had grown above the power lines, it was my job to scale the trees and cut off the limbs with a hand saw. This could be a challenge because some trees were very tall, reaching above seventy feet. Usually I took care of these limbs without incident, but there were a few very close calls. I became familiar with Winston Churchill's observation when his forehead was grazed by a bullet in the Boer War, "Nothing in life is so exhilarating as to be shot at with no result."

This was the summer I acquired the nickname that has endured. I am blessed with exceptionally high energy and tenacity and have always, in any context, been able to outwork others. In the TVA, there is a meaningful term: Extra High Voltage. Soon my initials, "EHV," became my moniker with added meaning.

Senior year started with an agonizing decision. For three years, I had been playing behind Jack Cain, the greatest tailback the school ever had produced. Because of my slight stature, I had endured tremendous physical abuse. On top of that, I had many other responsibilities senior year, including being class president. Miss Annie Laura had embedded "leader" in me in the third grade, and I was elected president of my freshman, sophomore, and senior classes. I also was the *Tattler* sports editor, co-chair of the HHS yearbook, and president of Beta Club, the scholastic society—a very full plate. In the locker room before the opening game, I asked Coach Taylor if I might talk with him privately. I explained my circumstances and he said, "So you're gonna quit, Vaughan?"

"No, sir, as I explained...."

"No, you told me you're a quitter!" He spit the word out like it was malignant.

After a few more harsh words, Coach Taylor put his hand on my shoulder and said, "You have taken a real beating these past three years and never complained. I'll tell you what. Just play Friday night and if you still want to quit, it will be with my blessing."

My mind was made up, but I would play that one last game. Friday night, for the first time in the history of the school, there was a power failure and the game was cancelled. Oh well, one more week. In what was supposed to be my last game, I became the unlikely candidate to lead us to victory. I ran for two touchdowns and intercepted a pass at mid-field for another. The Rotary Club named me "Tomcat of the Week" and honored me at their weekly luncheon. People all over town congratulated me and, even more, they congratulated Dad. I did not quit the team; it was a consequential turning point for me.

Years later, I saw Coach Taylor at Bozo's Bar-B-Q, the iconic restaurant in nearby Mason that had been the favorite of Dad, Uncle Earl, Brother Orr, and my family all my life. I told him what he had done for me: if he had permitted me to leave the team my senior year, it would have been easier for me to quit the next time and even easier the next time. Because of him, I learned never to quit and to develop perseverance that led to creating my own company and other accomplishments which I value.

During my senior year, a monumental, life-changing event occurred. Abraham Lincolnesque Judge John T. Gray, father of my gracious classmate Ora Louise Gray, was the most respected man in Brownsville and probably all of Tennessee. He infused me with the ambition to look over my local horizon by applying for a Navy ROTC Scholarship. Winning an NROTC Scholarship meant being able to attend any of the fifty best universities in America. Amazingly, in a nationwide competition of over 250,000 entrants I won one of the scholarships! It was considered the best scholarship in America, paying all tuition, board, books—everything—plus a $50 monthly stipend. All I had to give was three years of active duty and go on a "cruise" each summer. Judge Gray counseled me to attend Vanderbilt, and that is a double miracle that changed my life.

Many, many years later, in 1999, at Dad's funeral service at Brownsville Baptist Church, his minister of several decades said, "It is remarkable that a man can live in a small community for ninety-five years and I never hear an unkind word spoken about him."

The evening before Dad's service, while poring over family scrapbooks, I read almost the identical words about Papa when he died at eighty-seven. The Brownsville *States-Graphic* in an editorial had stated: "A neighbor of sixty years said he had never heard a negative word spoken about Dan Vaughan."

And my dear Mother. She was lovely, kind-hearted, intelligent, gracious, and completely beloved. For many years I continually heard, "Margaret was the sweetest person and best friend I ever had. I miss her so much."

This presaged why I moved from Brownsville after I finished high school—too much to live up to!

GENE VAUGHN

Gene Vaughn Wins NROTC Scholarship

Another high honor has come to Gene Vaughn, personable and talented son of Mr. and Mrs. Eugene H. Vaughn of Brownsville, with his notification by the Navy Department that he has been selected to partcipate in the Naval Reserve Officers Training Corps college program.

The program consists of a four year college course in which the Navy Department pays all of the selectee's principal expenses.

Gene was selected by a secret three-man committee, after he had passed exacting aptitude and physical tests. His application for enrollment has been approved by the Vanderbilt NROTC unit.

At HHS, Gene has been president of the Beta Club and the Senior Class, co-editor of the annual, sports editor of the school paper and an outstanding football player. He was a representative to Boys State last year.

What and where would I be if Judge John T. Gray had not seen something in me and lifted me to higher aspirations?

CHAPTER 2

Over the Horizon:
Vanderbilt and Commandant Ross Perot

There is nothing like a dream to create the future.

—Victor Hugo

In September 1951, when Mother and Dad drove away and left me on the steps of Old Kissam Hall at Vanderbilt, I felt I had left my world and entered someone else's. In later years, I thought deeply about what Mother and Dad, especially Mother, felt as they looked back at me on the Kissam steps. They did not have the opportunity to go to college and knew little about the world in which they were leaving their only child. And surely Mother must have known as she drove away there was a sizable chance she would not see me in this world again. Whatever Mother felt inside, she was a sunburst of loveliness with everyone she met at Vanderbilt.

The swirl started immediately. At that time they held pre-school Rush. Freshmen visited all twelve fraternity houses. I was thrilled to be invited back by eleven fraternities; I had liked every place I went. The truth is I did not know enough to be concerned or make an informed choice about which fraternity to join. In Brownsville, no one was referred to as a "Deke" or a "Tri Delt." I accepted the bid of Sigma Alpha Epsilon, keeping in mind that Uncle Earl was an SAE at the University of Tennessee, and felt great about it then and now. We had a terrific pledge class, including some of my best friends in life: Jack Caskey, Dewey Lane, and Dick Carpenter. It worked out well for me, but I vowed if I ever had any power at Vanderbilt, I would move Rush

16

from pre-school to the start of the sophomore year, when students have a better perspective of the actualities of varying fraternities.

School started in earnest, and I realized very quickly I was struggling in the deep end. Haywood High School had excellent teachers, but a high percentage of my Vanderbilt class had gone to prestigious prep schools. They, in effect, had their Vanderbilt freshmen courses in high school. I studied very hard and still felt like I was in quicksand up to my neck.

Carrying out pledge duty for SAE upperclassmen, being swamped by academics, and having virtually no social life meant my freshman year was going miserably. In the spring, every pledge of every fraternity had to run in the cross-campus, cross-country run. Brownsville did not have a track team, so I had no idea how I would do. To my enormous surprise, I came in third behind two varsity distance runners. "Herc" Alley, the wonderful track coach, threw his arms around me and said, "Eugene, I'm going to make you an SEC champion!"

Freshman year ended, and I set out for my first cruise and learned there was a whole other level of life. I was assigned to the USS *Missouri* (BB63). It was the most honored ship in the world. On its deck, five-star General Douglas MacArthur, signing for U.S. President Harry Truman, and the Japanese High Commander, signing for Japanese Emperor Hirohito, consummated the surrender of Japan on August 14, 1945, at the close of World War II.

Commandant of the 2,000 midshipmen aboard was Naval Academy Midshipman First Class Ross Perot, who would one day run for President of the United States. I admired him immensely. He continued to weave through my life. For a Tennessee boy whose closest exposure to water was TVA lakes, these six weeks were pure exhilaration. We sailed from Norfolk, Virginia, to Estoril, Portugal, and then to Portsmouth, England, where we had four days leave in London. Sailing, for me, was as much fun as the ports of call. Our bunks were hung three deep. Immediately below me was Bowden Wilson, Jr., a student at Rice University from San Antonio. Nearby was Jim Stafford, an SAE from the University of Oklahoma. We became close friends and enjoyed being together on and off the ship.

For a Midshipman 3/C, crossing the Atlantic was dominated by learning how to "holy-stone" the wooden decks at 6 a.m. and drills, drills, and drills. A holy-stone is an extra-large brick with a hole into which was placed a broom handle. Midshipmen had to develop dexterity in moving the broom handle back and forth quickly to sand the wooden deck clean. This was done in the dark with a fire hose going at almost full blast. We had gunnery stations, battle stations, abandon-ship stations, and countless more stations. There were sixteen levels from bottom to top of the Missouri. My gunnery station was in the powder room for one of the mighty 16-inch guns on the fifth level, and in the next drill I had a lookout station on the fourteenth level. There were no elevators. In ten minutes I had to navigate nine levels, same as a nine-story building, using ladders with traffic going rapidly in both directions.

Sunday was our favorite day. We still holy-stoned, but the rest of the day was ours. After chapel at 11 a.m., my friends and I usually spread blankets on the deck and played cards or read. Popular songs were piped through the ship. The Navy varsity football team practiced on the fantail; we did not keep track of how many wide receivers were lost overboard, much less footballs.

In the hottest weather we were permitted to sleep topside, the rolling sea rocking us to sleep. That was what I liked best, the simple joy of listening to the ship crash the waves, all around me the ineffable sounds of travel. Who would have believed a person could be so happy after days and days of having to holy-stone before sunrise and drills, drills, drills!

However, in the second week my idyllic cruise was interrupted in a bizarre way. In those days lobster, shrimp, and such crustaceans were not available in Tennessee. On Friday evening, fried shrimp was the entirety of the *Missouri* menu. I ate and became violently ill, missing two watches, a serious offense. I had to face Commandant Perot: "Midshipman Vaughan, you missed two watches. Why?"

I told him why, and he said, "I don't believe it. Five demerits."

I did not understand what had happened to my body, but it was clearly connected with Fridays. How could I know I had a shellfish allergy? I ate only bread the next Friday. That worked until just smelling the fried shrimp made me ill. I missed two more watches and was back before Commandant Perot: "I'm beginning to see you in my dreams, Midshipman Vaughan. What did you do to miss two more watches?"

I explained my dilemma and he said, "I still don't believe it. Ten demerits."

This was serious. Fifteen demerits put me in genuine jeopardy. Twenty demerits meant I lost my scholarship, so on Fridays thereafter I ate candy bars at the gedunk, Navy language for the concessions or snack bar.

Commandant Perot had quite a future ahead. Prior to his bid for the Presidency, Ross Perot went on to found Perot Systems, which he ultimately sold to General Motors, and became one of the most successful and famous men in America. In 1977, I presided at a Harvard Business School conference in Houston at which Ross was the keynote speaker. After I introduced him, a quarter century after my series of trips to Captain's Mast, Ross turned to me and said, "Midshipman Vaughan, I still don't believe it!" He told the story to thunderous laughter.

Fortunately, I was fit and healthy for our four-day leave in London. I felt breathless in the beauty of Sir Christopher Wren's St. Paul's Cathedral and Westminster Abbey. In Parliament, I imagined the great voices of Churchill, Disraeli, and Edmund Burke. My favorite place, oddly enough, was the National Portrait Gallery, where I looked into the eyes of men who had made history when "the sun never set on the British Empire." I found London the city equivalent of what I found at sea. Certain people can never get enough of the sea, and I am one. And I can never get enough of London and England.

By the end of the summer, this Tennessee boy knew that the sea and travel were permanently in my blood.

CHAPTER 3

"Gene, You Are My Very Heart"

The commitments that people make to values beyond the self are manifested in various ways—in their family and community life, in the way they treat each and all humans, in the goals and standards they set for themselves. These are people who make the world better by just being the kind of people they are.

—Dr. John W. Gardner

My six weeks' summer cruise left four weeks in Brownsville before sophomore year, and I made the most of it to earn money. To control cotton prices, the government limited the amount of cotton acreage each farmer could plant. My job was to measure the amount of cotton planted on farms. Shortly after sunrise, I would be at the front of a ten-yard chain, and the farmer would tend the end of it. Whatever the peculiar shape of the field, I could use trigonometry and my measurements to calculate the amount of acreage. I worked in the field until dark and then went home and worked up the measurements and paperwork. I was paid 15¢ per acre, $1 per farm. Working six days a week for a month, I netted over $1,000. That was big money at the time. Papa let me use his car, and I thought I would never be able to get all the dust out. I know he sure loved me a lot to let me use his precious Ford.

That summer was a period of encouragement after Mother's third operation. She continued to work and used some of her savings to buy me a dark blue cashmere sweater from Oak Hall, the top men's shop in Memphis. I wore that beautiful sweater for many years until the elbows wore out, and then I got leather patches. Ever since, I have owned a dark blue cashmere sweater, and it is my favorite. Each reminds me of how much Mother loved and sacrificed for me. I spent almost every evening with Mother and Dad that lovely summer.

Then it was back to Vanderbilt. The biggest change was that I now felt I belonged, particularly because I had made some great friends. I wrote sports for the campus newspaper, the *Hustler,* and loved following the football and basketball teams. I had an excellent job as dean's messenger and really enjoyed it because Dean Carmichael and his assistant were extremely nice, and I was the first student to know everything that was happening on campus.

Then, on October 9, 1952, there was a knock on my door; it was Jim Yates, the new pastor at Brownsville Baptist. Brother Yates was often in Nashville because he was dating a Theta at Vanderbilt and we had become good friends. I was about to make a joke that he was up so often he should get a room in my dorm; then I saw his expression.

Interstate 40 did not exist then and Jim set a speed record on old U.S. 70 to Memphis. We arrived at Mother's room in the Methodist Hospital about 8 p.m. She looked beautiful and was radiant when she saw me. Dad, Jim, Aunt Jo Peebles, R.N., and Aunt Elizabeth Morris, R.N., were there, but they left Mother and me alone most of the time. She wanted to know how school was going. I tried to ask about her, but she always pulled me close and whispered, "Gene, you are my very heart."

About 11 p.m. the doctor decided Mother needed rest and would be all right over night. Mother pulled me close again and whispered, "Gene, I am so proud of you. You are my very heart, you know."

Those were the last words I heard from Mother. She died during the night. Everyone said she was holding on so she could see me. Mother was only forty. My world came apart. I was not at all prepared for Mother to die; I thought she was getting better. I look back and know that I was diverted by school, and Mother would not allow Dad or anyone to tell me that after the third operation there was no hopeful report.

I made a lifelong mistake. Before the church service, we had an open casket at home. Mother looked so beautiful I leaned over and kissed her cheek. It was like stone. My heart burst. I still remember the terrible coldness all these decades later.

People from Haywood and surrounding counties as well as my friends from all around came to Brownsville Baptist Church. There were friends of all faiths; the pews overflowed. Our longtime friend Brother Orr came from Dyersburg and preached on "M-A-R-G-A-R-E-T," with "M" standing for "Mother."

There was an outpouring of love for Mother, privately and publicly. A *States-Graphic* editorial stated:

> Perhaps no other lady in Brownsville contributed more unselfishly of her time to things worthwhile or was more beloved by the people in general than this splendid lady. Her life and character were a benediction to those who had the privilege of knowing and associating with her. A lady of rare personal charm and possessing a radiant and happy disposition, Mrs. Vaughan made friends easily. Sincere in purpose she was possessed with the highest ideals of Christian living.... In her passing the community loses a splendid Christian lady, the home a devoted companion and mother, and the Church one of its most devout and earnest workers.

After a few days I had to go back to school, and it was extremely difficult on Dad to be alone. My parents' friends were wonderful, and both the Musgrave and Vaughan families encircled us, especially Uncle Earl, who was very close to Dad and me and had a gift for comforting. He had been a revered Army chaplain throughout World War II. Christmas break came at a good time. Dad and I could grieve together, but my returning to school that bleak winter was very hard for both of us.

Back at Vanderbilt, Jack Caskey urged me to take a course in philosophy taught by the galvanic Dr. John J. Compton, son of Nobel Prize–winning physicist Arthur Compton, who opened up the whole universe. Socrates, Plato, and Descartes were mere names to me before. Growing up in Brownsville Baptist Church, all my questions were answered fully. Now there came hurtling at me new ideas to challenge my mind and soul.

In the spring I was elected to the cabinet of the Student Christian Association (SCA), the largest organization on campus, so even with my new ideas I stayed close to my roots. Next, a rather amazing honor came out of the blue. "The Agrarians" were the most famous group of professors in the history of Vanderbilt. They included Robert Penn Warren, who wrote *All the King's Men*, Allen Tate, Merrill Moore, Jesse Wills, and other renowned authors and poets. During their time on campus they had formed the "Blue Pencil Society" for exceptional writing. My English professor, Dr. Bryant, was impressed by my writing and submitted a sample of my work. To my pleasure and surprise, I joined the fellowship of these prestigious poets and writers.

Mother was smiling on me.

As I set out in summer for my second cruise, to save money I hitchhiked from Brownsville, Tennessee, to Kingsville, Texas. By keeping my expenses far below my NROTC travel per diem, each summer I cleared about $1,200. Truckers were the best at picking up hikers, and long rides from city to city were optimal. But sometimes I had to take what I could get. That was the situation in Hammond, Louisiana. All I could get was an open-air ride to Houston atop a mountain of Black Diamond watermelons. Later, many people cheerfully observed (especially when introducing me as a speaker) that atop a load of watermelons (read: turnips) was a perfect way for me to arrive!

Kingsville, Texas, has its name because it is part of the famed King Ranch. It is so flat you can see a rattlesnake crawling on its belly a mile away. It seemed to be nothing but sky. And that is why we were there: to spend three exhilarating weeks deciding whether we wanted to become U.S. Navy aviators. I started flying the first week in the front cockpit of a trainer with the pilot in the rear cockpit. The second week he let me take the controls more each day while performing barrel-rolls, loop-de-loops, spiral dives, and featherings. During the final week, he let me keep my hands on the controls throughout all maneuvers, including take-offs and landings. I fell in love with flying—and with Texas—those extraordinary three weeks.

One of the great joys of Kingsville was that I was reunited with my good friends from the USS *Missouri*: Bowden Wilson Jr. and Jim Stafford. They knew Texas, so I was introduced to everything great about living in that robust land. I already knew about Davy Crockett, Jim Bowie, and Sam Houston from Tennessee, but they sat around campfires telling of the Alamo's "line in the sand," General Sam Houston's victory over General Santa Anna at San Jacinto, and the Texas oil wildcatters. They did not brag; they just told Texas history with pride, and it was hard not to want to live in that glorious land of independence and opportunity.

On our last Sunday before the double-airlift that took us to Little Creek, Virginia, for Marine training and took the Little Creek midshipmen to Kingsville, Bowden Wilson, Bill Wold, and I went to church together and spent the afternoon talking about our futures. Bill Wold was a basketball star at Rice and had been named All-Southwest Conference at guard as a sophomore. The three of us were marvelously happy and optimistic.

On Friday, the Vanderbilt NROTC midshipmen were loaded on a "Constellation-like" Douglas aircraft and flown directly to Little Creek, Virginia. We found our housing for the next three weeks was Quonset huts, "temporary" housing since WWII. Our Vandy contingent was first to arrive and got the pick of the double-decker beds. During the night a horrible rumor started that a "Flying Boxcar" had crashed leaving Pensacola Air Station. About one-third of the airlifts were "Flying Boxcars," with fuselages suspended between the engines sort of like a catamaran. Nobody had any idea who was missing or if the rumor was true. Sunrise brought the worst possible news. The "Flying Coffin," as it was subsequently called, carried students from several schools, including Rice and the University of Oklahoma. My good friends Bowden Wilson and Jim Stafford and new friend Bill Wold had died in the swamp around Pensacola. It was the worst tragedy in NROTC history. In all, thirty-nine midshipmen died. We sat around our huts in a daze, feeling this could not be true. This was the summer after Mother died. I had been living by faith. It all seemed unreal—hopes, dreams, and lives gone in an instant.

Understandably, under the circumstances, I did not like the Marines. Unlike Kingsville and the USS *Missouri*, which were totally organized with every minute utilized, the Marines mostly had us sit in auditoriums watching training films. Occasionally we got to practice landing invasions in barges.

Marine training at Little Creek excelled in only one area, leisure time, of which there was an overabundance. They organized comprehensive competitions in sports not requiring special equipment. I chose horseshoes. Competing were fifty or so midshipmen from all over the U.S. At the end of almost three weeks, the two finalists were from one university—Vanderbilt—one of them myself. We met in a best-two-out-of-three for the championship. I was really hot. I tossed several ringers, took the first game by a lopsided score, and was leading 17–7 in the decisive second game when a rainstorm broke. When we returned to the pits after two hours, everything changed. I only needed four points to be horseshoe champion, but I had lost my groove. The other guy got hot and won the championship. It was just horseshoes, but it taught me a lifelong lesson. When you have the lead, bear down; do not relax. A few years later I came across a statement by General Ike Eisenhower when he was president of Columbia University:

> In war, in politics, in fundraising—in everything—it isn't over until it's over—and then it may still not be over. Stay on guard.

When the chips are down, I always think of the horseshoe championship. "Kick it in!" became a lifetime moral commitment for me, and I passed it on to my children.

After that summer's grotesque NROTC training at Little Creek was complete, I returned to Brownsville, back to work meeting the farmers at sunrise. I had mastered trig and managed to clear $100 most days. Dad and I had a good time together, much of it spent at the family farm with Mama and Papa. The big news awaiting me when I returned home was a letter from Ormand Plater, editor of the Vanderbilt *Hustler*, asking me to become sports editor! I could hardly believe it. Being sports editor of a three-times-a-week campus newspaper was a big job, which I knew virtually nothing about. I had trepidation about being up to the challenge, but Dad urged me to try. And I knew Mother would want me to rise to the challenge and believed in me.

Of course, I would do it!

CHAPTER 4

Enthusiastic Flea

One enthusiastic flea can worry an entire dog.

—Old Tennessee saying

There are a lot of old Tennessee "truths," and I like the one about the flea. After all, fleas are indeed energetic and hardworking, and they cover a lot of ground. Once inspired, I always have been enthusiastic about covering a lot of ground with my "extra high voltage" and tenacity.

At the start of my junior year at Vanderbilt, armed with my experiences in two dormitories with "resident monitor" governance, and working for the dean of students, I asked Dean Carmichael why he did not put the responsibility on students to administer themselves in dorm life. After all, this would be consistent with developing college students to become responsible adults. I then learned a drawback of speaking up. Dean Carmichael said, "Great idea. Draw up a plan." I had many thoughts and contacted friends at other colleges to find out how they did it. The plan grew into a reasonably complex system that provided student-run self-administration throughout all the main campus dorms. With the Dean's backing, I spoke about the self-governing concept at campus gatherings. Before long I was elected president of the inaugural dormitory council. Today it is called Interhall, with dozens of dormitories, and is basically the same plan I dreamed up and executed.

At the same time, I was trying to master being sports editor. The first challenge, having to write three columns a week, I solved in high order by persuading Sheldon Hackney to become my co-editor and write one of the weekly columns. I picked well. Sheldon's future resume would include president of Tulane University, president of the University of Pennsylvania, and chairman of the National Endowment for the Humanities. The editor role was fascinating to me. I became good friends with "Scoop" Hudgins, the old-pro sports publicist at Vanderbilt. Scoop's pet peeve was to see "All-America" written "All-American." I still wince when I see it the wrong way in newspapers and magazines.

It was easy to recruit sports reporters for the *Hustler* because Vanderbilt was the school of the magnificent Grantland Rice, widely considered, with Red Smith, the greatest sports writer of all time. All I had to do was use the dean's records to locate former high school sports writers and invite them to join the staff using this Grantland Rice quote:

> For when the One Great Scorer comes
> To mark against your name,
> He writes—not that you won or lost—
> But HOW you played the game.

People signed on with the same zeal I felt about the ideals of sportsmanship and the same joy for writing about sports. Not surprisingly, with a heavy course load, job, fraternity life, and many extracurriculars, junior year flew by, and it was time for what would be a transformative summer cruise.

The Navy did a splendid job of giving every midshipman a great taste of the "Big Ship" Navy, Navy Air, Marines, and "Small Ship" Navy before asking us to choose. To my chagrin, myopia precluded my preferred Navy Air and explained my "sensational" style on punt returns of dashing for the ball at the last second and catching it on the run; I simply did not see the ball earlier!

My six weeks on a "Tin Can" changed my life in several important ways. Being on a Tin Can meant prioritizing, balancing, and managing a range of responsibilities, and making decisions, often more quickly than you would like. I loved it!

Our Tin Can was an old destroyer that gave me a taste of the real Navy. The mattresses were so full of bedbugs that each week we would drag the mattresses to the main deck and hang them over the lifeline for a day's airing and beating. The bed bugs thrived. A Tin Can is well-named; a battleship would be a Mercedes by comparison. In heavy seas, the waves swept over the forecastle with fire hydrant force. On the bridge, seawater crashed into lookouts on the wings. Standing a four-hour mid-watch with the ship bucking and rolling was exhilarating to me. Then, my favorite part: my bunk was next to the hull of the ship. I would lie awake and listen to the ocean crash and swirl against the skin of the ship, with frequent bumps of debris just outside my bunk. I was acutely conscious that only five-eighths of an inch of steel separated me from the sea. I can shut my eyes right now and my heart sings to the "ineffable sounds of the sea."

There were only a few of us to do everything, from chipping the rust on the hull and painting it with orange oxide paint in good weather to serving as chaplain on Sunday. In addition to keeping our Tin Can clean and standing watch for eight hours a day, each of us had five to ten collateral duties. And I was learning to navigate by the stars. Who could ask for a better life than this? Not me, and we were heading to Paris!

Ah, Paris! We took it all in—and it took in some of my friends. The Folies Bergère, the Moulin Rouge, Pigalle! I can't say the Louvre was our first stop, but we made it. Mona Lisa and the Winged Victory exceeded everything I had heard. Seeing the Impressionists up close ignited a lifetime love of this superlative school of art. My Brownsville parsimony prevented me from experiencing Le Grand Véfour or any Michelin three-star restaurants for which Paris is famous, but the cafes and bistros that lined the streets were elegant enough. I shopped the bookstores along the Seine and spent hours just walking the bridges. It is said that if you do not bring Paris with you, you will not find it there. This excited Tennessean did not bring much, but I left with a lifetime desire to return again and again to France and Paris.

The three-week cruise home to Guantanamo Bay was just as bone tiring and exalting as the first crossing. My summer cruise over, I arrived in Brownsville to an unpleasant surprise. Mother's friends had been nice to Dad, but none courted him out of respect for her. But another woman did not respect those boundaries. I felt she was everything Mother was not. Dad told me he was very lonely. Still, it hurt me terribly that Dad, less than two years after Mother was buried, was talking marriage to Marye Kinney. It broke my heart, but I agreed to be best man for Dad. I knew he loved Mother with all his heart. I also knew that with me away he was perishing from loneliness. It was confided to me that the town was staying neutral until they saw what I did. I decided to stand by Dad. There are certain times in life when you grit your teeth and get through it.

Then I left for senior year. The most positive high-impact change in my life at that time was moving into the SAE House. Four of us were in the prized corner room of the Great Gray Castle at Kensington Place overlooking the golden SAE lion: Jack Caskey, my best friend since freshman year; Dewey Lane, brilliant and the closest person to an Albert Schweitzer I ever have known; and Pat Hairston, a good old boy and drinking buddy of Jack's.

Dad gave me a car my senior year. It was a beautiful, baby-blue Ford with a cream top. I knew it was a gift to help win me over about his marriage. I did accept the car, with guilt. She was my Blue Beauty.

Every activity grew exponentially. SAE brother and close friend Dick Carpenter and I were asked by the NROTC Commandant to co-chair the first NROTC Ball in Vanderbilt history. He wanted it to be a big deal, so as one of the many special touches we ordered a beautiful cymbidium orchid for every lady attending. When I went to the Bureau of Personnel (BUPERS) at the Pentagon several years later and looked in my file, I saw I was cited for "Innovative, Distinguished Service" my senior year. It must have been the orchids!

This was my final track season. Coach Alley did not make me an "SEC Champion," but he nearly killed me trying. He did succeed in my becoming a stalwart, three-year varsity letterman. My first two years I had run the two-mile, requiring a strenuous, weekly, ten-mile run in preparation. Upping the ante during senior year, Coach Alley ran me in the mile at the beginning of some meets and always the two-mile in the final event. I won or held my own in two-mile races, called the "iron-man" events because they were the longest and most demanding. I loved track and I loved Coach Alley. He died while I was in the Navy, and I always have regretted not telling him what a positive influence he was in my life.

During my senior year I was startled to receive an invitation from Chancellor and Mrs. Branscomb to have dinner in their home when the illustrious Harold Sterling Vanderbilt and wife were staying with them. Instead of finding a crowd, I was surprised to be one of only five students invited. The special guest was the great-grandson of Commodore Vanderbilt, and this was the first time a mainstream member of the Vanderbilt family had visited, so it was a really big deal. Mr. Vanderbilt was engaging in a reserved way, and he and I really hit it off, mainly because I admired his feat of winning the America's Cup numerous times with his yacht *Ranger*, usually against Sir Isaac Lipton of England. His visit must have gone well because the following year he became vice chairman of the board of trustees, where he served for many years and established the splendid HSV Scholarships.

Funny what one remembers. Margaret Branscomb, a perfect hostess who could rise to any occasion, asked Mrs. Vanderbilt what she would like to do on the weekend. Nashville is known as the "Athens of the South" for its many aspects of culture, but Mrs. Vanderbilt immediately answered, "Grand Ole Opry." Margaret quietly responded, "It is said there are two kinds of fools in Nashville: those who have never been to the Opry and those who have been twice. By all means, we shall go." It was only much later, while viewing a statue of her on campus, that I realized her full name was Margaret Vaughan Branscomb!

Toward the end of school, my classmate Kay Russell said her father, Fred Russell, wanted to visit with me. Fred Russell, sports editor and co-owner of the *Nashville Banner*, wrote a nationally acclaimed daily sports column and was "Dean of Southern Sportswriters." I was astonished when Mr. Russell, who was held in highest esteem, akin to Grantland Rice, by me and many others, pulled out my articles, discussed them one by one, and offered me a job. With heavy heart, I told him about my three-year obligation to the U.S. Navy. I felt his offer was an utmost honor.

The legendary Mr. Rice died in 1954. In 1956, the year after my final column, the Thoroughbred Racing Associations established at Vanderbilt the Grantland Rice Scholarship (later renamed in honor of two of the greatest sports writers of all time to the Fred Russell–Grantland Rice Thoroughbred Racing Associations Scholarship), which is awarded annually to an outstanding high school senior with special interest and potential in the field of sports writing. This has produced Roy Blount Jr., Skip Bayless, and over sixty writers and broadcasters. In 2016 there were 621 applications for the four-year scholarship. I am proud, through Fred Russell, to have been an impetus for the prestigious program.

I love sports; actually, I love sportsmanship. Unbeknownst to me at this time, one day I would have the ultimate gifts: a son to share my love of sports and the incomparable joy of cheering him on as he played football and other sports, and a daughter who, along with playing field hockey and soccer among her many talents, would be a vibrant, crowd-inspiring varsity cheerleader. Sporting events would take on much deeper meaning in my future.

Then my milestone event arrived—graduation! For the first time in Vanderbilt's long history, in 1955 it rained on graduation day. Not a problem because the year before Vanderbilt had completed Memorial Stadium, at that time the foremost basketball home in the SEC. What a venue! I still revel in watching Vanderbilt's games in that stadium.

Vanderbilt completely changed my life and forever has stayed part of my lifeblood. One of my life's transcendent events happened in 1972 when I received a call from Chancellor Alexander Heard telling me I had been elected a trustee of Vanderbilt University. I was thirty-nine, and the legendary Dean Madison Sarratt told me I was the youngest regular-way trustee ever elected. (The other category to elect trustees is "Young Alumni Trustee [YAT]" wherein each graduating class elects a senior to serve a four-year term, thus assuring four YATs on the board at all times. This innovative YAT program started several years before my "regular-way" election in 1972.) It just so happens that Susan and I were in Louisville for the Kentucky Derby that day. After Chancellor Heard's phone call, we felt like "lifetime winners." It is hard for me to see any treasured aspect of my life that did not have its origins at Vanderbilt.

CHAPTER 5

A "Ter-rif-fic" Start in the Navy

Duty then is the sublimest word in our language.
Do your duty in all things.
You cannot do more.
You should never wish to do less.

—General Robert E. Lee

In June 1955, as a newly commissioned ensign, I reported for duty aboard the USS *Ross* (DD-563) at Guantanamo Bay, Cuba. Immediately I got very lucky. Aboard ships with long history, there are major rivalries among departments. It is not just good-natured rivalry but more like deep-seated jealousy and bitterness.

When new ensigns reported for duty, the heads of the departments got to select who they wanted in an order determined throughout naval history. Lieutenant Gene Brody was gunnery officer and immediately made me the first pick. That had status in itself, somewhat like professional sports drafts, but in this case it meant much more. Brody was a born winner who infused everyone around him with his confident, upbeat enthusiasm. Ask Lieutenant Brody in 1955, "Good morning, Mr. Brody, how are you?" and the answer came winging back, "Ter-rif-fic!" Not just good or great, Brody was always "Ter-rif-fic!" When asked that in 1970 as our lives reconnected, the answer was still a smiling, enthusiastic "Ter-rif-fic!"

The USS *Ross* was in Cuba for fleet maneuvers, gunnery practice, and, while I did not know it at the time, preparation for deployment to the Mediterranean for four months with the Navy's 6th Fleet. At night

Brody led his team to Santiago and Port-au-Prince and showed us the clubs and dives preferred by Hemingway and other celebrities of the day. People just naturally wanted to please and show off their best to "The Brode."

In the midst of this fun, I received orders to report to the U.S. Naval Station in Key West, Florida, for two months of Anti-Submarine Warfare (ASW) training. In eight weeks, we had to master underwater warfare. The Germans dominated the seas early during WWII because their advanced submarines torpedoed Churchill's mighty British Navy mercilessly and cut the vital supply lines from the U.S. to Britain by sinking cargo ships. German subs operated audaciously off the east coast of the U.S.

The history of ASW is filled with major technological break-throughs, so the advantage swept back and forth between subs and ASW ships, and so did the competition. I loved it! At Key West, our class learned how to operate the sonar equipment and developed the intricate, fine art of distinguishing among subs, significant water abnormalities, larger fish, and whales. We spent much time in subma-rines to get into the minds of the enemy and understand the peculiar psychology of submariners, who have to be prepared to be underwater for six months at a time and be perfectly still and silent while destroyers (DDs) release depth charges, hedge-hogs, and heat-seeking torpedoes all around them. I quickly decided I had no interest whatsoever in sub-marine service. If I go, I want blue sky to be the last thing I see. The star of our class was Lieutenant Demosthenes Ionidas, son of the chief naval officer of the Hellenic Navy. He was a great guy who spoke seven languages.

When I returned to the USS *Ross*, the ship was in full preparation to cross the Atlantic and spend four months in the Mediterranean conducting fleet maneuvers with the navies of other countries. ASW was to be a major part of the fleet exercises, as submarine warfare had mostly replaced big-gun shelling from twenty miles away.

My sonar gang was surpassingly excellent and expert at distin-guishing "schools of fish" from the real thing—and they had joy of life. Onshore they were constantly getting into trouble. Up I would go to the Captain's Mast to plead their cases. Captain Newbould, a wonderful officer, would say, "Mr. Vaughan, do you actually believe what your sonarman just told me?" "Yes, sir, Captain, he is a fine sonarman." The Captain would roll his eyes. Next week I would be standing before the Captain with another "innocent" sonarman. Captain Newbould finally shrugged and said, "Ensign Vaughan, Lt. Brody tells me you are an outstanding ASW officer, and you certainly are if your expertise is anywhere nearly as great as your loyalty to your sailors!" My sonar gang enjoyed "taking Ensign Vaughan's pants off," but they decided I was an okay guy and worked hard for me. In the Mediterranean, our gang distinguished itself.

All day and night we did intricate maneuvers with the U.S. 6th Fleet and then even more intricate, multi-national maneuvers. My most interesting assignment, however, was that every time we were in a port, and there were many times, e.g., Majorca and Rhodes, I was given a collateral duty called "Cultural Duty Officer." Simply put, this meant onshore I went with Captain Newbould everywhere—and made certain he got back to the right ship. The Captain said he could trust a Baptist! Captain Newbould loved a good time and was broadly informed. Together we went to operas, bars, churches, museums, bars, and bars. He always had a hilarious time, and what he thought was most fun was "losing" me. He would give me the slip, and I would spend until 3 a.m. or so searching every bar and sweating blood. We got along famously.

Another stoke of fortune! The *Ross* was at Piraeus, home port to Athens, at Christmas when the superlative Lieutenant Commander Demosthenes Ionidas married. He invited me to all the fabulous marital and Christmas celebrations. Never ever have I experienced such splendor of festivity!

It was in the Mediterranean that I became a Naval Officer. I was no longer the green ensign with bright, shiny brass. Green mold discolored my braid. And I had the Captain's respect as well as Lieutenant Brody's. Among the multitude of collateral duties, the Captain wanted a USS *Ross* newspaper for the Med cruise, and he assigned me editor. Using my Vanderbilt *Hustler* experience, I got it organized so we had reporters from every part of the ship. We had a sports section that even covered card games.

One part I secretly wrote myself. I had a good yeoman as assistant who clandestinely reported to me all the funny happenings, rumors, and endless odd things that were heard and seen among the crew around the ship. No one was spared. I covered the officers, and he covered the crew. My column was titled "The *Ross* Bilge" and it quickly became the hit and great mystery of the ship. The secret was maintained throughout the four months and curiosity grew enormously. It was announced the author would be revealed in the last edition. Pools were raised about the identity of the author. Captain Newbould asked me outright who it was. We had a quirky officer named Michael J. Lewis, who had become my roommate for the Med cruise. Michael was inept but genuinely funny. He once announced to the wardroom that, "Gene is Baptist, and he thinks my sleeping in the nude is sinful." When I told the Captain that my guess was Michael Lewis, he snorted. In the final column I simply signed it "EHV." People were nonplussed. My terrific yeoman revealed how he and I had worked together. I gave him huge credit, and he was a hero with the crew. Respect for the wardroom soared with the revelation that an officer actually had a sense of humor. Captain Newbould grinned at me and said "Michael Lewis, indeed!"

Captain Newbould had been sending his little newspaper to the captains of all the other ships in the 6th Fleet. By a combination of excellent gunnery/ASW performance and our newspaper, the USS *Ross* was the best-known ship in the Mediterranean Sea. The highest ranking admiral in the 6th Fleet sent Captain Newbould a personal message of congratulations for keeping up morale.

Life in the Navy was never dull. As soon as the USS *Ross* returned to the States, orders were cut for me to report to the U.S. Naval Gunnery School at Newport, Rhode Island. This was big time. Newport was home to the legendary Naval War College. Moreover, it was only ninety minutes from the Boston Celtics and the phenomenal Bob Cousy! Going to gunnery gchool also assured me I would be qualified fully to become gunnery officer on the USS *Ross*.

My gunnery school classmates seemed destined for fame or infamy. Every member was noticeably outstanding or a big risk. A distinguished Lieutenant Commander with a silver-handled walking cane had us all mesmerized with his knowledge and stories. Toward the end, we discovered he kept gin in the cane.

Lieutenant Marcus Aurelius Arnheiter seized on me, basically because he was marrying a girl named "Vaughan." I was incorporated into the wedding party at the Stork Club in New York and in the chapel at the U.S. Naval Academy. Marc was like a "bad penny." Eventually he became infamous, as told in *The Arnheiter Affair*, a bestseller.

A particular clean-cut Lieutenant (Junior Grade) stood apart from the rest and had "Admiral" written all over him. He was engaged to a Wellesley senior and asked me if I would like to meet some of her friends. Soon thereafter I was sliding down the slope to perdition. At a lovely, low-key party at Wellesley, a tray was passed with "water," slivers of ice, and an olive; I took it. My first sip of alcohol was a martini. I had skipped the minors and gone straight to the big leagues. I also saw how the other half lives! The "Admiral's" friend lived in Short Hills, New Jersey, exclusive home to the "Other Half."

I was finishing my indispensable time at gunnery school and getting excited about my return to the USS *Ross* when another BUPERS cable arrived with different instructions. I was to report to the U.S. Naval Shipyard in Charleston, South Carolina. This change in orders would have a profound influence on the direction of my life.

CHAPTER 6

The Sea and Solitude

I must go down to the seas again, to the lonely sea and the sky,
And all I ask is a tall ship and a star to steer her by,
And the wheel's kick and the wind's song and the white sail's shaking,
And a grey mist on the sea's face, and a grey dawn breaking.

—John Masefield, "Sea Fever"

In 1956, I had the incredible good fortune to put a brand new ship, the USS *Brister* (DER 327), into commission with a brand new set of officers and crew. My first nice surprise was that Lieutenant Paul Douglas, my best instructor at the Key West Sonar School, was executive officer. The captain was Commander Joe Cote, a down-to-earth guy from Harvard. All the bachelors at my level plus Captain Cote, whose wife was still in Massachusetts, lived in the BOQ (Bachelor Officers Quarters) across from the Officers Club, which was surrounded by an 18-hole golf course. They were a great bunch of guys. While in the shipyard we were on special work hours from 7 a.m. to 1 p.m. That meant we were on the golf course by 1:15. After golf, we went over to the Officers Club for a "Mr. Big" hamburger and table shuffleboard. We became so adept we could almost always "hang the disk" over the edge.

Charleston! My new roommate, Dave Moore, and I loved Charleston. As Naval officers, we were deemed appropriate enough to date classy young women from SOB (South of Broad). I already was acquainted with a Vanderbilt student, Sue Hagood, whose family was multigenerational SOB. Football at the Citadel was played in General Johnson Hagood Stadium. Her uncle was Admiral James Holloway, and the NROTC Scholarship was his idea; it was called the "Holloway Plan." As Chief of Naval Operations he was immensely respected and popular. Captain Cote was thrilled when I brought Sue on board!

I fell in love with the Low Country. Since then I have read avidly every book of the superlative Low Country chronicler and native Pat Conroy. Eventually our idyllic time of playing golf, enjoying society life, and exploring the wonders of the Low Country came to an end. From the mountaintop to the abyss! After a shakedown cruise, our home port became Newport, Rhode Island, but actually home was the middle of the horrific North Atlantic. In the mid-1950s, the Cold War was at its height, and America in both the Atlantic and Pacific had to fear invasion by nuclear air strikes and nuclear submarines. The USS *Brister* became an integral link in the DEW Line, the Distant Early Warning Line, which featured Super Constellations, loaded with high-powered radar, flying across the middle of the Atlantic Ocean. Under them were the destroyer escorts (DERs), loaded with radar and sonar, at 200-mile intervals. Our mission was to steam to our station on the DEW Line and for a month go back and forth in a thirty-mile-diameter circle. It was absolutely miserable duty. After thirty days on station, we would steam back to Newport for two weeks in port. The only good parts were the Celtics, Red Sox, and Boston Bruins. Then it was back to station for a month. Sometimes, instead of Newport, we went to the seaport of Argentina, Newfoundland.

In addition to the Celtics there was another very special attraction near Newport—Conn College (Connecticut College for Women, at New London). My "aw shucks," wonderfully resourceful roommate, David Moore, had a lifelong friend, Betsy Wolfe, who was a senior. She offered to get dates for three of us but did not want to pick favorites, so she and David devised a plan. Dave, Bill Phillips, and I arrived before dinner at Betsy's dorm. Bill sat down at their grand piano, and as soon as Rachmaninoff started wafting through the dorm, lovely girls streamed to the piano. Dave and I had to work very fast to set up three dates because Bill knew only a short passage of Rachmaninoff! It worked perfectly. I happened to invite the class president, a smart, funny, and wonderful girl. About twenty years later I visited the Houston home of a Harvard Business School suitemate, and there she was. Small, small world! I went over and asked, "Have you heard any good Rachmaninoff lately? We laughed and had a wonderful time reminiscing.

Ultimately, much of my time at sea was in solitude. My thinking during those long months of miserable weather, privation, and quiet loneliness far from mankind revolved around the big stuff: What did I deeply believe in? How devout was my faith? What were my fundamental principles and values? For what profession should I strive? What kind of man should I strive to be? That dreadful year in the North Atlantic was the most priceless period of my life for hard, uninterrupted thinking. A major transformation was taking place, I knew, but it took a while for me to recognize and act on it.

My deepest belief was a certainty. I believed in God and that He sent His only son to earth to be crucified on the cross for our sins. I could not imagine greater love, and my view of Him was an all-encompassing love. I had some questions yet to be resolved more fully, e.g., inerrancy; however, I was raised on faith and certain of my own.

Until my time alone at sea, I had spent little time thinking about my actual principles, beyond having good character. Papa believed business should be done on a man's word and a handshake, but I had seen Papa's next-door neighbor renege on an important handshake deal. That did not embitter Papa or Mama, but it was a raw deal that never was rectified. I decided I could not do business that way.

Racial discrimination was also on my mind. I barely had known it existed growing up, but I came to realize that Brownsville, Tennessee, reflected what might be called benign bigotry. I did not witness any physical abuse, but on Saturday night a whistle blew at 10 p.m., and if your skin was not white, you had to be outside the city limits by 10:30 p.m. or risk arrest. The schools were segregated. I saw it but did not understand the weight of it. By 1957, the issue of race relations was raging through America. When I confronted the issue at sea, I knew there was only one right answer. I believe we should all have equality of opportunity, although results must be earned.

While at sea, I read a lot. I loved history, especially American history. I understood the sacrifice it took to win freedom, and it was clear Americans must sacrifice again and again to remain free.

Finally, in these interminable months, it became gloriously evident to me that love was the all-powerful principle. In Corinthians 13:13, the Bible says "And now these three remain: faith, hope, and love. But the greatest of these is love." I knew that Mother's love for me made all the difference in my life. I resolved amid the darkness that if I were ever so fortunate as to have a wife and children, I would love them with all my heart. That winter in the violent sea and bitter cold when I felt I was alone with God, I prayed that I could become a man worthy of my parents and a family of my own.

Then there was the big question of what I should do with the rest of my life. From the day I entered the world, my family designated me to be a doctor. While I did not announce it, I had taken the required pre-med courses. I was on schedule to start medical school in 1958 upon discharge from the Navy.

I could not pinpoint when the change in me started. I expect it was serving under "The Brode." He was so admirable and enjoyable that it was hard not to want to emulate him. As I became a successful officer on the USS *Brister*, I began to envision the ship as a microcosm of the business world.

As I contemplated my future, a rumor started circulating that the USS *Brister* was going to be transferred from the North Atlantic to the Pacific. Rumors are a constant at sea, so fat chance, though the very idea temporarily diverted me from thinking about the future. About a month later Captain Cote went on the squawk box and announced the USS *Brister* was being transferred to Pearl Harbor.

The *Brister* went through the Panama Canal, the "path between the seas." Then, Honolulu! Waikiki Beach! Our first Sunday, a few of us rushed down to the famous Royal Hawaiian Hotel and bought ourselves matching swimsuits and shirts. We wore them out on the beach to the hilarious ridicule of the "beach boys," the islanders who are lifeguards. Our matching sets never appeared again.

Good luck compounded our good luck. The USS *Brister* immediately was put into the Pearl Harbor shipyard for many months. It had taken a terrible beating in the North Atlantic. So our schedule was to start work on the ship at 7 a.m. and be on Waikiki Beach by 1:15 p.m. We were the first men to arrive every day at Fort DeRussy, a beautiful part of the beach with Diamond Head in the background. It was owned by the military and available only to officers, families, and guests.

In the Ala Wai Canal Yacht Basin there were numerous houseboats for lease. Four of us *"Brister* Bachelors" leased a houseboat right across the pier from the *Groot Beer* (Great Bear), the magnificent and infamous all-mahogany houseboat of Hermann Goering. My ever-resourceful roommate Dave Moore, even at his young age, was commodore of the prestigious Watch Hill (Connecticut) Yacht Club, and he quickly instilled a genuine yacht club culture in "the Basin." Some houseboats were amazing; one adjacent to ours had a grand piano. Pretty soon we bachelors were invited to every party in the harbor, which tended to be continuous on weekends. I learned to sail in the "the Basin." One afternoon a photographer happened by just as I capsized. In the *Honolulu Advertiser* the next day, there I was in an embarrassing picture over the caption: "U.S. Navy Officer of the Deck Learning to Swim."

I arranged for my beautiful blue car to be shipped out, and I explored every part of Oahu. My favorite excursion was the Nuʻuanu Pali, where you drive a winding road to the volcanic ridge and suddenly before you, filling all your senses, are the magnificent greens of the mountains, dark blue of the ocean, and flawless blue of the skies. I was particularly awed by the Punchbowl, the National Memorial Cemetery of the Pacific, where white crosses fill a great green crater commemorating the lives lost at Pearl Harbor and during the war in the Pacific.

Probably because our "old salts" knew how to slow down shipyard work as well as speed it up, during my year in Hawaii the USS *Brister* went on only one DEW Line mission—to Kodiak, Alaska. But we had plenty of training runs, twice a week for months. I was thrilled being the gunnery officer in my crow's nest high in the superstructure, directing all the gun batteries and ASW. What fulfilled me the most, however, was being Officer of the Deck/Underway, especially on the mid-watch. At age twenty-four, two years out of college, I had a 2,400-ton warship and 250 lives under my command. Being Officer of the Deck at sea carries immense responsibility, but the zenith is smoothly bringing a ship in alongside a pier or another ship. You have to gauge the momentum so that the ship does not overshoot or embarrassingly die just short of "monkey-fist" throwing range. And there are a host of other challenges. Done correctly, you lay the ship in perfectly and everyone aboard the ship is proud because all eyes in a harbor are on a ship coming in. I had practiced so much in my mind that the first time Captain Young (who followed Captain Cote) said, "Mr. Vaughan, bring her in," I was able to lay her in perfectly. This won the confidence of Captain Young and the crew, as well as, most importantly, me. Getting it right this first time was invaluable.

My ultimate test came in the Pacific when our four-ship DER squadron was doing ship-handling drills. In this maneuver, we were to steam in a column, then the front DER would peel off to port or starboard, swing out and loop around and fall in behind the last DER. It may sound simple, but it requires precision timing, speed, and orders to the helmsman of exactly the right degree. The USS *Brister* was the last of the four DERs. I had the Conn (in Navy parlance, the one person who gives orders to the ship's helmsman [rudder] and engine room [speed] and stands in for the captain). When it was the USS *Brister*'s turn, I swung starboard, made the loop and was pleased to see that I had swung back into the column precisely correct. But something wasn't right. It flashed into my mind that we were closing far too fast on the ship ahead. The ship ahead was stopped! I went ice cold. My mind had complete clarity. I instantly said "right full rudder." We were going at twenty knots, so our "weigh-on" (momentum) carried us forward very rapidly. Our bow missed the stern of the ship ahead by less than two yards. A serious collision at sea had been averted.

The DER ahead of the USS *Brister* had gone dead in the water. When that happened, two "black balls" should have been raised as a distress signal, but that had not occurred either. My captain was in his chair on the wing of the bridge, and I had picked up the emergency and acted before he realized we were in peril. Captain Young was extremely happy because it only takes one collision to ruin a Navy career. There is a famous story about when Admiral Cat Brown ran the USS *New Jersey* aground. A nearby ship signaled "What are you going to do now?" Cat Brown immediately signaled back, "Buy a farm."

It was with this experience that I felt a unique, fleeting sensation that came from being in a highly responsible role, surrounded by exceptional cohorts, and our accomplishments outstanding. Once felt, it would never be forgotten. In the not-too-distant future, I would learn the perfect phrase to describe it.

Captain Young tried hard to get me to re-up as my three years ended June 30, 1958. I truly loved my life at sea. At one point I agreed to extend for one year, and the Captain recommended it, but regulations called for two years. I was lucky again. If I had extended for one year, I would have been tempted to stay because pay, prestige, and everything good would have happened in another year. I also was lucky that while there was global tension, my time in the Navy was a relatively peaceful period. Otherwise the *Brister* would have been on the first line of defense.

And even more good luck. As gunnery officer I had first pick among the fresh ensigns. John Stebbins ("Johnny Steb")—from Brooklyn!—won me over with his first smiling, "Hi ya, Gene." He was as kind as he was smart and made a wonderful officer—and lifelong friend. He married the daughter of a colonel, and together they produced "Pete" Stebbins who became an All-America soccer player at Clemson. Johnny passed away recently, and Pete, whose former teammate Jamey Rootes is president of the Houston Texans and recent chairman of the Greater Houston Partnership, came by our home for a deeply touching visit. Pete knew how close his father and I were.

I believe the best thing that happened to me in the Navy was being transferred to a second ship. First impressions are hard to erase, and on the USS *Ross* I could have stayed that green ensign a long time. But I went aboard the USS *Brister* with experience, molded brass, and confidence. Here I was the seasoned officer with command presence. I enjoyed being a responsible officer, learning to lead people effectively and—yes, maybe—commanding them around a bit. I began to feel a strong pull toward what I conceived as "business." I tried to fan the flames of medical school. At the University of Hawaii, I took music appreciation (for my humanity) and physics (for Maw-maw). As much as I hated not living up to the family dream of my being a doctor, that did not feel like the way my life was meant to unfold.

I took action focused on a future in business. I wrote the Chamber of Commerce of every sizable city in the mid-south and asked for their directory of companies, CEOs, and addresses. Next, I created a four-page brochure about myself. It included a picture of me in Navy Whites and crew-cut and listed my full credentials.

Then I mailed 2,000 of them.

I was seizing my future.

GENE VAUGHAN

In June I will be released from active duty by the Navy... During three years of commissioned service as a line officer, I have had much training and experience in administration of personnel and funds...With my military obligation completed, I want to channel this past experience into the field of management...I will not preclude any field which will offer challenging positions in publishing, public relations, or latitude for personal initiative and imagination...Here is what I have to offer...

Graduated June 1955 from Vanderbilt University with Bachelor of Arts degree...Completed pre-medical curriculum...Accepted by medical school but do not desire to continue after Navy service...Well based in chemistry, physics, biology, history, and political science...B average...Naval ROTC scholarship, augmented by Dean's Messenger job to earn 90% of total school expenses...Helped organize transition from dormitory monitor system to self-government and was elected first president of governing council of all men dormitories...Ranked 12th of 900 Navy ROTC and Naval Academy midshipmen in officer aptitude on senior summer training cruise...Two year member and Treasurer of executive cabinet of Student Christian Association, most active and largest organization on campus...Three year varsity track letterman...Three year officer of Sigma Alpha Epsilon social fraternity...Two year sport editor of campus newspaper

Education and Activities

High School

President of three classes and honor society. Three year varsity football letterman...Yearbook editor...Ranked number one man in scholarship...Voted "Most Outstanding Man"

LOCATION	SALARY	ELIGIBILITY
Favor mid-south but depends on opportunity	Open	Can begin job June 23, 1958

Would you hire this guy?

Navy Experience

Present rank Lieutenant (jg)...Graduate of Regular Naval ROTC program...Aboard destroyer USS ROSS one year as Anti-submarine Warfare Officer, in charge of thirty men, responsible for maintenance and effective use of sonar, torpedo, and fire control equipment...Volunteer editor of ship paper, recognized as the outstanding small ship paper of DesLant...Graduate ASW Officer and Gunnery Officer Schools...Was transferred in May 1956 to help place destroyer radar picket USS BRISTER in commission...Entailed complete organization and shakedown training of ship...Upon completion BRISTER operated out of Newport, R. I., as Early Warning Defense Line picket ship in Atlantic...In May 1957 became the Gunnery Department Head, in charge of two officers and fifty men...Primary duties include administration and coordination of two divisions, armament, anti-submarine ordnance, hull preservation, and management of funds allotted...Was one of select group offered instructor billet at Naval Academy but declined...In July 1957 BRISTER transfer to Pearl Harbor to assist establishment of similar Early Warning picket line across the Pacific necessitated the reorganization of department...Will be qualified as Executive Officer, second in command, in May

My good fortune to be transferred frequently to new places and challenging jobs during three years of shipboard service has afforded me excellent training as an administrator and organizer...The Navy presents an unsurpassed opportunity to develop skill in creating effective liaison between superiors and subordinates.

SHIP (Prior 15 May 1958)

USS BRISTER (DER 327)
Fleet Post Office
San Francisco, California

PERMANENT HOME

650 East Main
Brownsville
Tennessee

Civilian Employment

Made a two-month midshipmen cruise each college summer. After last two cruises measured cotton acreage, worked own hours sunrise to sunset averaging $20.00 per day...Previous summer work includes Tennessee Highway Department Junior Engineer, cutting right-of-way for TVA, and clerking in grocery store.

Personal Background

Single...5 feet 7...140 pounds...Excellent health...Age 24... Reared, attended elementary and high school in Brownsville, Tennessee, near Memphis...Father is postal supervisor, vice-president of medical clinic, Sunday School superintendant... Am active in sports, particularly golf and tennis...Enjoy writing, creatively and reporting...Have traveled with Navy in England, France, Italy, Portugal, Greece, Lebanon, Norway, Cuba, lived a minimum of two months in Key West, Florida; Charleston, South Carolina; Newport, Rhode Island; Norfolk, Virginia, and past year in Honolulu

I am eager to direct my enthusiasm and penchant for activity into a new career immediately upon release from active duty. If my qualifications fit your need, please write and describe how you think I can best be of help to you. If you are interested, let's set up a date to talk it over.

CHAPTER 7

Getting Down to Business

*Take time to deliberate, but when the time for action
has arrived, stop thinking and go in.*

—Napoleon Bonaparte

Flying from Honolulu to San Francisco, looking down at the flat solid clouds, I felt I was entering an unknown world. With five years of Reserves still to go, I mustered out of the active Navy in June 1958 on Treasure Island in San Francisco Bay. I took the long road home through Disneyland, Yosemite National Park, the Dakota Badlands, Mount Rushmore, and some of the beautiful ten thousand lakes of Minnesota. I followed the Mississippi River to Brownsville. It was great to be back, but no one could possibly understand what I had experienced. To my families I was the same Gene Vaughan who left. I looked the same, yet inside I was a totally different person with a completely new vision of my life.

Responses to my brochures had poured in by the dozens. In addition, the June crop of Vanderbilt graduates all had been placed, and Miss Ava Sellars, the superb woman who handled career placement at Vanderbilt, said she was making me her #1 prospect. The interviews and tests started. My anxiety eased somewhat when I missed only one question on my first qualifying test for Owens-Illinois Glass in Memphis, and they made me my first solid offer. Very early in the process I interviewed with IBM in both Nashville and Memphis and realized immediately this was a great company. The problem was they had filled all their places following graduation.

The really tough matter was Mam-maw. Her heart was still set on my going to medical school. She offered to pay my tuition anywhere if I would go to summer school and take medical courses to fan the embers back to life. I just could not say no to Mam-maw; I enrolled at Northwestern University. After several weeks of classes, I received a call from Bryce Ainslie, assistant manager of IBM in St. Louis. He extended an invitation to join the EDP (Electronic Data Processing) training program, but needed my answer the next day. I knew EDP salespeople were the "stars" of IBM. I immediately went to the bursar's office and found out that very day was the last day I could withdraw from summer school and still get half my tuition back. I took that as my sign of "Gideon's Wool" and never looked back. I called Bryce and was in St. Louis the next day. Mam-maw was really disappointed, but if she could only know how much I despise hospitals and the sight of blood, she would know how many lives were saved by my decision.

I loved IBM, and I loved the St. Louis Cardinals. Growing up in Brownsville, there were no major league baseball teams anywhere near us. The Cardinals were the southernmost and westernmost baseball team. I was a devotee of Harry Caray's pulsating: "It could be; it might be; it is—a HOME RUN!" And "Stan the Man Musial!" I took lodging with two older ladies on Vandeventer Avenue near IBM and alternated nights going to Sportsman's Park and playing canasta with my wonderful landlords.

IBM was dynamic, the most admired company in the world, and far beyond what I had imagined the business world could be. There were twenty in my training class and they all seemed brilliant. The course lasted for six months. We started by learning about elementary punch cards and later mastered the many world-famous IBM machines. IBM's newest and hottest break-through machine was the IBM 305 RAMAC. I studied especially hard for this exam because the new machine intrigued me. I was thrilled to make a perfect score!

An even greater triumph was just ahead. Mr. Pfansmidt, the St. Louis IBM general manager, called me into his office and said IBM just had made its biggest sale in history. The U.S. Air Force had seven commands, all using different accounting systems, and they wanted to unify them all on the IBM 305 RAMAC. I was appointed to serve on the five-person IBM Special Task Force to lead this conversion. He said all eyes at IBM were on this highest profile project. It was an amazing honor and opportunity. But I also knew something which nobody else remotely suspected: I had never had a course in accounting and barely knew a debit from a credit.

The "Elite Five," as we were dubbed, convened from all over the U.S. in Kansas City, where we would spend the next six months with select Air Force representatives. Each command sent an officer and an expert enlisted man, all with explicit instructions: (1) unify the accounting, and (2) make certain the system is the one at our command! I played my "junior" rank to the hilt, always deferring to my seniors and keeping my answers only to specifics about the 305 RAMAC. I was thinking hard all the time, lest I betray my vast ignorance in the one thing on which this task force was focused. The trickiest part was in the evenings and on weekends when we were together socially. Just as football players talk game small talk, these accounting experts wanted to talk mainly about the ins and outs of what they loved—accounting. Somehow I pulled it off. My hand was never called. Our Special Task Force received outstanding commendations from the top ranks of IBM.

However, I had one more major hurdle. Each of the five of us was assigned an Air Force Command to whom we had to teach both the new system and the 305 RAMAC. I was assigned Strategic Air Command (SAC) Headquarters near Omaha, headed by the legendary General Curtis LeMay. Now I was on my own for three weeks. On the first Monday, assembled before me were about thirty-five officers and enlisted men, the best of SAC. The first week was okay because I explained the new system and the intricacies of the complex 305 RAMAC, which I knew inside out by then. But from then on, hands were waving constantly, and I was the sole person to answer the questions. There was no side-stepping anything. These guys knew their stuff, and they still thought their SAC system was best.

I would stay up until 3 a.m. reading and thinking enough to stay ahead one more day, and at 6 a.m. I would skip breakfast and study more before the 8 a.m. class. I did not use jokes, but I had my "sea duty" and used just enough wit to get the class on my side. It always worked to kid the officers, and once word got around that I had been an Officer of the Deck/Underway in the U.S. Navy, that won the room. I do not know how I pulled it off, but with God's help I did.

Back in St. Louis, this member of the "Elite Five" was welcomed home as a hero, and I was ambitious to rise within IBM. However, something nagged at me: if I had not known something as basic as accounting, what else didn't I know? I had noticed that most of the top EDP salesmen and all of management had MBAs, most of them from Washington University in St. Louis. After asking my fellow IBMers for advice, I visited with the Washington University professor they recommended. The visit went well, and I told him I would sign up for the MBA course congruent with working at IBM. Then a career-changing exchange occurred. I was halfway out the door when he asked, "You didn't apply anywhere else?" I answered that I applied to Wharton. He said, "But you didn't get in?" I replied that I had been accepted. Then he asked, "Did you apply anywhere else?" I told him I applied to Harvard Business School. He asked, "But you didn't get in?" I said that I had been accepted. He said, "Gene, come sit down. We need to talk."

Harvard was my top choice, but I couldn't afford it. I wrote Harvard that I wanted to attend but needed financial aid. Incredibly, I was offered a J. Spencer Love Fellowship. J. Spencer Love, founder and chairman of Burlington Industries in North Carolina, credited Harvard Business School with his success. He loved the South and gave these outstanding J. Spencer Love Fellowships to Southerners, "not in obligation, but in the hope they would return and become leaders in the South." The Fellowship would not cover all my expenses, but it would be a critical help.

IBM was determined not to let me leave. I told them the absolute truth: I loved IBM and only wanted to get my MBA so I could do a better job for them. Dad thought I had lost my judgment. But, as always, we prayed about it, and Dad gave his blessings.

Meanwhile, my Vanderbilt roommate, Jack Caskey, had met a lovely girl, Sissy Rasberry, and I was invited to be a groomsman at their wedding in Shreveport. At the Friday night rehearsal dinner, I had scintillating cross-table conversation with a beautiful, auburn-haired Randolph-Macon student, whose sister worked for IBM. Fate was rearing her beautiful head. Susan Bolinger Westbrook, my future wife, was Sissy's neighbor and closest friend.

The stars that would light the rest of my life aligned that night.

CHAPTER 8

"The Visceral Feel of Entrepreneurial Greatness"

Mere survival is a so-so aspiration. Anybody can survive in one way or another. The trick is to survive gallantly, to feel the surging impulse of commercial mastery, not just to experience the sweet smell of success but to have the visceral feel of entrepreneurial greatness.

—Theodore Levitt, Editor, *Harvard Business Review,* and Harvard Business School Professor

With my car packed to the gunwales and having driven almost straight through from Brownsville to Boston to avoid leaving my filled car exposed at night, I had a flat tire about twenty miles from my destination. It is a good thing I do not overly believe in bad omens. It was pouring rain. I had to unpack my trunk to get my spare tire. Thus I arrived at Harvard Business School (HBS) in the fall of 1959 soaking wet and thoroughly subdued. At registration that day I was handed three thick cases to prepare for the next day's classes. Holy Cow! I moved into my room in Morris Hall and met my roommate, David Davies, an Englishman from Cambridge University.

Classes started the next morning, and the fear of God was struck into us when our professor, Richard Rosenblum, immediately cold-called the first person by name. He had memorized the application pictures. That set the pace. The first case lasted an hour and a half. A ten-minute break was followed by another chilling cold call and ninety minutes of case analysis. We did break for lunch, which was followed by the third case, another hour and a half. Then it was time to pick up the three cases for next day and start studying. I felt I was drowning.

THE FEEL OF ENTREPRENEURIAL GREATNESS

I had no idea what was going on. The thing is, nobody knew what was going on, but no one dared let on.

There were no lectures at Harvard. The case method was invented by HBS and Harvard Law School. In the foreword of my basic casebook were these words by Balzac, burnt into my memory, "It was the final, foolish hope of the dying man that he could pass along the accumulated wisdom of a lifetime to his only son. Alas, knowledge cannot be told."

Each case was twenty-five to forty pages. It was not that we did not have enough information. We were flooded with information, much of it irrelevant. I could see no obvious key to a case. There were 600 in my class, divided into six sections. During the cold-call response, ten to fifteen hands out of one hundred students per section would wave, each eager to shoot down what the previous speaker had said. I began to feel that I was back in the fourth grade. I prayed I would not be called upon. Every day was pure agony. We knew one of every six on average would flunk out. I was certain every student was smarter than I.

Intimidating! One section-mate from Atlanta was the son of the CEO of the largest bank. He grew up discussing capital budgeting theory like I did baseball scores. His biceps were like Popeye after a can of spinach. And he was highly articulate in an easy Southern way, e.g., the first week he referred to the CEO of a company as the "Daddy Rabbit." WOW. He was the real deal. His name is Jim Robinson, and early on he became CEO of American Express.

During Christmas break, I did not want to return to HBS. I'd just go back to IBM like they wanted. In the end, of course, pride made me return. Thanks to Coach Taylor, I was not a quitter. The second semester was again awful, but I was adapting. We had a study group of five which met at 11 p.m. At least the cases were beginning to make some sense to me, but my hand still never went up.

The dreaded WAC was worst of all—the "written analysis of cases." We were given Friday off to work on it, and it had to be typed and dropped in a chute by precisely 9 p.m. Saturday. They simply removed the "basket" at 9 p.m. Lines would form outside the chute to cheer on laggards. It became a ritual for my friends and me to drop our WAC down the chute about 8:45 p.m., join the last scene of terror, then walk the bridge across the Charles River and collapse joyfully in the Wursthaus just off Harvard Square. It was glorious beer, bratwurst, sauerkraut, laughter, and utter relief until 10:30 p.m. Then I would go to the newsstand in Harvard Square, buy a Sunday *New York Times,* return to the room and devour the *Times* until 2 in the morning. It was back to work Sunday afternoon.

During the first year, I took a very important, required complex course called financial controls, and near finals I knew I was in trouble. I asked for an appointment with Professor Neil Harlan. We talked a long while. He said, "Gene, ninety-nine percent of the time I tell my students they need to bear down. I have been watching you carefully. What you need to do is go fishing." We took a long walk together along the bank of the Charles River. I relaxed and scored well on the exam. Every time I drive by the Charles River part of my thoughts are on Neil's wisdom: "Go fishing." Neil and I stayed friends and communicated annually as long as he lived; he was an inspiring, honorable man in my career.

Mercifully, the school year ended. Forty percent of our study group (two of five!) were not invited back. I advanced to the next year with Theodore Levitt's words as my "burning bush." What I had tasted while saving the *Brister* from collision was, in Levitt's words, "the visceral feel of entrepreneurial greatness." That sense of something for which I did not have words in the Navy had pointed me toward the business world and on to Harvard.

After enduring a dreadful Boston winter, I wanted to work there in the summer because there had to be a reason so many smart people lived there. Through a series of friendship connections, I got an interview at Putnam Management Company and received their first-ever summer internship. I had no idea that this was to become a "transformational miracle" in my life. Putnam was pure magic. Product of an agrarian society, I hardly knew a dividend from a price/earnings ratio, yet now I was at the heart of one of the greatest money management firms in America. On my first day, George Putnam Jr. looked over my resume and said, "Vanderbilt! Sam Fleming's school!" I was off to a good start.

I was given a desk just outside the office of Walter Cabot. This serendipity was my best possible investment education. From 8:30 a.m. until 5 p.m., Walter was all Putnam, asking the blunt and incisive questions characteristic of the Cabots for time-honored generations. But I learned if I arrived early, Walter worked on his personal and family portfolios. It was phenomenal what I could learn. Walter's Uncle Paul, as treasurer, had put Harvard University into common stocks at the depth of the Depression. In Boston he is called simply "God." It is phenomenal that Walter, "God's nephew," and I began a close friendship that has spanned more than five decades.

To my enormous surprise, as a lowly summertime intern I was invited to every investment meeting at Putnam, including management meetings chaired by Charles Werly, Putnam's chairman and co-founder, and, even more incredible, to bi-weekly trustee meetings. Charlie Werly was a gentle, genuinely sweet man who had an uncanny feel for the market and stocks. That summer, between the trustees and the investment management team, I was exposed to a Mount Rushmore of investment executives.

And there was the remarkable Robert E. Riley. Bob Riley was Irish-Catholic, as far from "Boston Brahmin" as one can get. Bob was smart, really smart, a Harvard Business School graduate with no trace of Beacon Hill when Putnam hired him. I owe very much to the Putnam egalitarianism because it was Bob Riley who hired me for the summer of 1960 and full time upon my graduation in 1961. After my internship, I never had a moment's doubt that this was the profession for me. I couldn't wait to get back to Putnam and my new profession.

During my second year at HBS, I gained invaluable new insight into myself. The first week in the class of Dr. Sterling Livingston, one of HBS' most eminent senior professors, he passed out questionnaires without explanation. Three weeks later he introduced the psychologist/ author who carefully scanned the amphitheater of students and then stated, "There is a most remarkable person here who is so goal-oriented, persevering, and tenacious that if he missed his turn-off on the Los Angeles Expressway he would consider backing up. Will Gene Vaughan please stand up?" There was incredulity on the faces of many. I was a bit taken aback myself! But I also felt I now had permission for a boldness that I had sensed was inside to start to rise to the surface.

A couple of weeks later Dr. Livingston cold-called me. After five minutes, hands were waving everywhere. After ten minutes, only a few hands remained. After fifteen minutes, Dr. Livingston sat down. Later I was told I "opened" the case an unheard-of twenty-five minutes, after which Dr. Livingston then stood up and said, "I have only one question. Do you always prepare this thoroughly?" I said I did.

A lot of students gamed the case system. They would prepare only one of the three cases very thoroughly. During that one case they waved furiously to make certain they spoke, reducing the odds they would be cold-called later. I prepared every case every day very thoroughly. I knew I could game the system, but felt that would be a big mistake. I was paying a big price to be at this exhilarating school, and I wanted to learn all I possibly could.

During Christmas break, I had dinner with Jack and Sissy Caskey in Memphis. Sissy persisted (and it felt a bit awkward since I had a date with me) that I call her dear friend Susan Bolinger Westbrook, who had moved to Cambridge after graduation for a job editing publications for the head of Harvard's engineering school. (That was quite a bold move for a Shreveport girl—not many left the South.) I did not remember exactly who Susan was—in my mind I had her mixed up with another girl—but I promised, just to change the subject. I did not make that call until Valentine's Day 1961. The celebrated economist Dr. John Kenneth Galbraith was lecturing at Harvard University that night. I called Susan about 4 p.m. She was out, so I asked her roommate to go instead. Smooth! When we returned to their house on Chauncey Street, Susan opened the door. Susan! How could I have confused her with someone else? Standing in front of me was the beautiful Randolph-Macon girl who had captivated me with her wit and conversation at Jack and Sissy's rehearsal dinner. (Thank you, Sissy, for insisting I make that call!) Our eyes locked, and that was it for me. I guess her roommate just disappeared. Time evaporated while Susan and I talked rapturously, and then we lingered by the door holding hands. She told me she was leaving in six weeks for a long-planned, four-month trip to Europe and would not be returning to Boston. She promised her family that after her time in Boston and her European venture, she would return to Shreveport for at least one year.

Not surprisingly, Susan's dance card was filled the rest of that week and nearly full for the weeks preceding her departure. But there was something magical between us, and I was determined to see her as often as possible. I remember standing in my Cullen Hall room looking out at the Charles River and talking with Susan on the phone. I was laughing out loud. I thought Susan was the funniest and most delightful girl I had ever met. Then came Enchanted Sunday! We went to Harvard's Memorial Chapel to hear Dr. George Buttrick, among the foremost preachers of the times. And full of joy, we visited the very beginnings of America at Lexington and Concord, lingering at the "rude bridge." It is now somewhat vague to both of us, but we remember eating at the Colonial Inn in Concord—for several hours. We had no inkling of time. Love was happening!

Despite the stern rules prohibiting missing classes, I offered to take Susan to New York for her ship's departure. We managed to see a play, take a horse-drawn hansom carriage drive through Central Park, and watch the city-that-never-sleeps close down. At the dock, after I saw Susan waving to me from the top rail, I felt at peace. When the *Leonardo da Vinci* hove out of sight, I sent a Marconigram saying, "Susan, I love you!"

I drove back to Harvard to face the music. The music started immediately. Slipped under my door on official stationery was:

Mr. Vaughan, as you do not see me in class, please do me the courtesy of visiting me in my office at 2 p.m.
—Charles E. Bliss, Professor

Professor Charlie Bliss was one of the best. He was serious about kicking me out of school. Even in April of my second year, he had no tolerance for missing classes. I had missed two while taking Susan to New York (worth it!). We settled on my doing two extra white papers for him. While everyone else was basking in the spring sun and taking recruiting trips during the final weeks, I was writing excruciatingly complex papers for Professor Bliss. Worse, he was a personal friend of Charlie Werly and was incensed that his good friend was hiring an unserious "loser." I thought several times I saw a twinkle in his eye, but I diligently completed the papers.

That spring, Dr. Livingston invited me to be his associate the following year. This was an exceedingly high, one-of-a-kind honor. I already had accepted a position at Putnam, but the invitation from Dr. Livingston always has meant very much to me. IBM also offered me a position as an "elite" EDP salesman, with outstanding compensation, and applied almost irresistible pressure. However, I had turned down their kind offer to pay part of my HBS expenses just so I would not feel obligated to return. It was all very gracious. I had fallen so in love with investing that when Putnam offered me a full-time job, I did not ask how much they would pay me. My faith was rewarded when they paid me the average annual starting salary of an HBS graduate—$7,500— which translates to a current value of approximately $61,000.

It was clear to me that if you learn the core lessons that HBS teaches, you do not want to perform a <u>function</u> in a large corporation. You are taught how to <u>lead</u> a company. And if you really learn the foremost lessons of HBS, you want to be an entrepreneur, become a <u>founder</u>, a word that would resonate with me for life.

The colorful economist Pierre Rinfret put it more bluntly in an article: "If you have any wit or guts, what you want to do is implement your own g—— d—— ideas." Those words burrowed deep inside me.

During December of our second year, HBS gave us three days off and encouraged us to think exhaustively and draft a master plan for our careers. The essence was that I wanted an entrepreneurial career, my own company. I recognized that to reach this goal I lacked three essential things: experience, reputation, and money. My plan laid out how to achieve these three and a timeframe for doing so. In part, my plan stated: "It would be in a field in which I was proficient—either finance or marketing, preferably both. I must be convinced it would be of service to the country and to humanity in general. I do not expect my business to be my chief or sole interest; rather I intend it to be a base from which I promote causes in which I believe, e.g., service to my community."

Amazingly, just before my twenty-fifth HBS reunion, Susan, while looking for something else, found my "EHV Career Strategy Plan." Having long since forgotten about it, I was gratified to see I had followed my multi-phased plan faithfully and was a couple of years ahead of schedule.

I left Harvard Business School with more than an outstanding education, great knowledge derived experientially (often painfully) via cases, and a strategic plan. I also left with lifelong friends. Our "Section C" at Harvard Business School has stayed an especially close group because of Joel Schiavone. My 82 Revere Street roommate has shepherded us all with his enormous love and wit. While at HBS Joel learned a "trade"—playing the banjo! During the two years I lived with him in his Beacon Hill five-story house, Joel launched "Your Father's Mustache," a beer and banjo place that became instantly popular. Eventually he owned seven throughout the U.S. and played three times at the White House.

In 1986, Susan and I attended my twenty-fifth reunion at Harvard Business School. HBS went all out to make their reunions memorable mixtures of advanced learning and peerless fun. "The Fabulous Class of '61" was especially celebrated and honored throughout HBS-Land because our class leader, "secretary" Joel Schiavone, was the best known and best liked personality, arguably, in the history of HBS. In the HBS *Bulletin,* Joel writes hilarious, irreverent notes, especially for our own Section C. On the climactic final night, the tuxedoed '61 audience packed Memorial Hall, with Joel the major-domo in white tie and tails. I was among the earliest to be called to the stage. Joel made some typically pithy, scathingly laudatory remarks about me and hugged me. As I put my arm around Joel's shoulder I felt nothing but clammy back. I quickly realized I was in on the joke. As his penultimate act, Joel lavished praise on "the Fabulous Class." With that, his "ultimate" act was to turn his back and moon the entire audience! The legend lives on. We had so much fun, Joel-style.

Tom Broadus was a very special friend, a fellow Tennessean, from Knoxville, and brilliant. Tom's father had been #1 in his class at HBS. The first time I went into a Brooks Brothers store was with Tom in Boston. I could hardly believe people paid such prices. Tom invariably sat on the front row wearing a Brooks Brothers suit and tie with white athletic socks. I told Tom only a yo-yo would wear white socks with a suit. He liked that and quoted it a lot, but kept on wearing white socks. I was a groomsman when Tom and Libby married, and after Susan and I married the four of us became great friends. Another HBS couple Susan and I have enjoyed immensely is Dan and Dottie Blitch, of Athens, Georgia. Dottie followed Susan at Randolph-Macon, and when she found out we were dating, she excitedly exclaimed, "AM SAM!" This meant Susan had been invited to join the most honored and secret society on campus. Dan and Dottie asked us to go to Maine with them before our fiftieth HBS Reunion in 2011, and we laughed continuously; that says it all.

Over the four months Susan was abroad, we got to know each other even better through our writing. I had her itinerary so my letters reached her at every stop. I also sent her $10 worth of flowers with a note, "Don't eat the daisies!" Susan wrote that the flowers "filled" her room in Copenhagen. Susan's letters were beautiful; they captured her intelligence, grace, and wit. I'd run to the campus post office after my first class and for eight minutes sit under my favorite tree by the Charles River and read her letter. I fell deeper in love.

After my graduation from HBS in 1961, Susan returned to America. I met Susan's ship, and despite my having secured tickets to the hottest show on Broadway, we flew directly to New Orleans. Susan and I looked into each other's eyes and held hands the entire trip. Susan's family resided in Shreveport, Louisiana. Sadly, I never got to meet Susan's father, Charles Howard Westbrook Jr., who had passed away at age thirty-seven. Outstandingly beautiful and gracious, Susan's mother, Audrey Bolinger Westbrook, was a very special lady. She received her bachelor of arts degree with a major in mathematics from Randolph-Macon Women's College and was Phi Beta Kappa. Audrey took courses in accounting and oil and gas law and was deeply involved in the management of her family's business interests, including farming and timber. I remember being in her library and pulling a book by Dr. John W. Gardner, founder of Common Cause and distinguished professor at Stanford, and looking at the passages Audrey had highlighted. What a wonderful way to get to know my mother-in-law and meet the lifetime-inspiring Dr. Gardner.

Through Audrey, our family's roots are tied to Bollinger Champagne, a renowned champagne producer since 1829 and considered the elite champagne along with Krug. Bollinger is what James Bond, 007, drank. Naturally, a bottle (or several!) of Bollinger is present at every family special event. Similar to "Vaughan" and Vaughn," "Bollinger" and "Bolinger" are spelled differently in Europe and the U.S. Madame

Both Susan and Richard carry on the Bolinger name. We certainly enjoyed our "family" visits at Bollinger headquarters at Ay in the Champagne region of France. We have truly tested Bollinger—it is the best!

Lily Bollinger ran the estate from 1941 to 1971 and was famous. Her affection for Bollinger was often quoted:

> I drink my Champagne when I'm happy and when I'm sad.
> Sometimes I drink it when I'm alone.
> When I have company I consider it obligatory.
> I trifle with it if I'm not hungry and drink it when I am.
> Otherwise I never touch it—unless I'm thirsty.

And then there was Susan's amazing grandmother, Bum Bum, the fabulous matriarch who "ran the family" while Audrey "ran the business." Bum Bum read the *Wall Street Journal* every day and loved, she said, talking business with me. How fortunate for me that Susan grew up with business talk at the dinner table. One of the foremost regrets of my life is that the beloved head of the family and admired business leader, Susan's grandfather, John Corbin Bolinger, had died at age seventy-seven.

Susan's first cousin, Betty, married Clarence Frierson, who was the first male entering a family of very strong females after the sad death of Granddaddy Bolinger. Clarence set high standards for all things good; he took me under his wing, and I really took to him. We spent many enjoyable times together over the years—hunting quail on the banks of the Red River, celebrating enormous "Bolinger Christmas" gift exchanges with the entire family, and, as his family grew to four boys, engaging in football rivalries and spirited football games in the Frierson's big front yard. Clarence was like a big brother to me, whether serving on business boards together or engaging in marvelous, self-deprecating kidding. The Frierson "Boys" all grew up to be as admirable and staunch as Clarence and Betty, now deceased. The "Boys" and their wives are stalwart members of the Shreveport community. We rejoice that they, Susan, and I and our children remain close.

CHAPTER 9

Putnam Transforms My Career;
Susan Transforms My Life

Wheresoever you go, go with all your heart.

—Confucius

When I started full time at Putnam in September 1961, one of two hired, there was no authentic research anywhere, just statistical information. I was assigned airlines, railroads, and trucking, basically because they were the dregs and no one else wanted them; however, that turned out to be a big break for me.

As an embryonic research analyst at Putnam, I invented a technique akin to letting me take pictures of the "inside" of a company. I learned to take comprehensive notes on all research interviews with key company executives. By studying a series of them taken over time, a mosaic often emerged revealing a completely different picture from the snapshots upon which market prices were usually based. By April 1962 I had visited the top managements of every airline, and everyone believed the outlook was dismal. I projected the industry would lose a collective $31 million that year, and that day was planning on writing a negative report on the airline industry. Then, while shaving, it hit me that all the airlines had been adding a large number of planes. Yet I knew passenger-miles-flown had been increasing at a strong ten percent annually. Of course! Check when the new plane deliveries would stop because that would take the downward pressure off load factor. I walked quickly over Beacon Hill, past the Golden Dome of the State House, to 60 Congress Street, where Putnam occupied the two top floors. I became increasingly excited as the implications for earnings hit me. Things were beginning to click inside my mind. As I checked, I held my breath. Sure enough, plane deliveries already had stopped in the past two months. Stop expanding seat capacity and continue ten percent passenger growth, which equals huge increases in earnings per share.

I was thrilled, but I could not quite believe it. I was a neophyte analyst. Why did nobody else see this? What was I missing? I rapidly wrote my analysis and recommendation to purchase Delta and Eastern, but something bumped their prices two days before the trustee meeting, and instead I recommended Putnam purchase Pan American and Northwest. I told the trustees something must be wrong with my calculations, however, because the stocks were so cheap and everyone so pessimistic. Dr. Vannevar Bush tousled my hair and said, "By God, we have a real analyst!"

Dr. Bush, trustee of Putnam, was one of the most significant people in my life. Many historians say America would not have won WWII without Dr. Bush's scientific and organizational genius. It is averred that had his momentous inventions and discoveries occurred during peacetime instead of wartime, he would rank equal to or above Thomas Edison and Alexander Graham Bell. After the war, he served as chairman of Merck at its height and was considered the foremost graduate of MIT. Just to be in the presence of such a man, much less for him to like and believe in me, has been a lifetime inspiration.

After my airline presentation, we loaded up on the stocks. I had gut-gripping qualms when I learned from our head trader that the last big block of Pan American was bought from Fidelity across the street. Within a month, a *Business Week* cover showed a plane soaring out of storm clouds into a completely blue sky. All the airline stocks went crazy. My only mistake was that I should have bought them all, especially Delta, because it was the best of the bunch. It was thrilling to have the Putnam partners congratulate me. Mr. Werly invited me into his office—a recognized high honor—and told me I had done a tremendous piece of analysis to catch an entire industry turnaround. Actually, what I felt was relief because I had been there several months without making a recommendation.

My next big recommendation was in the emerging air freight industry: Emery Air Freight, before Federal Express and facsimile existed. (By then Susan and I were married and, with permission, together we interviewed John Emery, and she helped me write the report—she is an amazing partner in every capacity.) We made <u>many</u> times on this investment, even more than the <u>several</u> times on the airlines I recommended. After a slow start, I was establishing a reputation.

The Monday after President Kennedy was assassinated on November 22, 1963, America was "Closed," as a sign read on the door of a tailor's shop in Philadelphia, "for a death in the family." Mr. Werly called an emergency meeting of trustees and the investment team. Everyone was there, squeezed into the boardroom. The more junior people ringed the room, sitting in chairs with our backs against the wainscoting. Mr. Werly posed the question of overriding importance: What should Putnam do when the market opened on Tuesday morning—buy or sell? The debate was polemic and brilliantly articulated. Some argued that America had lost the leader of the nation and that the markets would be chaotic; the "first sale" on Tuesday would be the "best" sale. The arguments raged on. There were at least a dozen of the best investment minds in America around the table. I recall the powerful persuasion with which the opposing points were made. As a neophyte, I was persuaded from one side to the other. Mr. Werly presided coolly and brilliantly and seldom let any acrimony creep into the fierce debate, but voices were raised in exasperation as these highly intelligent men disagreed. They knew the peril to Putnam of being wrong.

Gradually it became evident that Mr. Werly believed the market would be positive. He gently sided with the arguments that JFK had taken action against the steel companies and felt Lyndon Johnson, as a very successful businessman himself, would be pro-business and that the market would read it that way. These were dramatic hours. Now that "BUY" was the on-balance, clear decision, the meeting turned to what to buy. No one had brought a list of current prices after the market had crashed on Friday. I spoke up and said I had Sunday's *New York Times* at home and could get it and be back in fifteen minutes. I had spent Sunday afternoon going over the NYSE listings in the *Times*, marking the stocks that seemed to me to be beaten down beyond reason and stocks I thought Putnam should buy. I handed the newspaper to Mr. Werly. He looked it over carefully and said, "Let's just use Gene's buying list." It was one of life's best moments for me.

Over the years I frequently have reflected on that Monday meeting as a dramatic indication of just how very tough is the profession of investment management. On Tuesday following JFK's assassination the market rose significantly. Yet, it was a long-debated, on-balance decision for a roomful of the smartest investors in America. When I chastise myself for not always being right in the markets, that JFK Monday debate helps me keep things in perspective.

Invitations poured in for Putnam to speak at clubs and organizations as mutual funds were born in Boston and Putnam Growth Fund was the best-performing fund in America. The partners passed the invitations to me, the junior man. I was soon introduced to "green lacrosse." In the midst of an earnest speech at a Kiwanis dinner I saw a "green flash." My audience had developed remarkable dexterity in using spoons to flip green peas to each other! It was easy to stay humble.

Speeches were a minor type of professional challenge. A different type of professional test, a very severe one, had come for me very suddenly in late 1961. Putnam partners had valuable sources in Wall Street brokerage firms. One week, compelling recommendations came from several creditable sources on E. L. Bruce Company, a stodgy, old flooring company that had been seized in a hostile takeover by a group headed by Eddie Gilbert and was undergoing major changes. Gilbert, 37, was a charismatic darling of New York cafe society whom the media dubbed "the boy wonder of Wall Street." The company was based in Memphis, so the partners decided to send me to do the research. They wanted me to go immediately because the stock was "moving." My research modus operandi then and throughout my career was to learn everything I possibly could in advance from written material and, once on site, to visit privately with four or five key members of management. Discerning different points of view was invaluable. The short time and lack of written information and the fact that Eddie Gilbert was not in Memphis at this time made my job far more difficult.

Like a lawyer picks a jury, I decided whom I wanted to interview, and, like a private investigator, I decided in what order. Of overriding importance to my process—then and throughout my career—was determining the <u>critical</u> <u>variables</u>. What were the five or so variables that made all the difference? Everything else was mostly "rabbit trails." In the case of E. L. Bruce, by the time I left after a full day of questioning five top executives, my "mosaic" was clear. I knew I did not want to recommend it to Putnam. The wrath of Wall Street descended on me. The brokers howled, "He's just a novice. You're missing a great stock. Send one of your senior people to Memphis." Putnam stood behind me.

It was front page news across the nation five months later, during the spring of 1962, when the market crashed and Eddie Gilbert absconded to Brazil taking $2 million from the E. L. Bruce till with him. He went to Sing Sing for fraud and larceny. I had done authoritative, in-depth research to get to the core of the facts and had the courage to stand up to the barrage of ridicule from the Wall Street brokers. I was a slow analyst, meticulous, and I did not make many recommendations. But when I did, they paid off in various ways. What I learned is that to be an outstanding investment professional, one needs to combine deep-digging, authentic, fundamental research with a warning instinct when things are not right. Courage to stand against the crowd is vital.

The early 1960s was more than just a time of transformation in my career; more important, my life was transforming through my relationship with Susan. True to her word to her family, Susan had returned to Shreveport for twelve months. The telephone bills proved it was too expensive for us to live in different cities, and we missed each other terribly. In 1962, Susan got a marvelous job as art editor at the distinguished textbook publisher Ginn and Company and moved back to Boston. It was wonderful to be together, to spend time with friends, and explore New England. We had fun all the time.

Of paramount importance to our life in Boston was John Poindexter. John took Susan and me under his wing and showered us with attention, support, and love. He infused me with his incomparable love of Vanderbilt. That John Poindexter, the nonpareil editor of the prestigious Houghton-Mifflin book publishing company, came from Mason, Tennessee—home of Bozo's Bar-B-Q—seemed a miracle conceivable only by God. We had a cherished friendship that spanned fifty years. I consider John my single greatest lifetime friend. I took his advice, zest, and passion for learning with me every step of the way.

Strange but true, all the time Susan and I were dating, the subject of getting married never came up or at least never came into focus. My heart assumed it would happen, but I wanted to be earning more money. Yet one Saturday afternoon in late 1962 while we were at Stop & Shop, using my plastic counter to keep track of the grocery bill, suddenly in my head a timetable developed. I should already have acted! Totally uncharacteristic of me, who likes to have everything perfectly planned and staged, I turned to Susan when we were back in my kitchen and said, "Susan, I love you. Will you marry me?" We were holding sacks of groceries. No kneeling, no romantic prose. Sudden joy filled us both! We called our families but asked them to keep it quiet so we could break the news to the wider family and friends when we came home for Christmas.

In addition to planning a wedding, we needed to find a place for us to live. We started our hunt, which at first was painful; what we could afford was small and ugly and offered no view. Then we struck gold at 75 Beacon Street, an apartment at the back of the second floor of the residence of Oliver Wendell Holmes Sr., the eminent nineteenth century writer (*Autocrat of the Breakfast Table*) and physician. Our entire apartment had been his cozy study, including the fireplace. It was small, but what character and charm. And the price: $125 a month! We fell in love with it. I installed pegboard in the "Tom Thumb" kitchen while my bride-to-be marveled at how dexterous a carpenter I was. We made a stand for books out of bricks and five planks.

My big mission was to find the perfect engagement ring. We looked at stones through a diamond scope at Shreve, Crump & Low in Boston—no luck, either too expensive, looked like a cracked mirror, or both. Upon return to Boston after spending Christmas in Shreveport, on the first day back when we met for lunch, we were standing at the corner of Tremont and Park, five blocks from our new home. I looked up and there was Trefry & Partridge, a 200-year-old Boston jeweler. Susan and I went in, asked for a diamond scope, and within a half-hour we had selected a gorgeous engagement ring—not big, but perfect!

The first week in May 1963 I drove to Shreveport in my second-hand Mercedes 180. By saving on plane fare, I had more money for our honeymoon. As I was driving down Line Avenue, calamity struck. I was driving slowly in the inside lane of the wide street and slowed further as I saw an elderly man crossing the street. I was at a full stop when he walked into my car. The offices lining the street were filled with people who suddenly evaporated except for a couple who helped me get the gentleman to a nearby hospital. I could find no one willing to be a witness. I stood convicted by my black car with a maroon Massachusetts license plate. When I went to see the gentleman the next day, he was asleep, but his wife and son informed me they were suing me, and they had witnesses. They would take every cent from "you !*!*! Yankee."

I could use the Bolinger family lawyers, but this would be a dreadful way to enter a marriage. I went to visit the gentleman again. When his wife started threatening me, he sat up and said, "This young man had nothing to do with it. I wasn't paying attention and I walked right into his car." He signed a statement, and it is only a memory now. Except for an honest man, my life could be very different.

The rehearsal dinner at the Shreveport Club, where Susan and I had met four years earlier, was marvelous. On May 11 we held our wedding ceremony at First Presbyterian Church of Shreveport. Dad and I had a tender moment, he saying how much Mother would like to be here and that she was. Rev. Benny Benfield, who had counseled us we were "entering a house with no doors and no windows," performed the ceremony. Everyone was thrilled we had found each other, in Boston of all places.

Then it was off to our honeymoon. The Grand Hotel at Point Clear on Mobile Bay is totally genteel, the Gulf Coast version of The Cloister at Sea Island, Georgia. Every member of the staff knows your name, and whenever you appear, your preferred drink is placed in your hand. We went sailing and played golf, and Susan picked up enormous pine cones, some of which we still have in our fireplaces. Perfect!

We followed the beautiful Blue Ridge Drive on the way back to Boston and our new home. Along the way we stopped at Camp Merri-Mac for me to be "inspected" by Macky, the founder of Susan's summer camp that molded her over fifteen summers. Bum Bum had given us a

Susan and I were already soul mates and consummate friends when we married.

full chest of silver; it was so precious that I carried it inside our cabin every night. It was that or sleep in the car! In Boston, our work was meaningful, our friendships warm; we were thoroughly happy. New England was paradise for Susan and me. The most special place was "Lobster Cove," the gorgeous home and grounds where George Putnam Jr. hosted the firm several times.

We went antiquing in Maine in the spring and spent summer weekends on Nantucket, utterly charmed. We had numerous favorite places. Among the best, we loved Tanglewood, the summer home of The Boston Symphony in the Berkshires, where we would spread a blanket and look at the stars while listening to the ethereal music.

One wintry evening, out our rear window, we saw a little boy pull his sleigh up a pile of dirty slush and then slide down it. It was in that moment that Susan, watching the child, made it very clear to me that if we were to have babies, they were going to be born in the South!

The "Newlyweds" in front of 75 Beacon Street. Oh, how we loved our beautiful, tiny apartment. The Boston Public Gardens were our *front yard!* We learned to ice skate at night on the Swan Pond. We wondered if *anyone* had ever been as in love or as fortunate as we. Our second-hand Mercedes 180 had red leather seats and air conditioning, affording us in the summer the pleasure of driving around before entering our hot apartment!

CHAPTER 10

DLJ of the South

The vitality of thought is an adventure. Ideas won't keep.
Something must be done about them.
When the idea is new, its custodians have
fervor, live for it, and if need be, die for it.

—Alfred North Whitehead,
mathematician and philosopher

In 1960, three Harvard Business School graduates—Dan Lufkin, Bill Donaldson, and Dick Jenrette—reinvented Wall Street research. Putnam was Donaldson, Lufkin, and Jenrette's (DLJ) first institutional client. DLJ's revolutionary in-depth research was soon followed by New York–based Baker, Weeks and Company and by Faulkner, Dawkins & Sullivan. But there were no in-depth research sources in the rest of the U.S. The idea of a regional DLJ began to build in my mind.

The 1960s marked the second decade of the Financial Analysts Federation (FAF), and an enterprising group of Houston investment bankers organized the 1964 FAF conference in their city. Putnam sent me. Held at the famous Shamrock Hotel, it was a splendid conference and put Houston on the investment map. To this day I run into attendees who are still awed by the Shamrock pool, so huge that a motorboat pulled water-skiers three abreast. On behalf of Putnam to promote our mutual funds, as was customary, I called on local brokerage firms, including Underwood Neuhaus.

Back at the office in Boston, I thanked Bob Riley for rewarding me with the FAF conference in Houston. Bob looked up with a puzzled expression, "Reward? Houston? If I wanted to reward you, I sure as hell would not have sent you to Houston!" But I loved Houston. The city was vibrant. There was "can do" in the air, and every person I met was so proud of Houston and happy to be there.

A few weeks later, Phil Neuhaus, of Underwood Neuhaus, called and asked if I would have lunch with him at the St. Regis Hotel in New York. Our lunch lasted until 4 p.m. He asked me to join his firm, founded in 1907 by his father, Baron Neuhaus. The offer was to head research, and by that he meant retail research. I told him I had no interest but gradually described the in-depth research I was doing for Putnam. For three years I had been conducting Putnam-quality in-depth research throughout the U.S. and had found institutional-quality research nowhere outside the East. I shared my vision of forming a cutting-edge institutional research team in the Southwest. For another couple of hours I talked about what would be needed in terms of quality analysts and dedicated salesmen.

Phil got excited. A few weeks later, his firm paid for Susan and me to travel to Houston. Our first evening, Susan and I were hosted by brothers Joe and Phil Neuhaus and their wives at the Bayou Club, the city's most exclusive private club. The only adornment in the main dining room was a portrait above the fireplace of Baron Neuhaus (looking quite stern), founder of the Club. They served crème brûlée for dessert, and Susan adored it. Ever since, she claims the reason we moved to Houston was for that crème brûlée! The next day I spent time with Phil and Joe as well as the firm's chairman Milton Underwood, a graduate of Vanderbilt Law School. They seemed to understand the concept of institutional research and that a significant investment would be involved. We negotiated and agreed on a salary and a piece of institutional profits. Very important, I got some ownership—not much, but the principle of being an owner was extremely significant to me. Moreover, I would be one of the seven directors of Underwood Neuhaus, one of only three non-family members and the only non-salesman. I did have a nagging concern: there already was a head of research at the firm, whom I did not get to meet despite several requests, but I was assured repeatedly he would not be a problem.

Putnam went all out to keep me. They understood our desire to be in the South to raise our family. The partners offered for me to select the city and they would establish a roaming research team around me. That had lots of appeal, but it did not fit in the strategic plan I envisioned for our future. When I left, Putnam held a luncheon in a prestigious private club in my honor. Horace Nichols, who always had been incredibly nice to me and was my investment mentor, handed me a bottle of Southern Comfort. Walter Cabot, who had served in the U.S. Army in Alabama and despised it, broke everyone up with his heartfelt, "You'll need it!" I have saved that bottle over the years, to be shared only by Putnam people. The brilliant Ted Lyman, who like George Putnam Jr. was a Baker Scholar at HBS, stood and said, "Gene, we want to give you some Northern Comfort as well" and handed me a large check. I was deeply moved. I was the first person ever to resign from Putnam.

Susan and I moved to Houston in August 1964. Moving to Houston in that sweltering heat is proof that our family does things the hard way. In the Navy, the USS *Brister* had a tongue-in-cheek insignia: a mighty arm rising out of a stormy sea, powerfully thrusting a sword skyward. The hand was grasping the sword by the blade, and blood was streaming down the arm. The ship's motto was "VIA NOSTRA DURA EST!" very loosely translated from Latin as "We do things the hard way!" Susan and I adopted this for our family crest. How fitting it has been!

In spite of the heat, we loved Houston from the start. Our new home on South Post Oak Lane took our breath away. We had watched emotionally as North American Van Lines (another of my successful recommendations to Putnam) drove away from our beloved 75 Beacon Street apartment, knowing all the ties we were leaving behind. But now we were moving into this paradise that looked out into a gorgeous virgin forest, with swimming pool, all for $170 per month. We could hardly believe our good fortune! The unit we most wanted was not available, and our two movers had virtually completed our move when the apartment owner told us our original choice had just become available. The senior mover laughed, "Charlie there, he don't see the humor in this!" This has become a wonderful catchphrase in our family! I made Charlie happier, and then we were looking into primeval forest. We named our new home the Bird's Nest and the woods into which we looked the Enchanted Forest. Houston embraces newcomers. We were welcomed with many invitations.

The big issue was the firm's former head of research, whom I had been assured would not be a problem. He was a <u>huge</u> problem! Things came to a head soon after my arrival when we were at odds over a recommendation he loudly made to buy a local company "on the move." My analysis was negative, and I refused to approve his report on Westec Corporation. Other brokerage firms were selling loads of the stock, as Phil Neuhaus regularly reminded me. My predicament was serious. I had just moved across the county and was the new guy. One Sunday morning before church, my "antagonist" called me at home and told me he would give me "one last chance" to change my mind before some big news was announced. He said he had met with James Williams, the chairman, that morning and was given "the scoop." I went to church and prayed hard for the Lord's guidance. That afternoon it became clear to me that I was a professionally trained research analyst, and if I was going down, I was going as a professional. I told Phil Neuhaus on Monday morning I would not approve the recommendation. Phil was not happy then, but he was very happy a few weeks later when that company was revealed as a sham. Chairman Williams was sentenced to fifteen years for manipulation and fraud. Other Westec officers and numerous Houston brokers and firms were fined. At a firm-wide meeting I was hailed as a hero who had "saved" Underwood Neuhaus while almost every other firm in Houston lost huge money and reputation. I thanked God for my research training <u>and</u> tenacity.

Soon I had a major break because Bob Grainger, an outstanding Underwood Neuhaus broker, had befriended Susan and me early, and Bob was good friends with Bob Allen, the CEO of Gulf Sulphur. Most sulphur companies are headquartered in the Southwest, and I had decided to make myself the most knowledgeable person in the investment industry on them. Bob Allen asked if I would like to visit the Gulf Sulphur operation in the Yucatan. Would I! The three of us flew down on the corporate plane and in three hours were in another world. By private boat we went up a jungle river. It seemed prehistoric. "Mexican Eagles" (buzzards) perched atop thatched huts. Half-naked women scrubbed clothes on stones in the river. Four miles away we knew we were near the Frasch-method sulphur plants. Anyone who ever has had a chemistry set knows what a stench there was. It was a great learning trip.

Another company, Freeport Sulphur, was a lot more complex because it had many operations and products to master. Their top management in New Orleans went all out to open the company to me. I produced in-depth research reports on each of the companies, including Pan American Sulphur, and our retail brokers sold sulphur. Our small institutional sales force put Freeport Sulphur in many major funds in America. Some moments linger forever. At a lunch in the Presidents' Room at the Houston Club with just Mr. Underwood and Joe and Phil Neuhaus, a prominent money manager said, "Reading Gene's Freeport report was like reading history in advance." Wow! I was impressed and so were they! Freeport was a large, high-quality company and, unlike some of its competitors, had no operations in Mexico. When the Mexican government suddenly took fifty percent ownership ("Mexicanization") of sulphur operations located in their country, Freeport's stock soared. It was a huge boost for our investment team.

A year-end project I started was to calculate individual performances of all listed Houston-area stocks over the prior twelve months. These were published in the *Houston Chronicle* the first weekend of the New Year along with an in-depth article I wrote about the "Top Fifteen." The *Chronicle* gave the article a Sunday Business Section full-page splash every year. Based on my work, a book was published entitled *The Money Tree Grows in Texas*. Thus, our research department was helping the retail brokers. I was laying the groundwork for the reason I came to Houston: to build a DLJ of the South.

In 1965 I had hired Robert Gray, a Tau Beta Pi graduate of The University of Texas and HBS who had a marvelous Central Texas sense of humor. In 1966 I hired Dick Nelson straight from HBS. That was also the year I was ready to launch the Big Idea. Our institutional research team did the seminal research on the offshore energy industry. We invited managers from the major investment management institutions in America to a three-day conference in Houston; over one hundred attended. We had decision-makers from the country's largest and most successful institutions—from Capital Guardian in the west to Putnam, Fidelity, and Massachusetts Investors Trust (MIT) in the east. We rolled out the firepower for them and featured future U.S. President George H. W. Bush, who headed Zapata Offshore. SEDCO (Southeastern Drilling Company) was represented by its CEO, William Clements, the future powerful governor of Texas. J. Ray McDermott, the largest and most popular offshore company, sent its executive vice president Alex Harbin from New Orleans. Large and small, our team held special research sessions on every publicly traded company in the offshore industry. To make the three days even more valuable to the attendees, we gave them access to a "who's who" of the energy industry, including a luncheon address by the famous wildcatter Michel Halbouty.

Of overriding importance was that no one was prepared for such sophisticated, high quality, in-depth, institutional-quality research. It had never happened in a region before. The conference was a soaring success. Highly profitable "Give-up" checks poured in. The reputation of our team skyrocketed and spread.

The FAF Conference had led Susan and me to Houston. In 1965, we attended the Philadelphia FAF Conference. En route by way of New Orleans, we saw that the Preakness was being run in Baltimore that afternoon. So we changed our tickets and went to Pimlico for the race. This launched our lifetime of avid traveling. Susan and I were well matched in our openness to adventure!

By a felicitous coincidence, *Institutional Investor* magazine originated at approximately the same time as our institutional investment team. The magazine hosted large conferences in New York, some with over 2,000 in attendance. They invited me to be a featured speaker and dubbed me the "Dean of Regional Institutional Research." Wow! Soon, each *Institutional Investor* magazine had a two-page centerfold featuring pictures of our team plus some "typically modest" Texas achievements. Our fame was spreading even more.

In 1968 I met Frank Scarborough at an HBS Club meeting and was

Fifteen of the sixteen reasons why institutional investors look to Underwood, Neuhaus for Southwest opportunities...

Steve A. Garrison, MBA, Harvard Business School; BSEE, U.S. Naval Academy; specialists in high technology, real estate, and construction companies.

C. P. Sanders, Jr., BBA, North Texas State University; Graduate School of Business, University of Texas; 5 years investment experience.

Kenneth L. Cochrum, BS, University of Texas; 8 years industrial and investment experience.

Darrell L. Vincent, MBA, Harvard Business School; BA, University of Oklahoma; 8 years industrial and investment experience.

Robert W. Gray, MBA, Harvard Business School; BS, University of Texas; Certified Public Accountant; 5 years analytical experience; specialist in petroleum and offshore companies.

Robert M. Stephens, MBA, BA, University of Texas; 6 years analytical experience; special situations.

J. Philip David, BSC, Ohio State University; 20 years experience in financial institutions; investment banking and institutional sales; Vice President/Institutional Sales.

Eugene H. Vaughan, Jr., MBA, Harvard Business School; BA, Vanderbilt University; Chartered Financial Analyst; 9 years analytical experience; Vice President/Research.

J. Frank Scarborough, MBA, Harvard Business School; BChE, Georgia Institute of Technology; specialist in retail conglomerates, chemicals.

William H. Murphy, Wharton Management Program; AB, Princeton University; 7 years industrial and investment experience.

Paul C. Talkington, MBA, Harvard Business School; BA, Rice University; 6 years analytical experience; specialist in utilities, transmission companies.

Richard L. Nelson, Jr., MBA Harvard Business School; BA, University of Texas; 4 years analytical experience; specialist in financial and technological companies.

Boyd R. King, MBA, Harvard Business School; BA, Rice University; 6 years experience in institutional sales.

John D. McStay, MBA, BA, University of Texas; four years analytical experience; oil, gas and special situations.

R. Jerry Falkner, B.A., University of Houston; special studies.

Underwood Neuhaus 15 Reasons centerfold ad in Institutional Investor *magazine.*

76

so impressed I hired him walking back to the office. So very fortunate. I was very proud of my team and continued to add smart analysts and MBAs. John McStay, a University of Texas MBA who later started his own fine firm in Dallas, and Paul Talkington, an HBS graduate, were major additions to our talent. Almost all was well, and even my "dire" problem resolved abruptly—and mysteriously—when I was out of town and returned to find him no longer with the firm. Even more on the plus side was Jennie Horton; I inherited Jennie as my assistant. She had a wonderful sense of humor and a gracious way with people. Jennie and I worked together for twenty years.

Around this time I had another dilemma. The Chartered Financial Analyst (CFA) program was started in 1962 under impetus by Ben Graham, of Graham and Dodd, the father of security analysis. For several years, the ICFA grandfathered experienced people, but beginning in 1966 you had to take three rigorous exams to be accredited. I was working hard to build my team and did not see how I could possibly study for these tough exams.

On top of that, and much more significant, we were getting ready for the birth of our first child. Margaret was born on June 1, 1966. I could not believe I was holding our baby. It was like it never had happened in the history of the world. How could I turn my eyes away from our beautiful baby girl in the bassinet?

But study I must. I—and my research team—would be humiliated if I failed the exam. I studied assiduously and passed Exam I. I went through the same agony in 1967 and passed Exam II. In 1968, I was committed to speak at both the FAF and Institutional Investor conferences. Truly, I had no time to do the tremendous reading and preparation for Exam III. But, having exhausted my internal arguments, it came back to one thing—I was a professional, and the CFA was the gold standard of professionalism. I took the test and passed, the first CFA in Houston to pass all three exams.

In May 1969 I was in St. Louis at an FAF Conference with plans to return in time for the birth of our second child. At 11 p.m. Susan and I talked, and everything was on schedule. At one in the morning, that changed. Richard was coming! But planes were grounded in Chicago.

Our next-door neighbors, Ben and Harriet Turner, stayed with Margaret while Audrey took Susan to the hospital. When Richard arrived on May 14, 1969, the nurse announced: "Is there anyone here for the woman who doesn't have a husband?" I arrived about noon. I do not recommend anyone missing the birth of his son! This subject has been a "roasting" topic at every family gathering, notably the rehearsal dinner at Richard's wedding. I weakly rejoined with the Navy dictum: "The father is necessary for the laying of the keel but not for the launching of the ship."

The best advice Susan and I received when we moved to Houston in 1964 was immediately to sign up our children, if any, for Helen Vietor's Pooh Corner. Thus we called immediately in 1966 and 1969 when Margaret and Richard arrived, so they, and ultimately our four grandchildren, joyfully have been Piglet, Tigger, Roo, Kanga, Eeyore, and Christopher Robin in the superlative preschool. We admire Helen immensely.

The regional institutional research concept was succeeding marvelously. We hosted a second Institutional Conference, which was even better attended and more successful in all ways than the first one. I had "laid the keel," and now I was feeling strongly it was time to "launch the ship."

In May 1970 I was invited by *Institutional Investor* to speak at its conference in San Juan, Puerto Rico. It was in the middle of a reasonably severe down-market and the main attendees were the forty-two speakers. Thus I had three days with some of the investment industry's best-informed professionals. Susan and I went immediately from there to a glorious week we had planned at Caneel Bay in the British West Indies. We spoke not a word of business during those idyllic days, but on the return boat I turned to Susan and said, "Now is the time."

Several factors, from growing family to job frustration with the conflict of interest inherent in even the best of brokerage firms, persuaded me that it was time to move to the third and most vital part of my strategic plan. After a decade of scrimping and saving and building knowledge and contacts, I, along with my HBS colleagues Dick Nelson and Frank Scarborough, made an amiable departure from Underwood

Neuhaus and launched our own firm. The Boston Company, on whose board my staunch supporter George Putnam Jr. served, was establishing a national network of money management groups and was eager to back our firm in a de novo start-up.

In June 1970, we rented a two-room office in downtown Houston and launched out into the deep.

CHAPTER 11

Launching "The Dream"

Every great achievement is the result of a heart on fire....
Each of us has a fire in our heart for something.
It is our goal in life to find it and keep it lit.

—Mary Lou Retton, Olympic Champion from Houston

The three principals—Dick Nelson, Frank Scarborough, and I—had seven children below the age of five. Although I managed a lot of client funds, I insisted on taking absolutely no customers from Underwood Neuhaus. Dating from the dark misery of the North Atlantic, this was the business creed by which I was determined to live. In this instance, I wanted to lean over backward to do right by Underwood Neuhaus. I admired Joe and Phil for their fine minds, and I purely loved Mr. Underwood. He had a magnificent personality and was wholly magnanimous. It hurt him when I left to form my own firm, but two years later he told me he would have done the same thing. He was an authentic entrepreneur at heart.

Thus, we had zero clients and zero revenue. It was audacious, yes, but our firm was based on years of carefully learning to conduct genuine in-depth fundamental research and a high degree of strategic planning. Our goal was not to be the biggest investment management firm but to be one of the highest quality firms. Our foremost founding principle, in writing, was: "Build Beyond Thyself." I had found this in the 1910 edition of *The Story of Philosophy* by Will Durant, and it summed up ideally what I believed our firm and I personally should strive for.

We were Harvard Business School graduates, so self-confidence, while not bankable, was a major asset. Well, maybe it was indirectly bankable. I had developed a relationship with Ben Love when we were both speakers at an event and laughed at each other's jokes. Now Ben was president and CEO of Texas Commerce Bank, the most powerful bank in Houston. He let it be known I was the kind of person he wanted to bank on. He always backed me in everything I did in Houston thereafter. In loyalty, five decades later, our family remains a client of his bank even though Ben is deceased, and I was a director of Encore Bank for over twelve years. Loyalty deserves loyalty. Ben and his wife, Margaret, were wonderful and loyal friends. Their son, Jeff, went to Vanderbilt as did their grandson, Benton. Jeff was a star on Vanderbilt's baseball team and held many hitting records that will stand in perpetuity because they were in the era of wooden bats. Jeff, like his father, is astonishingly adept at human relations. He is an exceptionally good friend.

Providence also was smiling upon us when Jim Baker (the Honorable James A. Baker III, who went on to serve in senior government positions under three U.S. Presidents, including Secretary of State under President George H. W. Bush) did the legal work to set up our firm. Jim was so gracious, coming out to our home to help us. He and John Cabaniss, who went on to become managing partner of Andrews Kurth, were an important part of our founding. They have remained cherished friends through the years.

The name of our firm was Vaughan Nelson & Boston, Inc. Two men and a city! The brochure concept had worked so well for me when leaving the Navy that I used it again; we mailed out 5,000. We conceived a classy format in which there was a picture and bio on each of us wrapped in the "best of both worlds" concept: the combined strength of Houston professionals backed by the strength of the century-old Boston Company with its tradition of trusteeship to families such as the Lowells and Cabots. Dick and Frank were the best possible partners. Our hearts were wholly invested, and so were our minds, bodies, and time. We worked very long hours and put our clients ahead of everything except our families. I devoutly believe, then and now, that compensation is merely a byproduct of doing a great job for our clients, not an end in itself, and we believed this degree of client devotion would shine through.

Introducing
Vaughan, Nelson & Boston, Inc.
Investment Counsel

"My advice to investors (who cannot give full time to a study of investments) is to seek out some trusted investment counselor. The emergence of this new profession of disinterested investment analysts, who have no allegiances or alliances and whose only job is to judge a security on its merits, is one of the most constructive and healthy developments of the last half century."

Bernard Baruch
My Own Story, 1957

EUGENE H. VAUGHAN, JR., C.F.A., PRESIDENT

Since 1964 when he joined Underwood, Neuhaus & Co., Inc., Houston, as Vice President/ Research, Gene Vaughan developed and headed an institutional research group whose in-depth research and analysis have over the last several years been utilized by financial institutions nationally. It is this same conceptual planning, emphasis on quality personnel, and knowledge of investment analysis that he brings to VAUGHAN, NELSON & BOSTON, INC. Prior to joining Underwood, Neuhaus he was an investment analyst from 1961-1964 with Putnam Management Company of Boston, managers of a spectrum of mutual funds.

A Chartered Financial Analyst, he is currently a director of the Financial Analysts Federation, the organization of 12,000 financial analysts and investment managers, and is a member of the executive committee and past president of the Houston Society of Financial Analysts. He is a member of the Investment Strategy Group of The Boston Company. His range of financial experience also includes having served as a director of Underwood, Neuhaus & Co., Inc., and currently as a director of the Founders group of mutual funds, Denver. He has been a speaker at institutional and other investor conferences.

A 1955 graduate of Vanderbilt University, he is currently serving as a director of the Vanderbilt Alumni Association and as chairman of Vanderbilt's national fund campaign. He is a past president of the Vanderbilt Clubs of Boston and Houston. He holds an MBA from the Harvard Business School and has been a director of the Harvard Business School Club of Houston since 1966. Gene served three years in the U.S. Navy as an officer on a destroyer.

We waited nervously after sending out 5,000 brochures. Guts, faith, and amazing wives.

RICHARD L. NELSON, JR., EXECUTIVE VICE PRESIDENT

Dick Nelson brings to the group an ability to translate his strong economic and analytical background into investment implications for individual industries and companies. A 1962 graduate of the University of Texas with honors in economics, he was awarded a Woodrow Wilson Fellowship. After serving as a company commander in the U.S. Army, he broadened his economic studies at the Harvard Business School. Receiving his MBA with concentration in finance, he wrote one of the early studies on variable annuities.

He was a research analyst at the John Hancock Mutual Life Insurance Company in Boston; and in 1966, returning to his native Texas, Dick joined the research group of Underwood, Neuhaus & Co., Inc. Drawing on his unique background, his approach is to identify important structural changes in the economy and assess their potential investment impact. In addition, he has conducted specialized research in a number of industries including finance, insurance, electronics, retail trade, apparel, and capital goods manufacturing.

He is a member of the Houston Society of Financial Analysts and the National Association of Business Economists. He is presently serving as a director of the Harvard Business School Club of Houston.

J. FRANKLIN SCARBOROUGH, III, VICE PRESIDENT

Frank Scarborough rounds out the balanced diversification of the group with his technical/business background. He is a 1964 graduate of the Georgia Institute of Technology, majoring in chemical engineering, as well as a graduate of the Harvard Business School with concentration in finance, planning and control. At Georgia Tech he was chairman of the Honor Board and a member of "Who's Who in American Colleges and Universities." He served in the U. S. Army as a lieutenant.

Prior to becoming a member of VAUGHAN, NELSON & BOSTON, INC., Frank had several years experience as a financial analyst. He applied probability theory to capital budgeting problems with USM Corporation, worked as a special situation analyst for a private investor, and was a member of the institutional research team of Underwood, Neuhaus & Co., Inc. Industries in which he has performed specialized in-depth research include chemicals, oil, food, and retail trade.

In addition to portfolio management and analytical responsibilities he concentrates on the special investment considerations of corporate pension and profit sharing plans, foundations, and other institutions. He is a member of the Houston Society of Financial Analysts.

This picture of James A. Baker III, hanging in my study at home, is inscribed: "To Gene Vaughan, a good client but, even more important, a good friend."

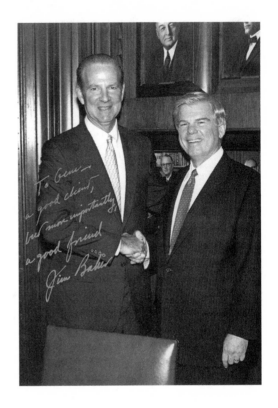

Several weeks after opening our doors, an oilman walked in and said he'd heard about the firm. We made a presentation (the "whole bale of hay!") and he decided on the spot to put money with us, becoming our first client. The next client came a very different way. From my first days in the U.S. Navy, I had my auto insurance with USAA, San Antonio. They were a great company, and their clientele comprised virtually every military person and family in America. At Putnam I had learned a lot about the burgeoning mutual fund business, so while at Underwood Neuhaus I wrote the famous chairman of USAA, General Robert McDermott, and requested a meeting. I recommended that USAA offer mutual funds. Our investment research team could be one of the research sources. The General seemed interested, but I heard no more—until he received a VN&B brochure. I received a call that USAA was building a mutual fund money management group and wanted me to make a presentation about our services. This long-planted seed came up at exactly the ideal time. The presentation went wonderfully.

Our first office was two small rooms, jigsaw cut to accommodate three principals, two secretaries, and, upon occasion, our precious Margaret Corbin and Richard Bolinger.

Vaughan Nelson was hired to augment the USAA research department until it was built. The fee of $50,000 (around $320,000 today) seemed to us a gusher akin to Spindletop.

We seriously needed more clients, and I went anywhere and everywhere to get them. Oklahoma was a particularly fertile area because there was lots of money but no investment counselors, and the trust departments were ultra-conservative. I discovered Ada, Oklahoma. I drove all night through a blizzard to be on time for an appointment. A man whose license plate simply said "BEANS" was the biggest bean grower in the nation. He became a client and brought friends with him.

Brick by brick, we put our firm together. We had wonderful help from Jim Bayless, the head of Rauscher Pierce Securities in Houston, a direct competitor of Underwood Neuhaus. Jim was one of the most well-liked and admired individuals in Houston. For some lucky reason, Jim and his family adopted Susan and me. He and his wife, Betty Lou, not only steered us to First Presbyterian Church, they literally drove us there. The magnificent Dr. Jack Lancaster, senior pastor, did the rest.

For decades, First Presbyterian Church was our tall-steeple church home, shaping and solidifying our Houston lives. I was fortunate beyond understanding to have Jack Lancaster as a pastor and close friend. As only children, we became not only brothers in Christ, but "brothers." Upon retirement Jack was followed by Dr. Victor D. Pentz, another superlative "man of God and man among men," who is one of my all-time favorite people. Vic has delicious wit, and we loved each other's sense of humor and working together in strategic thinking for the church and school.

Shortly after Jim brought us to First Presbyterian, he, as chairman of the investment committee, gave our firm the opportunity to manage the funds of the church. This led, years later, to my being asked to serve on the Philadelphia-based Board of Pensions of the Presbyterian Church (USA), which had the responsibility and honor of managing the retirement funds of all the ministers and missionaries of the denomination. Serving as long-time chairman of the Pension Board Investment Committee was the foremost volunteer job of my career.

Launched from Jim's shoulders, I became president of the Houston Society of Financial Analysts. Jim put the funds of Rauscher Pierce with Vaughan Nelson—not just the funds of the Houston office but all the investment funds of the prestigious investment banking firm. He also sent clients and friends to us. Jim was outspoken about stating widely that VN&B brought to Houston genuinely professional, in-depth investment research and money management talent. The next generation, Jim Bayless Jr. is made of the same stupendous stuff as his father and has been an abiding friend of our family.

In fall 1971, God did not just smile on us, he laughed out loud. The annuity board of the Southern Baptist Convention, Dallas, announced they were going to add a manager to the three they already had. What were the odds? Every investment management organization in the nation went after their business. Brother Robert Orr wrote a wonderful

Thrill of a lifetime! Richard and I "hanging a hull" on our beloved Hobie Cat off "Double Sunrise" in 1974.

letter telling about my Christian youth in Brownsville Baptist Church and his personal high regard for me. The annuity board headquarters were close to the Fairmont Hotel in Dallas, and nearly every month I took either Frank Durham, the executive director, or Davey Borders, his assistant, or both, to lunch at their favorite restaurant at the Fairmont. All my investment skills and the best-of-both-worlds concept and my HBS/IBM marketing skills were trained on the annuity board.

Just before Christmas, it was announced we won! We were in with the big dogs of the day: JPMorgan, Lionel D. Edie (headed by Luther King), and John P. Chase of Boston. The Baptists placed $25 million (around $147 million in current value) with us, by far our largest client. It was also a pacesetter client which made us eligible for other large clients. Ah, the spring of 1972! It was the richest I ever felt, before or since. We had been in business only twenty months and had broken even. New clients were seeking us out. Our performance was surging.

In the spring of '72, Susan and I purchased a front-row beach house at Bermuda Beach on West Galveston Island. It was one of the best investments of our lives and at the heart of our family. While living in Boston, one of the Putnam trustees told me their Boston home represented school and discipline to their children. Their Martha's Vineyard home represented the goodness of nature, family closeness, love, and fun. I never forgot those words. Our beach house, "Double Sunrise," is where our children grew individually and our family grew together. Our house got its name from the chapter in Anne Morrow Lindbergh's classic book, *Gift from the Sea*, and, in fact, we could see both sunrise and sunset.

Also that spring, George Bissell, head of Massachusetts Investors Trust, the oldest mutual fund group in America, called and asked me to become a director of the Financial Analysts Federation, which he chaired. Susan and I knew the organization fostered the quality of professionalism in which we believed. I was proud to accept.

After the mild bear market during which VN&B was launched, the investment environment was favorable. We had been watching, however, the emergence of the "Nifty Fifty." Increasingly, institutions across America concentrated their buying in these fifty stocks, and everything else was ignored. The fifty were then America's finest companies, such as IBM, Eastman Kodak, Black and Decker, Avon Products—all so-called "one-decision" stocks. Buy and hold forever. The increasing danger, in our view, was that the price/earnings ratios (PER) of the Nifty Fifty had skyrocketed while the rest of the market was getting cheaper and cheaper.

Our philosophy was more "Graham and Dodd," i.e., buy value and sell when it was no longer a value. The Boston Company had the same research philosophy, so we "doubled down." In August 1972 we went to our clients and told them our reasoning for selling our Nifty Fifty stocks and reinvesting the funds in excellent companies that were cheap. That was fine with everyone. They said, "That's why we hired you."

The danger came when the Nifty Fifty kept soaring. Institution by institution, and then the general public, capitulated, sold their value stocks, and put the proceeds into Nifty Fifty. There was a "geyser effect" on the prices of the favored stocks. The problem grew acute, then agonizing. While we were somewhat affected overall, we had a special crisis with the annuity board of the Southern Baptist Convention. They were our largest and most prominent client by far. The explicit pressure on us was that their other three managers were fully astride the Nifty Fifty sleigh ride, and their performance in the second half of 1972 was spectacular while ours was correspondingly lagging.

The problem was not unique to us. The most respected investment managers across America were having the same value versus growth problem as we were. I recall that Paul Miller, an outstanding investment manager, stated, "This is a market that makes the smart look stupid and the less smart look brilliant." It was truth, but it sounded like an alibi. I think the Baptist board was getting huge pressure from above (not God, but their other powers that be) because of the large performance differential. I made the most of our opportunities to present to the full annuity board. Our argument was accurate and compelling and that saved us early on. Next, I appealed to their common sense about the importance of diversification in managing funds as serious as the retirement funds of the wonderful Baptist ministers and missionaries of the South. I passionately argued that even if VN&B were wrong about Nifty Fifty stocks—and we were not—conscientious trusteeship dictates that at least one of their four investment managers be invested "with an anchor to windward." That saved us another quarter, but at year end the ax fell. We were terminated, and our funds were placed with a fourth Nifty Fifty management firm. We were achingly sick at heart. It was one thing to mismanage funds and underperform, but it ate your heart out when you knew you are investing wisely and wholly appropriately and got terminated.

Carol Loomis, by extraordinary synchronicity the wife of my Vanderbilt SAE big brother John Loomis and later close friend of Warren Buffett, was one of *Fortune*'s top writers. Her cover story in February 1974, "The Terrible Two-Tier Market," was the investment version of shouting, "The emperor has no clothes!" Her brilliant analysis and compelling conclusion suddenly penetrated the skulls of CEOs and boards across America. Nifty Fifty stocks plunged and never recovered. The devastation was dreadful. The annuity board's portfolio halved. VN&B was redeemed. We were proven totally right, but we were not rehired. Committees are exceedingly reluctant to admit mistakes on record. Moreover, the collapse of the best American-based companies precipitated the dreadful 1973–74 bear market during which the Dow Jones plunged forty-eight percent, the worse decline since the Great Depression.

We were not aware of it during the interminable two-year bear market because consultants providing quarter-to-quarter performance comparisons were not yet prevalent, but VN&B had performed extremely well comparatively during the crash. Because we had sold our Nifty Fifty stocks early, we had zero exposure to that disastrous group. And we held fifty percent cash reserves throughout the two years.

When word got around about our terrific defensive performance in 1973–74, clients began to migrate to us. We came through the two-year market plunge with a lot of agony but in great shape as a firm.

CHAPTER 12

Invincible Goodwill

Act well your part: there all honor lies.

—Alexander Pope

When George Bissell asked me to become a director of the Financial Analysts Federation, I had no idea how rapidly I would become deeply involved. Very quickly I was on the succession ladder to become chairman in 1973–74. The timing was terrible. In addition to the Nifty Fifty debacle and the worst market decline since the Great Depression, at the 1973 fall conference, the first at which I would preside, the New York Society of Security Analysts (NYSSA) agitated for more delegates. I thought they deserved them, given the size of their Society relative to their number of delegates, and I urged approval. It was fair, I believed. This concession made some societies around the country think I was soft, but it gave important insight into my character.

A nasty surprise was immediately ahead. Ted Lilly, full-time president of the FAF, and John Gillis, FAF legal counsel, called me the second week in January 1974 with shocking news. The NYSSA board had made a deal with the New York State Attorney General and members of the state legislature to put our profession under New York <u>State</u> regulation. Their clever plan was that every securities analyst who did business in New York, which meant <u>everybody</u> in the FAF, had to pass a state-administered test and register in New York. The NYSSA board would design the exam, so they, de facto, would be setting the standards for the entire profession. In their arrogance, the NYSSA board viewed New Yorkers as the real professionals and the rest of the FAF as Philistines.

It looked hopeless. Ted Lilly, smart but adversity-averse, immediately said, "They've got us." The New York Legislature was set to pass the bill in two weeks. In the middle of a horrible bear market and having lost our largest client, our fledgling firm was shaky. This disastrous distraction was the last thing I wanted. It was an agonizing decision that first night whether to let the NYSSA board win and let me focus on VN&B during conditions of turmoil in the markets. But once I reflected between caving to the NYSSA board and fighting for what I knew was best for our profession, it was clear that, as chairman, I had a responsibility to try to lead the profession through this peril. After the first hour of indecision, I never for a second thought about capitulating to the NYSSA. By dawn, John Gillis and I had developed a war plan. I mobilized a group of well-respected, smart New York heavyweights, including Walter Stern (Capital Guardian), Dave Williams (Alliance Capital), Donald Kurtz (Equitable Insurance), and Walter McConnell (Wertheim & Company), to delay the vote of New York State legislators. It turned out the NYSSA board had assured the attorney general and legislators there would be no opposition. In fact, they were brazen enough to say that the profession would welcome it.

My beloved pastor, Jack Lancaster, once advised me that when I encounter significant miscreants or betrayal I should "Always have invincible goodwill." That is powerful counsel, and I was drawing on it then.

I asked the redoubtable professional Walter Stern to chair a committee to create a self-regulation plan. Then I traveled around the country giving presentations to FAF societies (most of the forty-eight societies then extant) about the merits of becoming self-regulated. When put to a profession-wide vote, state regulation was opposed 5–1. The NYSSA board refused to accept the industry vote and said it was a NYSSA issue only. So we organized in New York, which voted 2–1 against the state-regulation plan. We did not stop there. We got highly respected Dave Williams to head a new slate for the NYSSA board. This slate won overwhelmingly—a complete win for the good guys.

In May 1974 at our FAF annual meeting in Los Angeles, Wally Stern, one of the single most brilliant men I have known in <u>any</u> profession, presented the self-regulation plan. Delegates overwhelmingly passed

A treasured picture of a laughing and beautiful Susan with Bob Hope comparing his ski-jump nose with mine. He concluded, to the delight of the large audience, he had only the third-worst nose, behind Jimmy Durante and Gene Vaughan!

it. With minor changes, it has been the core of FAF regulation ever since. At the climactic Saturday evening dinner, Bob Hope entertained a ballroom packed with jubilant delegates.

It was a very tough, prolonged fight over five exceedingly difficult months. My decision at that fall conference to take the side of NYSSA in seeking more equitable delegates laid the basis for the NYSSA delegates and members believing in my fairness in the subsequent state regulation battle. I was told afterward that the NYSSA delegates trusted me more than their own board. The vital battle also taught me that John Gillis, FAF legal counsel, was a foxhole buddy who could be counted on.

Back at VN&B, our staunch performance in a tough market continued to draw new clients. When I was at the monthly meeting at The Boston Company in June 1975, CEO Bill Wolbach was very complimentary and told me that our worst monthly new business reports were better than the best reports of any other affiliate. By that time there were affiliates in San Francisco, Los Angeles, Seattle, Louisville, Boston, and Florida as well as Houston. *Business Week* did a highly complimentary article on the affiliates entitled "String of Pearls."

Bill said TBC "would like to help VN&B more," but they owned one hundred percent of the other affiliates and wanted to purchase the rest of our equity. I reacted indignantly: You let us fight our way through this terrible two-year crash, and just as we are coming out of it and making good money again, you want to take away our upside! They clearly had rehearsed this and suggested I negotiate with George Phillips, CFO, on a fair price.

The truth was that Frank, Dick, and I, while legitimately protesting, were not at all resistant to getting some capital. We had young families with mounting expenses and had been financially strained a long time. I needed to call upon a lot of Jack's "invincible goodwill." George Phillips and I negotiated continuously the rest of 1975. At Christmas, we had arrived at a plan to spread the transaction over two tax years, dependent on papers being signed by December 31. We nailed down the final details, and The Boston Company lawyer was to fly to Houston with the papers the morning of New Year's Eve. I would sign, he would fly back to Boston with the papers, and the deal that had taken over six arduous months of tense negotiation would be consummated.

When the call came, I let out a primal scream. To this day, Margaret and Richard remember December 31, 1975, as "The Day the Boston Lawyer Missed His Plane!" He had played tennis that morning and missed his flight. Six months of work down the drain!

Yet that missed flight ended up being fortunate. I went back to the negotiating table with renewed determination. George Phillips was a superb negotiator and was later to become chairman of The Boston Company, but it was "my dream" to me and "just money" to him. Our negotiating was tenacious, but we ended up making a cleaner deal, uncomplicated by putting future profits in the formula. Upon completion, as hard fought as it was, it was a wonderful feeling to my colleagues and me to have substantial capital for the first time in our lives. Something else valuable I stored away was the knowledge that we were in business with very smart people, but we could not quite trust them. Later, I heard that George Phillips had remarked, "Gene Vaughan is the most honest person I have ever negotiated with." I'm not sure if that was "smart negotiating," but I was true to my "North Atlantic" character.

That year America celebrated its Bicentennial. With happy spirits, Susan and I purchased a Cadillac Seville and went to my HBS 15th Reunion. God Bless America! VN&B continued to prosper and now had important clients in Houston, San Antonio, Austin, and Dallas, and all over Oklahoma, New Mexico, and Louisiana, with some exceptional clients in New Orleans. I was on the String of Pearls operating committee, and at one of the monthly Boston meetings, Nate Garrick, executive vice-president, took me aside and, halting and embarrassed, told me TBC wanted to establish a de novo affiliate in New Orleans. I was stunned. Since the beginning, affiliate territories were sacrosanct. We had worked out special arrangements when personal relationships crossed affiliate lines, and Nate always handled these fairly. This was breaking our original covenant and a direct violation of our agreement. Reneging on a promise was not acceptable. We original affiliate CEOs saw Nate Garrick as a rock-solid man of character and strength, and to us he was The Boston Company. But I knew something substantially was amiss when I got the subsequent call from Nate saying we were never promised New Orleans as our territory. I told Nate I knew this was not his fault. He chokingly said, "Thank you, Gene." I soon learned the personal events that landed trusted Nate in this compromised position. He had divorced and remarried and was approaching retirement so financially weakened that they had leverage over him—a lesson to be remembered.

Shortly after that, I received an odd phone call from Boston saying they wanted me to also run their Los Angeles affiliate. Perhaps this was supposed to make up for New Orleans; it did not. I had no desire to live in or travel to LA, but fortunately I found just the right people to make things work there.

Spring 1977 was Vaughan Nelson's turn to host the String of Pearls conference and we chose a resort near Phoenix. The Boston Company announced Nate Garrick was not coming, but Bob Monks would be there. All my instincts told me that something was seriously wrong. We had seen Monks while in Boston, but he never spoke. At the conference, Monks dominated the meeting. It emerged that it was his money that had bought controlling interest in The Boston Company. As chairman of the conference, I asked Monks to lay out his plans for the affiliate system. Oh, he had plenty, which he expressed in ad hominem fashion!

After the conference adjourned, the affiliate presidents convened informally. We were all shocked and extremely upset. The consensus was the String of Pearls was endangered. Back at the office, I reviewed the conference insights with my colleagues, and we all concluded that we needed to start negotiations to buy ourselves back from The Boston Company. Knowing how much the previous negotiation had diluted me from work, I asked someone else to negotiate for us. That was a mistake. The next months were scary, tumultuous, and miserable.

Timing was not great on the home front for this turmoil. Susan and I, needing more space for Margaret and Richard, had been thinking about building an addition to the house we had purchased on Avalon Place in 1966. We loved our Avalon home, which was directly across the street from the exceptional River Oaks Elementary, which Jeff Bezos, the founder of Amazon, attended. Our realtor suggested we look for a new house instead as the real estate market was soft. We resisted several lovely places but when we stepped onto the front porch at 3465 Inwood Drive, we fell in love! The house had four white columns and looked into a forest of oaks draped in lovely gray Spanish moss. We purchased it at a very good price in late April 1977. We priced our house on Avalon Place aggressively, but it did not sell, which meant in May we owned two houses. Again, Ben Love, our dear friend and banker, backed us without hesitation and did not even ask for a signature. Several years later when introducing Ben at a civic meeting, I told this anecdote. Ben rose to his full 6'4" stature and said, "Gene, you didn't have any collateral except your two children and I could not foreclose on them!" One could never top Ben, even in praise!

Meanwhile, Monks replied to my request to buy back Vaughan Nelson & Boston with a vengeance! He would send people from Boston to run it. Someone must have advised him Texans and Southwesterners would not like the idea of their funds being managed by Yankees. So

In April 1977 we fell in love and continue to cherish our home on Inwood Drive in River Oaks, from which we can see a forest of oaks draped with lovely Spanish moss. Photo by David Shutts Photography.

Monks had another idea. He would terminate me and keep the rest of the team to run the firm. To their immense credit, Dick and Frank sent word to Monks that if I go, they go. I do not know what Monks would have done next, but the following Monday's *Pensions & Investment* front-page headline read:

THE BOSTON COMPANY PULLS COMMANDO RAID
ON SEATTLE AFFILIATE

Duff Kennedy left the String of Pearls conference with exactly the same decision I did but chose a different way to handle it. He leased an office just down the street and proceeded to move everything to it. Over the weekend, Monks personally led the commando raid that caught Duff in the act. This was sensational news, and reporters, while not entirely absolving Duff, were extremely sympathetic. Monks and The Boston Company were put in a very bad light. The next phone call I received from Boston was startling. Dwight Allison, president and CEO, whom I highly respected, said they wanted me to move to Boston and head up the entire affiliate organization. I said we were very happy in Houston (I did not mention that we were so happy we had two houses at the moment, actually three counting the beach house), and I was certain Susan would not move.

The next day Dwight called back and said he had been thinking and believed the way to do it was for The Boston Company to have a Boston-Houston axis: I would head the String of Pearls system from Houston, and they would run the rest of TBC from Boston. He added big financial incentives. If there were no Monks, this would have been quite attractive because I always had admiration and fondness for Dwight. But Monks was a fact of life, and I asked Dwight to expedite our one hundred-percent re-purchase of VN&B. After a couple of weeks, the deal was done.

My partners and I now owned one hundred percent of our company (and I managed to sell our Avalon house at near asking price). It had taken me from 1961 to 1977 to complete the strategic plan I wrote at Harvard Business School; this was an extraordinary moment of fulfillment.

CHAPTER 13

Best of <u>One</u> World

Investment management, properly done, is a ministry.

—Sir John M. Templeton, CFA

The reality facing us was that our clients had hired Vaughan Nelson & Boston as the best of <u>both</u> worlds, and we did not know how much value they placed on "Boston." It turned out not much. We visited our clients, and every one signed the required change of control papers. One of the major strengths The Boston Company bequeathed Vaughan Nelson was the image-ideal slogan: "Serious Minds for Serious Money." Our investment team was all CFAs, steeped in in-depth fundamental research and known for hard work, commitment, and perseverance, so the slogan was appropriate.

It also was appropriate that we find the right new office space for our best-of-one-world firm. Gerald Hines not only built the classiest buildings in Houston—and eventually the world—he was a marketing genius. He distributed six-inch models of his upcoming seventy-five-story Texas Commerce Tower. I was fixated on mine for months, and while our firm was pitched by several other excellent builders, my heart became set on Ben Love's building. Word reached me Ben had told the realtors he wanted Gene Vaughan in his building, "Give him what he wants." Ben was forever my friend. We selected the sixty-third floor, looking out across all of Houston with Hines's exotic, award-winning, twin-towered Pennzoil Place in the foreground and the preeminent Sky Lobby just below us. When construction reached the sixty-third floor, my daughter and I went up on the outside elevator as the workmen were coming down at the close of day. We walked on the sheet metal to where my office would be and peered over the edge. In the eerie quiet, cars on the street below appeared as toys. There was nothing overhead. It was one of my life's most exquisite moments. "My" City. "My" Firm. Shared with Margaret. It was exhilarating to my core.

I did not think we could work harder than before, but debt, to a family that thought borrowing for anything except a mortgage was sinful, is a huge incentive. For many months, I had been working hard to get United Energy Resources (UER), which occupied the elegant seventy-fifth floor, as a client. We were up against heavyweights from across the U.S. After a tumultuous and exceptionally strenuous year, at Thanksgiving Susan and I took the children to Padre Island to play amidst the enormous sand dunes. On the Friday after Thanksgiving, CEO Hugh Roff personally called to wish us a "Happy Thanksgiving," then added, "By the way, you have been selected to manage UER's funds." To this day, I think Hugh Roff is the single nicest person in Houston!

Investment management consultants, which in more recent years have grown into an industry, did not use The Boston Company affiliates, so I had zero experience with them. Meidinger Consultants (now William M. Mercer-Meidinger-Hansen, Inc.) had emerged as one of the big five. When Meidinger invited me to make a speech to their consultants from throughout the U.S., I accepted. Fortunately my message landed on target. Immediately, Meidinger started placing our firm on its short list for searches. Once we got to the finals, we knew how to win. I worked diligently to become a student of final presentations. For final presentations, I was always on the ground the night before because Texas weather is capricious. We won several times because we cared enough to be there early. When weather detained competitors, sometimes this early arrival also gave me an opportunity to meet the decision-makers. I devoutly believe the adage: they don't care how much you know until they know how much you care! The secret was we did care more. And we worked harder. Through Meidinger searches we soon had sizable clients throughout the Southwest, Denver, Kansas City, Chicago, Atlanta, and points in between. From the time our newly independent VN&H (Jim Hargrove joined us after serving as U.S. Ambassador to Australia under President Gerald Ford) shot out of the gate, our performance was terrific, and the consultants jumped aboard.

In the *Institutional Investor* 1979 "Pensions Olympics," our nascent firm placed third among the entire industry in new equity clients won. We caught energy stocks exactly right, along with value stocks, and they propelled our performance. In mid-1979, Ed Barksdale, CEO of a leading consulting firm, flew to Houston to tell me in person that our firm had been selected to be one of their "twelve money management firms of the 1980s!" This was highest praise for a firm only nine years old and independent for only two. It meant our little firm had just received its official invitation to the Major Leagues.

In addition to our devout belief in authentic fundamental research, our overarching investment philosophy came from the Rothschild Family. The Rothschilds said their fortune was built on letting some-one have the first twenty percent of profit and someone the last twenty percent. They contented themselves with the "sixty percent in the mid-dle." Likewise, our firm's investment philosophy could be capsulized as the Middle 60. It was and is, in my opinion, the most outstanding philosophy over the long term. It is impossible for anyone to predict the bottoms and tops of markets and/or industry runs. It is basic Graham and Dodd that markets and industries go from undervalued to over-valued (and overshoot) and back again, with an upward trend line. The discipline that makes our philosophy work is willingness to leave some profit on the table. In my personal investing, Rothschild works because it does not bother me to suffer opportunity loss, but capital loss is a real loss. The difficulty is that clients sometimes do not see the value of willingness to leave something on the table.

In 1979 and 1980, energy stocks went higher and higher and follow-ers continued to jump aboard. The energy industry started drinking its own whiskey and made wild predictions about oil prices. The highly respected CEO of Exxon was a Vanderbilt trustee, and he confided his personal projections for the price of oil as far above general expectations. This was exactly the kind of raging market emotionalism the Roths-childs had in mind. V N&H did very careful research and in August 1980 decided, while some overvaluation was the normal pattern, the energy group was substantially overvalued. The performance of energy had been so strong our average portfolio holdings were approaching forty percent energy. We went to each of our clients and showed them our reasoning for reducing their energy holdings to about ten to fifteen percent. Of course, nowhere was the energy choir more fervently singing than in the Southwest.

Energy stocks dipped in early September and we felt great, but later in September, when Iran invaded Iraq, oil shot sky high. In early October, hostilities between Iran and Iraq intensified as they fought for control over key ports and oil fields. Oil shot up higher. Energy stocks soared. Our "one world" crashed quickly. Consultants turned on us immediately and their clients left us. Energy stocks crashed in November, but the damage was done. As with the Nifty Fifty, we were accurate but early—at great cost. Over my long career, it has been a truism that the finest long-term investment managers say their worst miscues came from "being wrong for the right reasons."

The energy industry was devastated. Houston, having ridden through the Great Depression in fine shape, was hit hard by the Energy Depression. During the economic devastation of the early 1980s, Houston lost its great banks. The exception was the bank led by Ben Love, brilliant on offense and equally brilliant on defense. He sold Texas Commerce to Chemical Bank, which parlayed Manufacturers Hanover, Chase Manhattan, and J. P. Morgan into the colossus now known as JPMorgan Chase. As far as I know, the only good thing that came out of that dismantling of most of Texas's longstanding banks was that Carolyn Ross joined our firm as my executive assistant. She and I immediately became a team at Vaughan Nelson, and she remains my valued and trusted assistant today.

It was a heartache time in Houston and at Vaughan Nelson. We had added people to our team and were committed to most of the sixty-third floor in Texas Commerce Tower. We were close to break-even again, going the wrong way. Then a "gift from above." My "brother," Jack Lancaster, had asked me to join his four-person Morning Prayer group. One member was David Hannah, a canny Scot in real estate, who loved space. David, as fully recounted in articles featured in *Reader's Digest, Texas Monthly,* and numerous other magazines, successfully launched a rocket from Matagorda Island. I was invited to watch the launch. On the boat I met a fine couple, Buddy and Ethel Carruth. The next week I received a call from Buddy that changed the course of our firm forever. Buddy was chairman of the Gus Wortham Foundation, third among Houston's big five private foundations. He wanted me to manage the entire foundation and for our firm to manage his personal funds as well as his wife Ethel's. This large client and its superlative radiant power had major ramifications for our firm.

Shortly after being hired, I was moved to go alone to our beach house for contemplation. Over the course of several days and nights, with the solitude of the Gulf and the sound of the waves as my backdrop, I thought and wrote and changed the firm completely. I knew God had sent Buddy and Ethel Carruth to me for a reason, and He wanted Vaughan Nelson to be substantially different from what it was—and better.

I have no doubt God guided my hand as I wrote that we would no longer seek clients through consultant organizations. "Consultant clients" belonged to them, not us, and could be taken away at any time. I wrote about the kind of clients we would seek: stable, long-enduring clients such as foundations, endowments, pensions, and wealthy individuals. Moreover, within these categories we would accept only quality-of-life clients that brought positivity and uplift to our team. We would seek and accept only clients we could reach by short hauls on Southwest Airlines, which we labeled "The Company Plane." Spending time with our families was a priority. We would no longer manage hot, aggressive funds. We would rededicate ourselves to strong, fundamental research and seek only uplifting and enduring business.

Curious how a shard of a thought can change one's life. Years earlier, while half-listening to Eric Sevareid on television talk about Walt Disney, I heard him say, "There are three kinds of people: Well Poisoners, Lawn Mowers, and Life Enhancers." Susan and I had made a firm decision to eschew Well Poisoners and surround ourselves with Life Enhancers. This "principle" had already dramatically improved our personal lives, and I decided to implement it in our firm's life.

With a bit of apprehension, but mostly with pride, everyone at the firm embraced these principles and values. I had a peaceful mind and

An unexpected break during busy times. The week before my fiftieth birthday, Susan contrived to kidnap me and take me to Grindelwald, Switzerland, for my milestone birthday. Stupendous! Here we are happily dining after descending from the "First," the fabulous mountaintop overlooking Grindelwald with a stunning vista of the Alps.

knew this was our path to the solid top tier as a firm. Vaughan Nelson in the future would grow more slowly but more solidly. We would spend more time with our children.

After the Energy Depression, our research was conclusive that the market was <u>historically</u> <u>underpriced</u>. We "fully invested" in cheap stocks. It was the natural perversity of the market to refuse to go up. Impatient clients began to kid us that "the end of the tunnel was… New Jersey." After what seemed an eternity, things began to break our way. At New York City's Harvard Club, after a meeting with a Kentucky client, Frank and I rejoiced on Friday, April 13, 1982, to see the stock market was flying up! It turned at 777 on Friday the 13th, a numerologist's delight, and the long bull market was launched. Glory Hallelujah!

These were incredibly busy days for me and extremely high-pressure times for the firm. Without using consultants as sources, we had no one to recommend us for the finals and were always competing against firms that had the strong support of consultants. Vaughan Nelson was a welterweight slugging it out with heavyweights, yet winning more than our share.

Anheuser-Busch is a prime example. I had met Marty Burns, their internal fund director, and cultivated him over a period of time. When Anheuser wanted to add another firm, he called and invited us to compete. I will never forget the presentation at the preliminary screening meeting. I was alone and awoke with severe neck pain; when I returned home, I learned that a bone spur had jutted into a cervical nerve. Miraculously, whatever I said through gritted tee[th must have impressed] the screening committee. Maybe they interpre[ted my anguish as] ordinary caring because Vaughan Nelson [was one of the three firms] selected to present to the entire Anheuser [Busch board of directors].

The aptly named August Busch Jr., CE[O at the head of an] awe-inspiring board table with twenty-two h[igh-powered directors]. He chaired the meeting and was wonderfull[y ... glances. I was on] the fence! I started off with "It might be...it c[ould be...it is! Home] run! Holy Cow!" This signature line of Cardi[nal sportscaster Harry] Caray brought a great response. I explained I h[ad grown up listening almost] every summer day to the Cardinal Baseball Network. My heroes were Stan Musial and Enos Slaughter. I had their attention and made the most of it. Against all odds, we were hired. Of course our excellent performance undergirded our qualifications.

Halliburton was a big client that took much ingenuity to land. On one of my trips to Dallas I met their treasurer, the highly influential chairman of the investment committee. We hit it off, but it was difficult to follow up because he lived in Duncan, Oklahoma. You have to get creative to just "be in the neighborhood" and drop by, but I managed it over the course of two years. Gradually I convinced him and the investment committee that Vaughan Nelson cared more about Halliburton than any other investment manager, and with their large subsidiary, Brown and Root, in Houston, it made good sense for them to have a Houston manager. When Vaughan Nelson presented to the investment committee against five strong competitors, we had won before we went in the room.

One aspect of this level of high-pressure competition is that frequently it came down to a final two or three firms, and the chairman of the selection committee would say, "We could throw a handkerchief over all three of you." Seemingly there was no payoff whatsoever for coming in second. You invested the same amount of time, hard work, and "self" as the winning firm. As Queen Victoria famously said about the Battle of Cowpens, "There is no second place." I believed in learning from a loss and being smarter and more determined next time. We won numerous clients after the winner had stumbled.

When I went to the beach to redesign Vaughan Nelson, I decided the most stable and enduring clients and the most satisfying in the sense of a "ministry," in Sir John M. Templeton's noble meaning, were endowments and foundations. We developed an excellent reputation for managing these funds with particular expertise. Being a trustee of Vanderbilt University and on its investment committee played a big role; in fact, I did know a lot more about endowments than most investment managers.

An ideal example to me of investment management as a "ministry" has been the Wortham Foundation. From our offices on the sixty-third floor of Texas Commerce Tower, all the personnel of Vaughan Nelson had the exultation of watching the construction of the Wortham Center. One of my all-time moments of ecstatic pride was when I was leaving a meeting of Wortham trustees and Chairman Buddy Carruth said, "Hold it. I want to say to your face what I have been saying behind your back. We could not have given the money to make the Wortham Center possible if you had not managed our funds so well!" A God-given "ministry" to us—YES! (The Foundation had given $30 million to anchor Wortham Center.) Later the venerated trustee chairman Fred Burns elevated my life for many years with his public expressions of gratitude.

With the highly respected Wortham Foundation as a positively radiating client, we added other foundations. Among them was Houston Endowment, the funds of Jesse H. and Mary Jones, the largest private foundation in Texas.

Trinity University in San Antonio came to us through its new president Ronald Calgaard. He had interviewed at Vanderbilt for provost and after arriving at Trinity sought me out. A very intelligent man of wide-ranging interests and knowledge, he introduced me to his trustees and, after a year of steadily working to convince almost all of the board, not just the investment committee, we won out over heavy competition.

Later in the 1980s we were hired by Texas A&M. This set up one of the most dramatic moments of my career. After a long bull run from April 13, 1982, we became convinced the market had far outrun itself by mid-1987, and we went very defensive, using both cash equivalents and conservative stocks. That is, we were letting someone have "the last twenty percent of profit." On "Black Monday," October 19, 1987, the Dow Jones fell 509 points, 22.6 percent, $500 billion in one day. People were in shock. I remember chairing our investment meeting that day and thinking, "God, why now? You know we meet with the Texas A&M investment committee on Thursday!"

On Thursday, not only was the entire investment committee present but so were deans and most of the board itself. Usually a convivial group, there were no pleasantries anywhere. We went straight to the conference table. I said nothing except "I know what is on your mind. Turn to page one." It showed:

Week of October 19, 1987

Dow Jones	Texas A&M Endowment
−22.0%	−5%

A roar went up. People were slapping each other on the back. Admiral Robert Smith, chairman of the Houston Federal Reserve Board, took the floor. He said, "Gentlemen, you have saved our university! We will never forget this!" Aggie Spirit is not excelled anywhere.

At the University of Houston, their new chancellor, Arthur Smith, and his wife, June, invited Susan and me frequently to their home. Arthur was a high-caliber leader and enjoyed talking with me about university matters because of my experience at Vanderbilt. Eventually, we were invited to meet with their powerful investment committee and were hired.

Among our most all-time satisfying clients was Tuskegee University in Montgomery, Alabama, the historically black university of Dr. George Washington Carver. Steve Canter, chairman of the investment committee, called and said he thought we would be a great fit. The finals pitted four excellent firms. Frank and I were returning from

Montgomery at the airport in Dallas when I called Steve and learned that we had been selected. It was a wonderful relationship; they treated us just like trustees, always including us for dinner the night before board meetings at the chancellor's lovely home, "Grey Columns."

Another exceptionally satisfying client was Austin Presbyterian Theological Seminary. We managed their funds for over a decade, and each meeting was a blessing. When a consultant became involved and we were eventually terminated, the CFO drove from Austin to my office to tell me in person, and we cried together.

And then there was The Board of Higher Education of the United Methodist Church in Nashville, which managed collectively the smaller endowments of Lambuth College and other Methodist colleges in the Mid-South. It was chaired by the matchless Gus Halliburton, the treasurer of Vanderbilt, my longtime friend, and one of my favorite people in the world. He possessed a superb personality and a warm and gracious heart. When he was dying, Susan and I went to see him in the hospital. Gus, still a great storyteller at ninety-two, kept us spellbound and laughing. Moments like those make me feel sorry for people who are in this profession only or mainly for the money.

One of the toughest—and absolutely intriguing—clients was The University of Texas Law School. On the rotating board of UT Law were two dozen of the most successful and renowned lawyers throughout the State of Texas. They were all tough and had great wit, mostly at the expense of each other. This was a very difficult client to attain and keep because almost all the lawyers had their own idea of the investment manager or bank they resolutely wanted. In our quarterly meetings we mostly skipped the presentation and started immediately with Q&A. These men were used to talking, not listening. It was highly satisfying that several members of the UT Law board engaged Vaughan Nelson to manage the funds of their own firms.

By 1981 our continuing growth led us to conclude that it was time to add a strong partner. Over two weekends I went through every name in the FAF directory, creating A, B, and C columns. At the very top of column A was Walter McConnell. At first he declined—saying there were rumors Wertheim would sell and he would leave too much money on the table—but months later he called saying he had regretted his

My philosophical beacon, Dr. John W. Gardner. When he spoke at the Houston Forum, with me presiding, the feeling in that roomful of 1,100 was electric, and my heart soared.

decision every day. I said, "Let's talk." Within a week, Frank, Dick, and I invited Walter to join us as a named partner—Vaughan, Nelson, Scarborough & McConnell. Walter was tremendously respected for the quality of Wertheim & Co. research and was an authentic white hat on Wall Street.

From year one of our firm, I sent out letters of heartfelt gratitude to our clients at the end of the year (EOY) between Christmas and New Year's Day. I shared some of my favorite quotes and readings and somewhat bared my soul in these letters, even though I was aware of how cynical some people can be. The night after they were put in the mail, I was like a playwright waiting for the first review of the critics. Dr. John W. Gardner was by far the person about whom I received the most appreciative letters. John Gardner is the single person who has most shaped my philosophy of life, and he became my philosophical beacon. A highlight of my life came in 1993 when, while chairman of the Houston Forum, I invited Dr. Gardner to speak and introduced him to a capacity audience and then spent an electrifying, life-lifting day with him. We became friends, and when Dr. Gardner died in 2002 at the age of 89, I dedicated my entire EOY letter to him. I have read many dozens of books about leadership, and his *On Leadership* (1990) is the best ever, in my opinion.

I wrote EOY letters for thirty-one years, over time expanding the mailing list to several thousand people. One year, I was particularly nervous about an EOY letter I had crafted. I became more so when I was told Arthur Temple was on the phone. Arthur Temple was CEO of Temple Industries, which owned a massive amount of East Texas timberland, and he had a reputation for being one tough man. So I was prepared for him to say something like, "How dare you send me that crap?" Instead, he said my letter was one of the best things he had read in a long time. He went on to comment on specifics and ended by inviting me to come for a visit to Diboll, Texas, his headquarters. This led to our being hired to manage the funds of Temple Industries and, later, his wife. Mrs. Temple was charming. She came into our boardroom one afternoon, spun gracefully and said, "I don't feel nearly as good as I look!" This favorite witticism has been employed by each member of our family!

The firm kept on rolling, signing excellent clients. In May 1990, I attended a two-day institutional investor conference in New York. On the second day, the main speaker was Gene Sit, the brilliant founder and CEO of Sit Associates in Minneapolis. He was in the middle of his speech, and after naming the characteristics he believed were essential for an outstanding firm, he said that the most outstanding large firm in America was Capital Guardian, of which Wally Stern was chairman. I agreed totally. Next he said of the middle-size firms, the most outstanding was Miller, Anderson & Sherrod, Philadelphia, of which the renowned Paul Miller was chairman and CEO. Again, I agreed.

Just at that moment the person sitting next to me asked me a question, and I turned to whisper an answer. In the next instant, everyone was applauding and looking at me. Someone told me, "He just said Vaughan Nelson is the most outstanding smaller-size firm in the nation."

I was dumbstruck. From an ultimate podium in New York, from one of the most respected men in our industry, to be in the company of those other names whom I revered was beyond my wildest dreams. At that moment, I knew for certain what it was like to have the "visceral feel of entrepreneurial greatness!"

When I returned to Houston after the conference, the Dallas-based *Financial Trends* did a major, multi-page feature on our firm, leading off with what had been said about Vaughan Nelson in New York. I was quoted as saying, "This is what I want on my tombstone!"

On top of this recognition, the firm was on an all-time winning streak. Our cumulative performance over the long-term was outstanding. Near-term, from mid-1992 through all of 1993, we won ninety percent of our marketing competitions, and thirty percent would have been considered exceptional. Each victory was well-researched, hard fought, and sweet.

An invisible but major factor in our firm's winning so much throughout its history under my leadership is the recurring statement quietly confided by many of our competitors: "If we don't win, we hope Vaughan Nelson will." We never spoke ill of a competitor, in a field rife with undercutting. We supported the profession. Four of us were presidents of the Houston Society of Financial Analysts. Ultimately, three of us were directors of the FAF; we were "white hats" professionally and personally. CFAs all, we personified professionalism and honor.

Also during this period there started the wonderful, month-long family trips by car which over time included the Lower West (Grand Canyon, Disneyland, and Knott's Berry Farm); the East (Randolph-Macon, Washington, D.C., New York, and Boston); and the Upper West (San Francisco, Yosemite, Yellowstone, and Tetons); and later, Britain, France, Kenya, and Russia. All were superb. Were I to pick the single most life-changing event from a multitude of such exhilarating experiences, it would be "The Great Pillow Fight." On our first trip, when Margaret and Richard were about eleven and eight, we drove to San Antonio, the Grand Canyon, and the kids' paradise of Los Angeles. We had a great time, but there was some restraint. Daddy was still a reserved businessman. Then, suddenly, at the Pine Inn in Carmel-by-the-Sea I whacked each of them with a pillow. They were startled, looked at their mother, looked at me who was winding up to whack them again—and they whacked me. The "Great Pillow Fight" was on! It changed our relationship completely. From then on Daddy was fun! He told silly jokes. We found everything was marvelously fun together, and from that moment we "grew up together."

CHAPTER 14

"The Merger"

Press on. Nothing in the world can take the place of persistence.
Talent will not; nothing is more common than unsuccessful people
with talent. Genius will not; unrewarded genius is almost a
proverb. Education will not; the world is full of educated derelicts.
Persistence and determination alone are omnipotent.

—President Calvin Coolidge

As far back as 1973, when I was chairman of the Financial Analysts Federation (FAF), I had said that having two voices speaking for our industry was confusing and counterproductive. I believed the FAF and Institute for Chartered Financial Analysts (ICFA) should merge. However, the ICFA board was adamantly opposed to merger. Virtually no progress had been made in the intervening years, when I was asked to join the ICFA board in 1986. When I agreed, I quietly promised myself to find a way to get the merger done. Having been a hands-on leader in both the FAF and ICFA, I stayed close to the ground and knew both memberships wanted the merger badly. One by one, I made progress with other members of our twelve-person board. By the time I was becoming chair of the ICFA in 1989, my number-one priority was to unify the profession.

It was a contentious period, but there were no bad and good people, just honorable people (for the most part!) with very deeply held opposing points of view. This actually speaks to the seriousness with which they took their profession and professional organizations.

In 2010, on the occasion of the twentieth anniversary of the founding of the CFA Institute (a name change from Association for Investment Management and Research, AIMR), as founding chairman I was asked to give the keynote address. In attendance were almost all the ICFA board members who were at the August 3, 1989, crucial vote, the founding board of the CFA Institute, and the current members of the CFA Institute board of governors. My speech helps tell the dramatic story of the birth of the CFA Institute.

Fellow Charterholders: This afternoon we members of the founding board were filled with immense pride and astonishment when we participated in the current board of governors meeting. Yes, we worked immensely hard back 20–25 years ago, and, yes, we had a noble vision of what professional unity could accomplish, but what the CFA Institute has become now—the reality—is beyond our greatest dreams at the time!

It is fittingly symbolic we gather tonight in the beautiful New York Yacht Club, surrounded by models of Sir Isaac Lipton's sleek craft and Harold S. Vanderbilt's lustrous *Ranger*, whose international races for the America's Cup elevated both the skills and sportsmanship of international sailing. Symbolic because the current board is profoundly elevating our profession globally by making the CFA—the gold standard—international, even in China! Friends, we aspirants of two decades ago give you our profound thanks and applaud you for what you have achieved and will achieve.

This room is filled with heroes. We are all immensely proud of what the FAF, ICFA, AIMR and CFA Institute have become. We are proud that two decades ago when it was our turn to step up to elevate our profession, we did not shrink from that duty and opportunity. We are proud that in the time of crisis our "over the horizon" vision and steadfastness advanced the entire profession and most particularly enhanced the eminence of the CFA Charter. A shining moment commending the merger occurred in 1991 during the wonderful healing and "coming together" at the St. Louis annual conference when Sir John Marks Templeton stated: "There is no professional title more honorable than the title of Chartered Financial Analyst."

In 1989, when there were only 15,500 CFAs, this was the miracle for which we hoped and dreamed! Who would have believed in 1989 the membership of the CFA Institute would be 100,000 today! One of the proudest moments of my life was when our son, Richard Vaughan, earned his CFA.

The merger on January 1, 1990 was historic. It united our profession. It unleashed profound creative power for advancement of our profession. With remarkable synchronicity the collapse of the Berlin Wall occurred on November 12, 1989, coinciding with the vote for the collapse of the "wall" between the FAF and the ICFA.

There are several heroes who are not in our midst tonight. I want to single out one. In doing so, I will recall a monumental day and night in which several of us here this evening were eyewitnesses to history. The day was August 3, 1989. The place was the historic Boar's Head Inn, across from then-ICFA headquarters in Charlottesville. The occasion was the final showdown vote of ICFA trustees to approve merger or not. There were sixteen persons present, including twelve trustees, ICFA "negotiator" Dan Forrestal, legal counsel Mike Dooley, vice president Darwin Bayston and CFA director Tom Bowman. After sixteen years of sporadic merger talk and two years of valiant hard work by the ICFA, FAF, and society leaders, and intense—often contentious—debate profession-wide, this was the climactic showdown.

In September 1987, two years earlier, Charlie Ellis, present tonight, had conceived a vital strategic breakthrough with a new organizational structure he believed should be done. Some words you never forget! In Charlie's classic style, he remarked, "I think you should do this, but my thinking remains plastic and supple!"

On May 11, 1989, two-and-a-half months earlier, the FAF membership had already voted in favor of combination by 62 percent to 34 percent. The NYSSA board was opposed, and the New York and Boston Societies had voted against on balance. Rancor—and some bitterness—swirled pervasively during the quest for the birth of our unity.

The atmosphere in the room was electrified. The meeting's tone was set by the opening statement of Presiding Chairman Gary Brinson. He declared, "I am unalterably opposed to merger, and were it to pass, I will resign!" So much for neutrality from the chair! Jim Vertin, the superb professional and keeper of the Blue Flame of CFA Purity, added that he was not only implacably opposed to merger but he also was opposed to asking the charterholders to vote. For several hours, every trustee joined in the ardent debate, eloquently and passionately.

Some trustees worried the financially stable ICFA would be hugging a drowning man and would be pulled down. I rejoined that ICFA and FAF are Siamese twins. Others feared a merger would cheapen the CFA Charter. Some argued the charterholders did not want a merger. The opposition of the NYSSA Board (and their threat to withdraw) was a concern.

Merger proponents reiterated that our profession was too small to be represented by two organizations. In 1989 the membership of FAF was 30,000. It was confusing to employers, regulatory authorities, the media, and the public.

In 1974 we barely averted state regulation by arduously mobilizing the membership. But, as FAF Chairman at the time, I well knew the debilitating cacophony of two organizations speaking to and for our members. Dan Forrestal, Jim Dunton, Ted Muller, and I argued that despite the risks, combination would make possible the elevation of the profession. Mostly we pleaded for vision to consider the powerful possibilities if the energy and focused creativity of a unified organization were unleashed for the future of our entire profession.

But the highly articulate, persuasive opponents included some of the most respected leaders in our profession, such as Gene Sit, Rossa O'Reilly, Jim Vertin, Gary Brinson, and George Noyes. As you can imagine, they held sway. At Charlie Ellis's recommendation, we all had read the little book *Getting to Yes*, but Jim Vertin and Gary Brinson had written the encyclopedia on Staying at No!

The opponents were strategically astute. They challenged that Pete Morley, who was full-time CEO of both the ICFA and FAF, and Jim Dunton, on the ICFA board as the president of FAF, should not have a vote because of their affiliations with the FAF. Legal Counsel Dooley ruled they could not vote. One-and-a-half votes for merger evaporated! I said "half" because Pete Morley was a mysterious case. No one knew how Pete would eventually vote. Early on, he was strongly for merger. Of late he had been spending much time with Jim Vertin.

Another unexpected development: B. Milner and Dan Forrestal were designated negotiators for the FAF and ICFA, respectively. They were both superb—intelligent, honorable, skilled, and highly respected. During the fervent debate, Dan became highly frustrated by what he believed was "reneging" on the part of some opponents and suddenly left for his home in St. Louis. Dan was not a current trustee and had no vote. But merger proponents were deprived of a fluent, highly informed voice.

However, there were surprises on both sides. Trustee Elliot Williams, at Travelers in Hartford, worked with Chairman Gary Brinson. We assumed he would vote with Gary. To our immense relief, Elliot spoke up persuasively for merger. Finally, after four hours of intense debate, every argument had been exhausted—and certainly every participant. Now the strained hush of voting.

The vote was announced: five to five. Defeat. After all this effort, the merger would not go forward. Ballots would not be sent to charterholders. Utterly frustrating, draining defeat. In 1973, when I was incoming Chairman of the FAF, we brought up merger for the first time. The ICFA trustees were vigorously opposed. Outgoing ICFA Chairman Frank Block said, "Give it time. The ICFA will absorb the FAF." Sixteen years later the answer from the ICFA Board was still no.

During the break, I was still in my seat, exhausted, dispirited. Then an astonishing thing happened. I had agreed to serve as AIMR chairman only the first six months in 1990 to finish my year as chairman of the ICFA. The ICFA and FAF would alternate chairmen.

Gene Sit came over and whispered to me that he would switch his vote if I would agree to be the AIMR chairman for the first one-and-a-half years. He was completely serious. In a stunning reversal, a new vote was taken and the vote in favor of merger and sending a ballot to charterholders was 6–4. By that small margin, history moved forward.

The ensuing vote by charterholders was an overwhelming 83 percent in favor of merger. That is 83 percent! If not for that courageous change of vote, the 83 percent would have been denied a chance to vote. Except for that one vote, the history of the past twenty years would be quite different.

You know the rest of the dazzling story.

In happy truth, the brilliant critiques of Jim Vertin, Gary Brinson, George Noyes, and Rossa O'Reilly—and their subsequent loyal support—made the merger far stronger than if it had sailed through. With the chivalrous example set by leaders, the rancor and bitterness of the split began to heal swiftly. Because of the caliber of the first governors, the pervasive spirit of the inaugural board meeting, on January 16 in Los Angeles, was gallant. I asked every governor to express their visions for the CFA Institute (AIMR) in a go-around. The visions were uplifting, far-sighted, wise, and realistic. It is surpassingly gratifying that most of the members of the inaugural board are present this exalting evening to see their visions come true. In addition, the wisdom of Wally Stern and Ted Muller pervades this room.

Earlier, I said there is a person not here whom I want to single out: Gene Sit. It was Gene Sit's courage to reverse his vote that made the CFA Institute possible. Gene loved this profession and relentlessly pushed for betterment of the Institute. Gene died suddenly a short time ago. Within the last months of his life, he was still calling me about improving the CFA Institute—he still held me responsible—and, Jeff Diermeier and John Rogers, I know he was calling you, also. Gene lived to see the majestic elevation of our profession his single vote change made possible.

We had a crisis of opportunity twenty years ago, and we have another kind of crisis in our profession now. The greed and outrageous deeds of "Wall Street Extended" recently have brought shame to the investment field and tarred us all. The overriding truth is that the CFA Institute has a responsibility and opportunity as never before.

Present tonight is an outstanding CFA Institute board with responsibility, opportunity, and a compelling purpose. My

In our suite at the annual conference in St. Louis, after the successful completion of my chairmanship of the newly merged CFA Institute, I gave my signature right arm upward thrust and a deep-throated, exuberant "A-A-A-H!" It was a moment of exultation, my taste of élan vital!

friends, this is your time. The sublime opportunity of the inaugural board was twenty years ago. I believe they rose magnificently to that challenge. We now proudly pass the torch to you.

What a privilege to spend our careers in this splendid profession. Tonight we link arms—all of us in this room and fellow stalwarts of the past, present and future. We link arms to dream, act and, yes, to give a portion of our life's blood for the ascension of our splendid, noble profession.

At the AIMR annual conference in St. Louis in 1991, our first year as a combined organization, as chairman I was asked to give an extemporaneous speech to the long-suffering spouses of our delegation. Many of them had lived with the merger frustrations for a very long time, and this conference was the culmination and reward. I was under tremendous pressure to come up with a few special words. Suddenly there came into my mind this line from Tolstoy: "One can live magnificently in this world if one knows how to work and how to love, to work for the person one loves and to love one's work."

I told our spouses I understood the anguish they had been experiencing during the zealous effort to uplift our profession through merger, and I thanked them. When the conference was over, surrounded by Susan, Margaret, and Richard, I felt the embrace of their love and support.

As the keynote speaker at my request, Sir John M. Templeton in St. Louis was accorded a new honor, "The Award for Professional Excellence." His speech was not about investing strategy. It was about responsibility and the profession. After stating his deeply held belief that investment management, properly practiced, is a ministry, he stressed that to help others create and maintain prosperity was a goal worthy of a great profession. "**There is no professional title more honorable,**" he concluded, "**than the title of Chartered Financial Analyst.**"

It made me proud to be in the same profession as Sir John. He was a profound thinker and a deeply religious man, who yearly gave the "Templeton Prize for Progress in Religion," which was financially greater than the Nobel Prize. I have been privileged to know many truly great investors, and, while it is difficult to compare generations, I believe Sir John is the greatest ever, including the Oracle of Omaha. Sir John pioneered international investing when there was no research or regulation or accurate accounting available. He did it calmly, brilliantly, and spiritually. I was honored to introduce him three times to large audiences. The first time was in June 1990.

> It is conceivable that in every field there is a person or two who is so much more gifted, or better-trained, or harder-working—or something magical—that they so far excel the common lot as to

defy credulity. I can remember that thought occurring to me here in Houston in 1972–75 when Ken Rosewall and Rod Laver held their annual series of incredible battles in the finals at the River Oaks Tennis Tournament, volleying at the net toe-to-toe, three to four feet apart, hitting and returning one impossible put-away shot after another, sometimes stringing a dozen or more impossible volleys in a row, until you <u>knew</u> you were witnessing something superhuman.

One saw it in basketball in "Dr. J." whose soaring sky-walks defied human capability and inspired the next generation to elevate their own striving to an entirely new level of achievement. We <u>see</u> it most clearly in sports—in the beautiful, unmatchable levitation of a Michael Jordan—but this kind of phenomenon does exist upon occasion in other fields.

Sir John Marks Templeton occupies that position of mastery to the point of wizardry in the investment management and research profession. Let me cite a small part of the evidence: this week I asked the Lipper Analytical Securities Corporation, which is the keeper of performance statistics in the mutual fund field, to conduct a computer search to ascertain the best performing fund in the 30-year history of their database. The answer, hands down, is The Templeton Growth Fund, which grew a phenomenal 8,602 percent during the three decades, a sustained growth through good and bad markets of 16.01 percent yearly. This was five times the average cumulative added value of the other 141 mutual funds in existence over the period. It is 50 percent better than the fund in second place.

Sir John's professional life has been an inspiration to countless younger investment managers and analysts. He has stood for highest quality research analysis, was one of the early advocates of the formation of the Institute of Chartered Financial Analysts to foster high standards of professionalism, and himself became one of the first to earn a Chartered Financial Analyst designation.

He was a pioneer in global investing, decades ahead of his time in seeking out values throughout the world. Sir John <u>is</u> a deeply religious person. In conversations with him—and there can be few pleasures to equal having tea and conversation with this eminently

Sir John M. Templeton came from his home in the Bahamas to be keynote speaker when I was given the Humanitarian Award by the American Jewish Committee in 1993.

genteel, gracious person and his charming Lady Templeton, with us today, in their lovely home called "White Columns" in Lyford Cay—it is totally clear that he attributes his success not to his Yale Phi Beta Kappa and Oxford Rhodes Scholar intellect but to bringing his life into harmony with God's Will.

Please join me in welcoming a farm boy from Winchester, Tennessee, who has been knighted by the Queen, an authentic investment genius, but, beyond that, one of the truly great and noble men of our times—Sir John M. Templeton.

As chairman of the now-named CFA Institute in 1990, it was my pleasurable duty to represent North America at the European Federation conference in Stockholm that summer and the Asian Federation conference in Bangkok the following spring. Susan and I had both loved Bergen, Norway, on separate visits before we married and now rejoiced in going there together. We were enchanted by the fjords and stayed at lovely little towns, such as the charming and historic Mondal, ancestral home of Walter Mondale, U.S. presidential candidate. On a "summer day," June 15, we were in the first car to drive through the newly plowed roads to Stockholm. Snow banks were fifteen feet high on either side. In Stockholm we were treated like Nobel Laureates—at least, we were accorded all the pomp if not the circumstance. In fact, we visited with the president of the Nobel Foundation. At our conference, the Japanese representative was so arrogant—their stock market had risen crazily and was at fifty to sixty times earnings—that we all were offended but did not let on. Susan and I finished our trip by taking a ship to Finland and then made a marvelous visit to Copenhagen and the beautiful Tivoli Gardens, where Hans Christian Andersen wrote many fairy tales, including *The Emperor's New Clothes*, which had become highly significant to me!

In Japan the "arrogance" was completely reversed by the overwhelming graciousness of Mr. Gentaro Yura, the full-time executive managing director of the Securities Analysts Association of Japan (SAAJ). He arranged Kabuki Theater, tea at their best teahouses, and business meetings for me with heads of their major brokerage houses, and he accommodated us in the luxurious Imperial Hotel, the best. He also arranged for a bullet train trip to Kyoto, one of our favorite places in the world. We will never forget the lanterns on the stairs in their Sacred Garden. Breathtaking! A thrill of a different sort was when Susan and I ate at a horseshoe-shaped table in a popular restaurant. We were talking so animatedly to each other that when we heard applause we were completely startled that the entire room was looking at and applauding us. We had been eating with our chopsticks! It was not our dexterity but our effort they appreciated!

Mr. Yura asked me to write a forecast of the Japanese stock market for publication in the *Japan Analyst Journal*. On a tour I had been shown a "creaking floor" as a warning device and used this analogy to "warn" that the Japanese stock market was highly vulnerable. In actuality, their "arrogant" market declined for over two decades! Mr. Yura was proud of my forecast and sent me reminders.

On to Singapore, where we were again overwhelmed with hospitality by George Teo, the foremost international broker who was the leader in the professionalization of the Far East, and his lovely girlfriend, Dottie Shaw, niece of the famous Run Run Shaw who owned the largest chain of movie theaters. We were served lemongrass soup the first evening, and every imaginable delicacy followed. George had hosted our son, Richard, and his Princeton friend, Todd Baur, several years earlier and was our guest during the joyful annual conference in St. Louis. George has remained a good friend ever since. Todd was a member of the "Houston Rodeo Gang," along with several other SAE fraternity brothers (Richard was Eminent Archon [president] of SAE at Princeton and national Eminent Archon), teammates from "lightweight" football, and other Princeton friends who made an annual "pilgrimage" to be our guests at the exciting Houston Livestock Show and Rodeo. All are lifelong friends of Richard and our family. In addition to Todd, they include Pat McKee, Jeff Ramseyer, Collins Roth, Henry Smyth, Randy Winn, and longtime Houston friends Andrew McCullough and Ernie Miller.

Bangkok produced a spectacular conference, but it was somewhat anticlimactic for Susan and me after all the amazing hospitality to which we had been treated. The traffic jams exceeded any I have seen anywhere else. But everyone was wholly hospitable at the "Shangri-La," as we called the happy and successful conference.

Our brief side trip into China was horrid. In the best restaurant in Canton (now Guangzhou), cockroaches were crawling on the walls. When we were departing at the airport, our luggage was searched and they found a speech I was to give in Bangkok, a speech which they claimed was "capitalist propaganda." They detained me for several hours before "U.S. cash" solved the diplomatic impasse!

With its many highs and a few flairs of drama, I was proud to represent my profession worldwide. After the fierce merger battle and successful healing in the aftermath, many professionals called me the "Father of the CFA Institute." Years later, that title was made official by my colleagues, and I have to admit it was nice to see it in print!

To commemorate the fiftieth anniversary of the creation of the CFA program, in 2012 the CFA Institute published the outstanding *The Gold Standard: A Fifty-Year History of the CFA Charter*. I was among those interviewed for the book, which includes some of the flavor of the merger struggle and much more. I urge members of my profession, or anyone considering it, to read the book. One of my quotes from that book is: "The matter of overriding importance was to have faith in an over-the-horizon vision of what the profession could become if we united our talent, energy, and resolve."

I'm glad we had faith. Currently, with over 150,000 charterholders worldwide, growth is everywhere but is most rapid in China and India. It is good to be on the right side of history in something so invaluable to our profession.

CHAPTER 15

I Hear You, Edmund Burke

*The only thing necessary for the triumph of evil
is for good men to do nothing.*

—Edmund Burke

In 1986 I decided I would throttle back a bit. But while I was in Chicago for ICFA board meetings and suiting up for the merger battle, the phone rang in our hotel room. It was my dear pastor, Dr. John Lancaster. For some time, he had wanted a school at First Presbyterian Church and believed this was the time to do it. He asked if I would serve on the school study committee. Rushing out with my family to hear keynote speaker George Plimpton, I quickly said, "Yes, of course."

Yes, of course, is my answer to someone I respect and love as a brother—and to a cause I fully believe in. James Ewell Brown "Jeb" Stuart always concluded his letters to Robert E. Lee with the phrase "Yours to count on." I have tried to be that kind of person with people I love and admire.

Little did I realize how deeply that "Yes, of course" to Jack Lancaster would affect me. The first surprise was when I returned to Houston and, reading Jack's study committee letter, learned that I was actually chairman of the committee, not just a member. I really did not want to commit this kind of time. But Jack could count on me, and we set to work. The meetings, starting in August, grew longer and complex. There were financing issues, major discussions on the caliber of person to head the school, and debates on educational standards. On top of that, there

125

was eventually revealed a secret plan by a fundamentalist faction to take First Presbyterian Church out of the Presbyterian Church (USA) denomination and into a fundamentalist Presbyterian organization. They were not successful, but the faction included many potential parents and even an assistant pastor who taught Sunday school classes with the most potential parents. It saddened me that all this contentiousness and unkindness was taking place in our church home.

But we persevered. We worked through the issues and recruited an outstanding, albeit intractable, headmistress from a top school in New York City. Presbyterian School became a huge success by every measure. Our board set three principles: we would (1) be Christ-centered, (2) have strong academics, and (3) require parents to be actively involved. With me as chairman, Presbyterian School opened in fall 1989 for early childhood and lower school education. In August 2000 the middle school opened with sixty students in fifth and sixth grades, and in June 2003 the first class of eighth-grade students graduated. In 2005, a fourteen-acre property located off Loop 610 South was purchased to become the school's Outdoor Education Campus (OEC). It opened in spring 2008. There are now 550 students attending Presbyterian School, and graduates are excelling in Houston's finest high schools and America's prestigious colleges. Significantly, Presbyterian School is not only Christ–centered and focused on academics but also nurtures good, caring citizens who are interested in the world around them and contributing to its success.

In 2009, on the school's twentieth anniversary, I was honored by the announcement of the "Eugene H. Vaughan Academic Enrichment Center of Excellence at Presbyterian School." The Center is designed to help all students succeed, whatever their needs may be, from tutoring to help with learning disabilities. Another wonderful school memory: I had the utmost joy of presenting Sir John Templeton to my Presbyterian School students as a "real knight." So, as it turned out, my role in creating the school was well worth the early tumult.

Serving in a leadership role means taking a stand, and that can be very lonely. I can think of no instance more illustrative of this personally than my experience with St. John's School, where I was a trustee. Just two or three times in my life has everything inside me cried out to do nothing, but because of my belief in the truth of what Edmund Burke said, I did act. Timing for this particular Edmund Burke moment could not have been worse; it was happening at the same time as the merger was fraught with complications and we were planning for Presbyterian School. But there was no choice. Because of certain policies and the environment at St. John's, the morale and self-esteem of many students and parents were being drastically affected. Susan and I were chairing the annual giving campaign during the "Energy Depression," so we had to listen—and listen—to unhappy parents. St. John's policies reduced the chances of seniors getting accepted into top-tier universities. In the final analysis it came down to ranking seniors in their college applications, which the college counselor insisted on, backed by the headmaster and chairman of the board. Through research, I learned from the admissions officer of Columbia University that no high-quality high schools in the East and very few in the nation ranked students. To understand the issue, imagine a St. John's senior class of four students, all of whom are future Oxford Scholar caliber. But now two are in the bottom half, and one is in the hopeless fourth quarter. Elite colleges would not touch a ranked student below the top ten percent, but they would accept non-ranked applicants when convinced. St. John's was doing an injustice to its mostly elite students by ranking. Morale at the school was so low it was heartbreaking to witness.

Board meetings were at 7:30 p.m., ten minutes from home. At 7 p.m. I would decide that I simply would not go. I was just one trustee of many over the years, and why was it my responsibility to correct the wrong? At 7:10 p.m., I would decide I would attend but not say anything argumentative. At 7:20 p.m., Edmund Burke invariably would kick in. If I were to have self-respect and live by my personal code, I had to go and I had to speak up. Some very unpleasant things were said to me by the "control" group. Eventually I carried the day and ranking ceased. Since 1990, many more students have gotten into the colleges of their choice. Some trustees still apologize every time they see me. I smile and say, "Thank Edmund Burke."

During this distressing time at St. John's, our son, Richard, was a student there. He was not personally affected by the policies, and as a top student had been approved to spend a year at Fettes School in

Edinburgh, Scotland. This was a huge honor because no one from St. John's School had ever been permitted to attend. Richard had started school a year early, so he had what we called a "year of enrichment" to be used in some worthwhile way. Richard also was one of several students who qualified to participate in the "Junior Transfer Program," wherein he could spend a semester at any of twelve top high schools in America. He chose Princeton Day School and fell in love with the roundtable method of Socratic teaching, as opposed to the usual lecture style. He decided to forgo Fettes and seek a roundtable school. He found his "miracle" at St. Andrew's School in Delaware and spent his year of enrichment there. The first person he met was Tad Roach, a wonderful English teacher who became a superb headmaster. While we were thrilled for Richard, it nearly broke the hearts of Susan and me for our beloved son to be 1,500 miles away. After leaving him on campus, we found the lumps in our throats so painful that we had driven to almost halfway home before we could talk about him.

As we knew he would, Richard thrived at St. Andrew's, and it provided him his pathway to Princeton. During Richard's two football seasons at St. Andrew's, every Friday I flew to Philadelphia, rented a car, and spent the night at the DuPont Hotel in Wilmington. Next day I drove to St. Andrew's for the 1:30 p.m. game. Richard and I did not talk before the game, but he knew I was there, and so did his teammates. I became kind of their talisman. After the game Richard and I would meet for about ten minutes under the trees, hug, and then I would drive 80 mph to Philadelphia. I never missed a game. I wanted to be nowhere else. As a St. John's faculty member wrote, Richard was "an electrifying runner."

Richard was elected student body president and was, as the headmaster stated, "a leader of the best kind, where it is conferred." An unexpected bonus and a favorite memory: George Plimpton, who became a good friend, adopted Richard's St. Andrew's class and gave the graduation address. George, the best-known and most beloved raconteur in America, had so much charisma he could be seen from outer space. He also loved fireworks and was "The Fireworks Commissioner of New York City." When he told me he would like to do something very special for graduation, I knew there would be fireworks involved. He said if I

A happy respite in 1986. The "Vaughan Boys Out West!" Dad, Richard, and I cut the heart out of San Francisco, Los Angeles, and Big Sur. It was Dad's first trip so far west and the first time the three of us spent a week together "on the road." The tableside session with B. B. King at the Fairmont Hotel vied for the highlight.

would pay for the fireworks, he would get the "Gucci Brothers, First Family of Fireworks" to donate their time, and he would donate his time. Thus, just after dark by the gorgeous, two-mile-long lake, George, in collaboration with Richard in his role as class president, intoned the individual name of each spectacular firework with a poem or joke about every graduate just before it exploded magnificently over the water. It was an unforgettably marvelous experience for everyone. Richard has been a stalwart trustee of St. Andrew's since 2005 and chairman of its vital investment committee for over a decade. He and Headmaster Tad Roach love and inspire each other in thrusting St. Andrew's ever upward. This thrills Susan and me.

The unique challenges with Presbyterian School and St. John's helped prepare me for even more that I would encounter in later years at the Texas Medical Center. When Dr. James Willerson, the renowned president and CEO of The University of Texas Health Science Center and superstar of medicine, asked me to become chairman of his board of development, I agreed. I was very excited about this opportunity to

129

take on a leadership role in Houston's illustrious medical center. At last I was coming in proximity to the dream of Mam-maw.

Almost immediately, however, Dr. Willerson informed me Dr. Denton Cooley had elicited a promise years ago that when he retired as CEO of the Texas Heart Institute, Jim would replace him. That time was now! Thus my first day as chairman I met privately with Dr. Larry Kaiser on his first day as the new CEO. He asked me to "forget being a cheerleader." He wanted me to be a fiduciary chairman. We spent two extraordinarily ambitious years together in tackling immensely challenging situations and advancing the institution internationally. Within the world's largest medical center, there was a plethora of competition among health institutions, which is a good thing, but some competition went so far as to be destructive. Dr. Kaiser eventually returned to his native Philadelphia for family reasons, but we did a tremendous amount of hard and enduring work, including successfully rebranding The University of Texas Health Science Center. The name was so complex there was no elevator ride long enough to explain it. The new name, UTHealth, has a logo that is strong and a beautiful burnt orange. Most important, the name change created a new and vibrant image for the institution. And it became the board to serve on. UTHealth reached its celebratory zenith at a classy first-ever gala, "A Celebration of Transformation and Hope," honoring Dr. Denton Cooley and the Honorable James A. Baker III. River Oaks Country Club's ballroom was overflowing, fulfilling the goal of spreading the word broadly throughout the region that the excellence of UTHealth had risen to a new and exhilarating level. Denton and Jim, both highly admired and popular, engaged in witty banter. Dr. Kaiser wove a powerful message about the accomplishments and ambitious goals of UTHealth, climaxing with a surprise announcement of a scholarship in my name.

My Med Center experience also gave me the chance to work closely with Marc Shapiro, esteemed banker and civic leader and the best financial mind in Houston and far beyond. We became close. Another bonus was becoming close and admiring friends of Phil and Suzie Conway, previous chairman of UTHealth and chairman of the nursing school board, respectively. We regularly get together for dinner and always have a serious agenda written on a cocktail napkin. They are world champion people. Additionally, my admiration deepened for the preternaturally inspiring head of MD Anderson Cancer Center, John Mendelsohn. MD Anderson, under his leadership and the amazing graciousness of him and Anne, was perennially named the #1 cancer center in America. This great institution was transformed by Dr. Mendelsohn with his expertise and graciousness, inspiring its 20,000 employees into his "image." His logo is the best I have ever seen: "Making Cancer History" with a red slash through "Cancer."

Every time I have said, "Yes, of course!" I have gone into the situation realizing there could be major challenges and rough seas, but each time I felt that what was gained far outweighed any loss. I also have gone into every situation and made every decision in life with Susan beside me. She has encouraged me and has been my partner in every sense. How could I not stand tall when Susan is by my side?

CHAPTER 16

On Hallowed Ground at Vanderbilt

*One thing I know: the only ones among you who will be really
happy are those who will have sought and found how to serve.*

—Albert Schweitzer

The invitation I received in May 1972 to serve on Vanderbilt's board of
trustees was life-changing and life-enhancing. Alexander Heard, the
chancellor of Vanderbilt for nineteen fertile years, was one of the men
I have admired most in my life. Alexander and Jean Heard were the
best husband-and-wife leaders I ever have known. During his years
of leadership, they invited us to stay at the mansion for most trustee
meetings. "The Chancellor" (I could never accept his invitations to
call him "Alex"—after all, he was not only head of Vanderbilt but was
also concurrently chairman of the Ford Foundation) assigned me to
many of his most important special committees. Even more, we had a
marvelous friendship that endured. The matchless climax of our friendship was when they invited us to vacation with them in the Galapagos
Islands to celebrate Chancellor Heard's seventy-fifth birthday; we
"Rambo-snorkeled" together around the perimeter of a large sunken
crater, surrounded by beautiful black and gold "Vanderbilt" fish and
benign seven-foot sharks. Our families also traveled together to Russia.
Our time together was pure gold.

William S. (Bill) Vaughn, CEO of Eastman Kodak, was chairman
when I was elected to the board of trustees. While I was unaware of it
when I went on the board, it slowly became evident to me the Vaughns
have played significant roles at Vanderbilt over three generations. The

This memorable 1978 Vanderbilt board of trustees photo includes Chancellor Heard (front row, fourth from left); the matchless "Mr. Vanderbilt," Sam Fleming (front row, fifth from left); and William S. Vaughn (front row, second from right), CEO of Eastman Kodak, past chairman of the board of trustees, and the man I believe to be the single best leader under whom I have ever served.

grandfather of Chairman William S. Vaughn was William J. Vaughn, said to be a true polymath. A mathematician by training, he could read a dozen languages, including Sanskrit and Russian, possessed a history library of 6,000 volumes, and helped introduce Phi Beta Kappa on campus in 1901. "Miss Stella" Vaughn, chairman Vaughn's aunt, was Vanderbilt's first female instructor, persevered relentlessly for the admission of women, and was "unofficial Dean of Women." She became known as the "grand old lady" of Vanderbilt. Bill spent much of his youth growing up on campus in what later was voted "The Vaughn Home," and in his words, "I inhaled Vanderbilt with every breath I took." He graduated with a record of all As, was awarded the Founder's Medal, named Class Poet, and attended Oxford University as a Rhodes Scholar.

Undergirding my judgment that he was the best leader under whom I ever served—which says a lot indeed!—he was known as a quiet and unassuming person of vision, wit, and unfailing good manners. Chancellor Heard wrote of him, "His tenure as chairman included extraordinarily difficult years of campus tension, during which his poise, wide-ranging experience, intellectual power, and sagacity made him of prodigious value to Vanderbilt, and especially to me."

I am profoundly grateful that I did not debate with this great man how our name should be spelled!

My delight serving on the board multiplied when Bill Bain and Gene Shanks became trustees. Bill and I went way back. When I was at Underwood Neuhaus and Bill was vice chancellor of alumni and development at Vanderbilt, Bill would end the day in our home after Houston development calls, and we would dream of someday having our own companies. Eventually Bain and Company had over 7,000 consultants worldwide—almost as successful as Vaughan Nelson! When Gene Shanks, president of Bankers Trust, became trustee, the three of us gravitated together and had rare rapport and much fun. Gene hired our son, Richard, to work at Bankers Trust and, I believe, gave Richard the impetus toward an exceptionally high level of business acumen and ambition. Tom Barry, my admired friend, completed Richard's "MBA" when Tom started a new company and Richard had the invaluable experience of ten start-up years with an able and noble businessman. Richard has been exceptionally fortunate because, since moving to Houston in 2006, he has been associated with Cockrell Interests, headed by Ernie Cockrell, a third-generation Houstonian whom I believe is exceeded by no one in honor and business astuteness, and by the laudable Bobby Hatcher.

Gene and Susan Shanks (we call ourselves "Gene and Susan Squared") became closest friends. We traveled together to Las Vegas—he was a mathematical genius and taught me how to win!—and we always have laughed continuously when together. Gene was, in my judgment, one of the two or three best trustees over my three and half decades on the board.

Being a trustee of Vanderbilt University was itself an unexpected, existentially enhancing aspect of my life from age thirty-nine onward. I was soon to learn it also brought myriad bonuses. One of these occurred during a break at an early trustee meeting. A distinguished gentleman walked over and said, "You look like a good Tennessee Squire to me!" It was trustee Reagor Motlow, president of the Jack Daniel's Distillery and son of the famous "Lem Motlow, Prop." which appears on every bottle of Jack Daniel's. Soon thereafter I received a "Tennessee Squire" certificate of membership and a deed to land (a square foot) in Moore County, Tennessee, home of Jack Daniel's Distillery. That started a never-ceasing flow of happy surprises, such as invitations to coon hunts in Moore County, Tennessee Squire glasses for sipping whiskey, annual calendars with pictures of people and places in Moore County, and humorous letters telling me of "goings on" in Moore County—all delightful. In obituaries, I sometime see "Tennessee Squire" among achievements. Not an achievement in my case but surely a pleasure.

Among the bonuses of Vanderbilt are the friends who have enriched my life, such as the Roger Reynolds family of San Francisco. Roger is an astute lawyer and influential thinker. He and his lovely wife, Debbie, with their outstanding children, Zach and Jen, visited us in Houston en route to Vanderbilt, and it has been my privilege to correspond regularly with Roger every month or so on an intriguing variety of subjects and issues, including his beloved Giants and Oakland Warriors. We are friends for life.

On rotating years, every Vanderbilt trustee had the opportunity to host the Friday Night Black and Gold Dinner, very formal and festive. Every trustee wore a black tuxedo with the gold cummerbund presented upon becoming a trustee. One of the years in which we hosted, due to illness I could not attend. Our daughter, Margaret, graciously shared the duties with Susan. The event took place at Cheekwood Museum, a classy venue, on a dark and stormy Shakespearian night. In front of this distinguished crowd that included a good number of Fortune 100 CEOs, Susan rose and said, "I am told there is an old Tennessee saying: Don't plant more cotton than your wife can hoe." The place exploded with laughter. For decades that line has regularly been quoted to and about heroic Susan.

In 1994, I was presented the Vanderbilt Distinguished Alumnus Award. It was presented by my dear friends, John Poindexter (left) and Bill Bain (right). Both toasted and brilliantly roasted me.

Although I served on key committees such as executive, investment, administration, and building and grounds (the Vanderbilt campus was honored as a National Arboretum), the role I cherished most as trustee was serving as chairman of the student life committee, which I did for twelve years. I believed—and often said—I had the best job on the entire board. Interacting with the students directly was tremendously stimulating. Until my chairmanship, the administration created an agenda for the trustees' student life committee meeting, which featured students and topics that invariably reflected well on everything at Vanderbilt. I set firm policy that each trustee student life committee meeting had to present a balance of campus problems as well as positive issues and events. I encountered a lot of resistance, but I held my ground. For instance, cheating was a huge problem across the nation, and I held an entire trustee committee meeting focused on that issue, including the national perspective, the specifics at Vanderbilt, and what was being done about it. Alcoholism was another horrific issue. Binge drinking was starting in high school and compounding at college. I remember the trustees getting very engaged because the student life committee started opening up issues they had not seen before. At the time, the most controversial trustee student life committee meeting I held was on "Homosexuality at Vanderbilt." No punches were pulled. Several students and professors told their stories. One student came out during the meeting. Margaret helped me tremendously in preparing for this meeting. I believe bringing these campus issues into the light improved student life and enlightened the trustees tremendously. Attendance by trustees grew larger; they had the alternatives of attending the academic affairs committee or going to play golf or taking a nap at the hotel. So I took rising attendance as a genuine compliment.

After seventeen years focused primarily on improving financial structure and endowment assets, we entered a Golden Age at Vanderbilt with the arrival of Gordon Gee as chancellor in August 2000. He arrived with 600 bowties; off-the-chart energy; invincible zest for faculty, students, and alumni; and ideas flying like Christmas sparklers of yore. The atmosphere on campus changed instantly. He knew his stuff. And everyone knew he knew his stuff. Gordon not only opened his chancellor's office door to students, he went to their Greek houses, their dances (Gordon loved to dance), intramural games, and the Rand Student Cafeteria. In no time at all, students took him to their hearts and dubbed him "The Gee."

Houston was one of the first Vanderbilt cities outside Nashville where Chancellor Gee spoke to the alumni. I introduced him and, in part, said, "Gordon Gee is going to be for Vanderbilt's future what Spindletop was to Texas. He has come roaring in as a fabled gusher, and nothing ever is going to be the same again!" Gordon wowed the large audience. As we left, we hugged, and our friendship only deepened from that moment.

Early in Gordon's tenure, the trustees gathered to honor Susan and me for our major donation to help restore the Dean Madison Sarratt Student Center. Dean Sarratt was a towering institution at Vanderbilt and an inspiration. Hanging in the lobby of the Sarratt Student Center was the admonition for which he was famous: "Today you are going to take two examinations. One is in geometry. The other is in honor. If you fail one, let it be geometry."

Provost Tom Burish suggested it would be appropriate for the Vaughan Plaque also to hang in the lobby across from that of Dean Sarratt. On November 3, 2000, Chancellor Gee said very nice words about Susan and me and asked me to speak. In part I said:

This is, in fact, hallowed ground and a hallowed moment for me. It was but 110 miles when Mother and Dad drove me to this campus in 1951 from Brownsville, Tennessee. Brownsville is a west Tennessee suburb of Mason, a tiny town without a red light and Bozo's Bar-B-Q, John Poindexter would remind you. But the round trip of my life from that first step on this campus back to this spot, this moment, is indeed for me a flight through the "Smoke Screen of Impossibility...."

Vanderbilt made everything possible for me. It elevated my vision. It equipped me to dream. Vanderbilt gave me life-long friends. One of those friends introduced me to Susan. Robert Frost talks about the road that made all the difference; Susan has been the Autobahn that has made all the difference! And indirectly, therefore, Vanderbilt also gave me Margaret—our double-degree Vanderbilt graduate—and Richard. So Vanderbilt has made possible almost everything I treasure most in the world....

I augmented my NROTC Scholarship by working those years as Dean's messenger, so I saw a lot of Dean Sarratt. He was the first person I ever heard in just ordinary conversation speak William James' magnificent words: "The best use of life is to spend it in something that outlasts life." Once you hear those words, they burrow down inside you and you can never get them out and they itch you all over until you, trying to do something about it, end up standing on some hallowed ground like today....

Dean Sarratt was no doubt astonished and highly pleased that I became a Vanderbilt trustee. He had six years to work on me before he died in 1978. But he would have been immensely pleased that I became chairman of the student affairs committee because during those six years Dean Sarratt constantly admonished me to "Remember what the university is about is students. All the rest of us are scaffolding...."

There is a perfect symmetry to today. God and Vanderbilt have granted my dream—to nurture the institution which has so nurtured our family and me—by permitting us to play a small role in re-creating the building that is at the center of student life at Vanderbilt University, one bearing Dean Madison Sarratt's name.

Gordon and I were close friends and I his confidante; he tested ideas on me. When I came to trustee meetings alone he always asked me to sit with him—just the two of us—at basketball and baseball games, during which he told me some of his problems and hopes. Susan and I were always invited to stay at "Braeburn," and we became privy to the marital problems which led to divorce. I adored Gordon. More than any person I have ever known, he possessed a "merry heart."

In "transient" Boston, I was elected president of the Vanderbilt Club, and when we first moved to Houston, I was elected president of the Houston Vanderbilt Club. My big idea was to hold "Vanderbilt Comes to Houston." On a Saturday morning, Chancellor Heard led a team of Vanderbilt's most distinguished professors. We had a sizable audience of not just alumni but of parents who were eager to hear more of this excellent school which was "not in Texas, but close enough to Houston." I believe this event radiated rapidly through Houston so positively that it touched off the large flow of students from Houston to Vanderbilt which has continued unabated. Alumni in the area have climbed from several dozen to over 3,000 currently. I have been interviewing applicants and writing recommendation letters for fifty years. Among the honors I most cherish is that I am told I have been called "Mr. Vanderbilt" in Houston in recent decades!

In culmination of my service to Vanderbilt after I became an emeritus trustee at age seventy-five, our family gave the Eugene H. Vaughan Family Scholarship for Entrepreneurial Excellence. It is to be used for worthy applicants from Haywood High School in Brownsville, Tennessee, or YES Prep Public Schools, St. John's School, or Kinkaid School in Houston. So far the scholarships all have gone to the Houston short list. I still hope to encourage someone else from Brownsville to attend!

Margaret was with me at the climactic dinner in 2008 when Chancellor Nick Zeppos thanked me for my thirty-six years of service as a

Margaret's first visit to Vanderbilt.

trustee and welcomed me as trustee emeritus. He presented me with a meaningful, hand-carved trustee bowl, the lid of which was made from the original "Vanderbilt Oak." It was a tough night for me, and the real celebration came back at the Vanderbilt Plaza when my beloved, double-degreed Margaret presented me with a bottle of Gentleman Jack, which we shared with an outpouring of precious memories.

*Margaret at her graduation ceremony from Vanderbilt in 1988
with her exceedingly proud "Trustee Daddy."*

Margaret and Vanderbilt are nearly synonymous to me, both beloved and at the center of my being. Margaret had been traveling to Vanderbilt with Susan and me since about age six. A perennial honor student, class Prefect, varsity athlete, and cheerleader at St. John's School, Margaret was a leader in her class. On her official admission visit to campus, she emphatically stated, "I love Vanderbilt. But, Daddy, that is your school. I want my school." She had been accepted and was being aggressively pursued by outstanding Davidson College near Charlotte, North Carolina. All indications were that Davidson would be her choice. Heartsick, I backed off and went mute on the issue, waiting for the final announcement of her decision. The evening before the acceptance deadline, Margaret announced to Susan and me that she had decided on Vanderbilt. At the eleventh-and-a-half hour, by some miracle—to me—a recent Vanderbilt graduate whom Margaret particularly admired had taken her to dinner and persuaded her to go to Vanderbilt.

The obstacle course was just beginning! Susan, Margaret, and I drove to Nashville, and at registration Margaret seemed abnormally subdued. Soon it was verified that she had full-fledged mononucleosis. Everyone knew this was incompatible with starting college. Her advisor, the dean of students, and her doctor, Dr. Andy Spickard, a classmate of mine, told her to delay a semester to start. So did Susan and I. Margaret never wavered. She resolutely said, "Daddy, you can't tell me all my life not to be a quitter and now tell me to quit." She was hospitalized for several weeks, and it was awful for her, but she refused to quit. I was torn between frustration and admiration. She struggled, but she persevered. Margaret was elected to the prestigious Honor Council her junior year and was vice-president of the council her senior year. She pledged the Pi Beta Phi sorority, like two generations of Bolinger women before her and, incredibly, upon graduation was the recipient of the Excelsior Award, an honor so high that it was awarded only once every few years to "a student who rises above all others."

I can close my eyes now and see a co-ed walking across campus with swept-back blonde hair, wearing a purple and white Haywood High Tomcat letter jacket, and suddenly, in a blinding flash of recognition and pride, whispering to myself, "That's Margaret!"

CHAPTER 17

The Visceral Joy of Friendship

*A friendship founded on business is better
than a business founded on friendship.*

—John D. Rockefeller

The smiling cherubic face on every can of Campbell's soup we saw growing up belonged to Mike Feeley. In adulthood he was just as pleasant and honorable as he looked on the can. Mike was a Harvard Business School graduate working for the prestigious investment banking firm of Brown Brothers & Harriman when he showed up at my office. I did not know him well, but he arrived with an idea that elevated my professional and personal life. Mike told me he recently had dinner in New York with Don Kurtz (Equitable Insurance Corp.) and Steve Canter (Dreyfus Mutual Funds), and they warmed to his idea of a small group of CEOs of investment management firms getting together periodically to discuss investing and personal issues. I liked the idea a lot, and on my next trip to New York, Mike, Don, Steve, and I had dinner to develop the concept. I suggested Wally Stern (Capital Guardian) and Walter Cabot (Harvard Management Company) would be ideal members and agreed to contact them. We added Tom Barry (T. Rowe Price, followed by Rockefeller Co.), who suggested Ed Mathias (The Carlyle Group).

We thought nine would be an ideal number and named it the "Group of Nine." I consider the Group of Nine another miracle that has enhanced wonderfully the lives of Susan and me. Beginning in 1986, we met every nine to twelve months with rotating members taking responsibility for the venue and hospitality and other members handling the high-quality

143

program agendas. Over the span of three decades, we have grown to trust each other completely. Susan and I consider these couples to be among our closest friends in the world. We know we could call on Pat and Tom Barry, Carol and Steve Canter, Dorsey and Walter Cabot, Betsy and Wally Stern, Ed Mathias and George Roche (T. Rowe Price) and Don Kurtz (whose wonderful wives sadly have died prematurely), for anything, anytime, and they would respond. Susan and I would do the same. Along the way, the Nine made the decision that we liked each other so well, that camaraderie and trust had grown so deep among both the CEOs and wives, that we would add no more. We realize the Group of Nine has been a precious gift.

Our gatherings were not boondoggles in any sense, but we did meet in splendid places and had memorably good times around the work. There was a trend: July meetings were in places like Nantucket and Mohegan Island, and winter meetings in sunny resorts like Key Largo. Susan and I hosted the February 1991 meeting in Lyford Cay, Bahamas. The legendary Sir John M. Templeton, who had become my good friend, invited us to stay at the Lyford Cay Club and hosted us at his nearby White Columns home.

The Vaughan Family had many wonderful road trips, and we did not consider it a true vacation unless we spent the first night at La Mansion del Rio in San Antonio. So when Susan and I chose San Antonio as the Nine site in 1993, we knew how to show everybody a great time. The group loved the Alamo and "Tennessee heroes" stories. The barge rides on the river and many superb Mexican food restaurants along the River Walk were unlike anything they had seen before. One night we took them "a few miles down the road" to Gruene Hall, Texas's oldest and continually operating dance hall, built in 1878. The dance floor was wavy from wear. The band that night, "Asleep at the Wheel," later became famous. Memorable!

June 1998 brought us to Auberge du Soleil in Rutherford, California. This is our absolutely favorite venue. Susan and I worked months ahead to make certain we could show our friends the best of the area. This included an incomparable nine-course dinner at Thomas Keller's famous French Laundry, where Susan had to make reservations six months in advance.

In 2010, we celebrated the group's twenty-fifth anniversary in New York City, followed by several unforgettable days in an inn in Northampton. The gorgeous lavender wisteria outside our window frequently appears on the immersion plates of our minds. We honored Mike Feeley for "making it all happen." Unknown to us, it would be a timely tribute; our dear Mike died the following year of throat cancer.

Lasting friendships coupled with lasting business relationships are precious. That makes losing a friend and colleague of many years so heart-wrenching. On the morning of January 10, 1994, my dear friend and partner, Dick Nelson, came into my office and said he did not feel well, an upset stomach, and agreed when I urged him to go home. Within thirty-nine hours of coming into my office Dick was dead.

No one was remotely prepared for this tragedy. The foremost infectious disease expert in the Texas Medical Center—and a personal friend of the Nelson family—concluded that Dick had died of "infectious disease of unknown origin." To this day, he says it is one of the most baffling cases he has encountered. (His best guess is the infection was contracted in the Baikal Region of the USSR the previous summer.) We all did whatever we could to help Dick's family. The next morning I met with Barbara Nelson and their two children at the safe deposit section of their bank to discuss how to proceed. Dick was fifty-four; his death was so sudden that there were no plans whatsoever. Frank picked out a cemetery and gravesite. Susan met with the pastor at Memorial Presbyterian Church and fully planned the funeral with him. I wrote his obituary.

It's hard to press on at a heartbreaking time like this. Frank and I sat down and carefully organized the firm. We personally called each of Dick's clients and ultimately personally called all our clients, understanding that the sudden loss of a name principal was unnerving and sorrowful. We all needed the comfort and reassurance of communication.

I knew I had to bring in a principal or two. I made my mind up immediately about one. Margaret Buescher was a Vanderbilt graduate and a key person in the trust department of Texas Commerce Bank. Margaret—gracious, lovely, smart, and a CFA—was admired and well-liked by everyone who knew her. Now I had to go tell my staunch benefactor and friend, Ben Love, that I wanted to hire away one of his stars.

I played my ace. I knew another bank was trying to hire her. Ben said, "Well, Gene, if I am going to lose Margaret, I had rather lose her to you."

In addition to dealing with the loss of our partner and friend, in my case a relationship that spanned twenty-eight years, we were striving to put fingers in the numerous dikes that were springing leaks. Competitors come at you when you are weakened, and consultants especially moved in. We felt we needed to invest conservatively during this period of vulnerability, but the great growth market of the 1990s was taking off. "Value" investing was giving way to "growth" and "momentum" investors, firms whose philosophy was to buy only stocks that were on the move and making new highs. This was anathema to our "value" investing. Brokers were becoming "smarter" than professional money managers because they felt no constraints of responsibility.

It is a notable tribute to how hard our team worked individually and as a group that we did so well to meet the challenge. In 1995, I added another Vanderbilt graduate—if one looked closely one could spot a trend! Someone called it "Gene's academic nepotism." Lee Lahourcade, also a Harvard MBA and CFA, became a principal. This solidified our team during a sad and highly pressurized period.

In the 1994 EOY letter, I wrote that Dick Nelson was zestfully investing and punning—he loved and excelled at both—through his final day at work. In every aspect, Dick went out vibrantly on top. In honor of Dick, I quoted these words which hang in Deener Matthews's The Swag, our favorite retreat in the Smoky Mountains of North Carolina. Deener's husband, Dan, was the Dean of Trinity Church at the foot of Wall Street.

> It is hard to see where we stand right now as Holy Ground. We are a people so caught up in the process of living that we find it impossible to live in the present moment. Almost everything in our society lures us to dream of the future. Everything will be better, we think, when things are different than they are right now. The very best God can do is what God is giving us today. Not only is the ground we stand on Holy but each day is a gift.

In a eulogy for a dear friend, Nobel Laureate Seamus Heaney said, "He would walk into my mind as if it were a town and he a torchlight procession of one, lighting up the streets." These words are embedded

Out of the blue, Matt and Ellen Simmons invited Susan and me to be among their guests at Kincardine, the magnificent country mansion near the Royal Family's Balmoral Estate in Scotland. With kilt-dancing and pony-trekking on the Queen's horses, the trip featured non-stop hospitality and fun.

in my mind because they are exactly the way the Matt Simmons Family entered our lives. Matt and Ellen both had unlimited energy, stamina, and yeasty minds. They came to us at a large party in the mansion of the chancellor of the University of Houston and forthwith invited us to be their guests at Kincardine, a Downton Abbey–type ancestral home of young friends in Scotland, about ten miles from Balmoral, the magnificent country home of Queen Elizabeth II. The dozen spirited and congenial couples were from all over America, Italy, and Norway, elated to be in this rapturously picturesque land, a fabulous time of non-stop hospitality. Matt was a true genius. He literally knew more than anyone in the world about oil and was constantly in demand to speak world-wide. Moreover, he was a true renaissance man, not unlike Churchill in that he was a splendid artist, historian, orator, raconteur, author, and world traveler. Ellen, another outstanding graduate of Conn College, was always at his side yet raised five superlative daughters to perfection. I facilitated the oldest, Wheeler, in transferring her sophomore year to Vanderbilt; she graduated summa cum laude. Matt and Ellen became our consummate friends, and we were frequently together at their home when they were in Houston and at their magnificent "Little Women" Alcott House in Rockport, Maine, one of our favorite places on earth.

Tragedy struck. While swimming alone in their pool in Maine, Matt had a heart attack. Susan and I went to Rockport for the funeral, gathered with L. E. Simmons and Matt's other accomplished siblings—there is an endowed chair at Harvard Business School for the family, all of whom are graduates—and ached with grief. We have loved their precious girls, from watching them "bake cookies" of rocks when they were very little through their marriages. They are family to Susan and me. It was a treasured tradition that Matt was the merry center of every Christmas and other gatherings in their home. Matt and L. E. are brothers of a remarkable Renaissance family. They embody Brilliance, Goodness, and overflowing Generosity.

L. E. and his wife, Ginny, are among the most gracious and generous people we ever have known. They invited us to be guests at their beautiful wilderness home on the Snake River in Wyoming. L. E. often told me, "You are part of our family." Without preface, L. E. performed one of the single most inspired acts of generosity in my lifetime. Soon after Richard and Ann married, Susan and I went to Kiawah Island alone. L. E. had no way of knowing my body would fail me during the trip but—out of the blue—he offered his private plane to take us to and from Kiawah. This act of kindness seemed to "divinely" presage what developed into a dire physical need. L. E., a devout Mormon, is a major business and moral leader in Houston, having chaired Texas Children's Hospital and the Jesse H. Jones Graduate School of Management at Rice University, among many other worthy endeavors.

God has gifted Susan and me with friends from esoteric sources, one

*With two of my fellow "October Boys"—Joe Hafner (center) and
Jeff Love (right).*

being the births of Margaret and Richard. The common experience of
preparation for birth, the hospital stay, and our children growing up
together has fostered our friendships with John and Marilyn Holstead
and Ewing and Kay Werlein. The men were outstanding partners at
Vinson & Elkins, and Ewing Werlein became a respected federal judge
and chairman of the Houston Methodist Hospital System. For many
years the six of us spent every New Year's Eve together and glorious
repartee abounded. Probably excelled only by our tented safari Kenya
adventure was our whitewater expedition on rafts down the Middle
Fork of the Salmon River with the Holsteads (Will, Rand, and Scott,
plus Margaret and Richard). The five-day excitement was compounded
at the end by a forest fire—which prevented our stopping to camp
overnight—and salmonella attacks!

Being born in October long had been a handicap (youngest, smallest
in class), but all that has been completely compensated for by becoming a charter member of the "October Boys Luncheon Club." Joe Hafner, Jeff Love, and I have had "lunch in October" for many years and
have recently been joined by Tom Amonett. Joe and Merrill Hafner

are closest friends. Joe was long-time CEO of Riviana Foods, big-time rice products, which led to a running joke that he had to be served rice (in lieu of potatoes, etc.) everywhere we went. We have served on many boards and always have had a rollicking time whenever together. Merrill is a beautiful, gracious, admirable New Orleanian, and she and Susan uphold the reputation of the South for charming, elegant women. Jeff Love, Joe, and I are replete with long-running humor and dearly love being together anywhere, anytime. Jeff, a master wordsmith (especially of words five syllables and more), emceed a Vanderbilt event honoring me in 1994.

When Susan and I moved to Houston in 1964, I gravitated to Rice University because it and Vanderbilt were so similar in size, academic quality—even football struggles. When President George Rupp arrived, we became great friends. When I resigned from the St. John's School board after Richard transferred to St. Andrew's, I filled him in on the issues, and George, who had two children at St. John's, did a magnificent job as a trustee of speaking with knowledge and moral authority. In fact, I think George is the single most articulate person I know.

My already high regard for Rice soared when its chairman of the trustees, Jim Crownover, and his wife, Molly, invited Susan and me to a small luncheon in their home for incoming Rice president David Leebron and First Lady Ping Sun. They both are truly extraordinary and have elevated Rice, Houston—and me. They are warm personal friends and have been gracious hosts to us in their home. Ping is luminous and serves as an invaluable board member of Center for Houston's Future. David has been elected president of the ultra-prestigious American Association of Universities (AAU). Again, I am amazingly fortunate. Rice spawns greatness. Current board chair Bobby Tudor and his glowingly dynamic wife, Phoebe, who is a moral force for good, are Houston's unrivaled couple on multiple uplifting fronts.

It is an incomparable gift to have a friend whom you cherish with all your heart and who reciprocates in full, and beyond. Such a friend to Susan and me was John W. Poindexter, who "adopted" us in Boston in 1963 just before we married and was our family's best friend the rest of his extraordinary life. With a breaking heart I gave his eulogy in Benton Chapel at Vanderbilt in 2011.

JOHN POINDEXTER MEMORIAL SERVICE
BENTON CHAPEL, VANDERBILT UNIVERSITY
MONDAY, FEBRUARY 7, 2011

How does one celebrate John Poindexter, the Michelangelo of celebrating the lives of others?

All who have heard John give a tribute or eulogy—as he did for Chancellor Alexander Heard a few months ago here in Benton Chapel—would agree only John Poindexter possesses the eloquence to do justice to John Poindexter.

Nashville's splendid Historian Ridley Wills called me in Houston to make certain I knew about John. I thanked him and told him I was coming up and would speak. Ridley exclaimed: "I just told Irene I wonder what poor soul is going to try to do justice to John!"

I cannot do justice to John, but here are some qualities of this magnificent man you may recognize. Qualities such as: unique— in all the world sui generis unique!; erudite; urbane; noble; perfectionist; unfailingly kind and polite; perhaps thrifty; profoundly and relentlessly inquisitive, his mind forever learning; a consummate True Gentleman; a connoisseur of breathtaking scope; an arbiter of perfect taste; compassionate; exacting; an epicure; superbly sophisticated wit; and always a friend and good company without peer.

Finally, John was incomparably eloquent about that which he loved with all his prodigious heart: Vanderbilt University.

It has been sixty years since I first walked as a student on this glorious campus. In those six decades and as a trustee for 39 years, I have never heard love, loyalty, and devotion for Vanderbilt expressed so unfeignedly and eloquently as by John. Over the years, there are certain distinctive voices which personify Vanderbilt: Dean Madison Sarratt, Chancellor Alexander Heard, and John W. Poindexter are three of the foremost.

Despite our shared West Tennessee roots—Mason and Brownsville—John and I met in Boston. Long a distinguished editor at Houghton Mifflin, John in Boston was "Mr. Vanderbilt." He searched out all Vanderbilt alumni who worked there, those who were graduate students at Harvard or MIT—or, we kidded him, those who just wandered through Boston—and instilled in each of us a lifetime of love, devotion, and service to our alma mater.

John "adopted" Susan and me the year we married, and we have been closest friends for half a century. We quickly discovered the uniquely "epicurean" John. The Boston Vanderbilt Club met in our home and, while guests waited, taxi after taxi pulled up in front with no people but loaded to the gunwales with delicacies from Boston's gourmet grocer, S. S. Pierce. Each driver said, "Mr. Poindexter sent us." Compliments of John, the alumni guests were given dozens of Southern treats such as Jack Daniel's-flavored figs and what John enjoyed calling "Hatchie River Catfish Caviar!" Don't you believe it!

We began to suspect the extraordinariness of John when that same year we went to the new Four Seasons Restaurant in New York City, then in its third year, when it was the most famous restaurant in the world. John asked so many knowledgeable questions that halfway through the meal, the executive chef himself came out to see what manner of man was this. He and John hit it off as kindred spirits, and he cooked the rest of the meal table side. John had this effect on experts in many fields.

Our friendship quickly ripened, and thus we soon met the mar-velous Judith, destined to be John's human equivalent and love for 37 years. She too was a star of the publishing world as the admired, and somewhat feared, director of personnel at Houghton Mifflin. John and Judith were, without question, Boston's most proper "Proper Bostonian" couple! The four of us gathered frequently, including to watch the burial of President Kennedy amidst the all-engulfing grief in Boston.

John was beloved by all of us who passed through Boston, and he inspired hundreds of us—and thousands during his Vanderbilt career—to emulate his service to our alma mater.

Susan and I moved to Houston in 1964. In 1971, in a stroke of customary genius, Chancellor Heard asked John to become Vice Chancellor of Alumni and Development, thus beginning "The Golden Age of Poindexter" at Vanderbilt. John was in huge demand to speak at Vanderbilt clubs around the country. His unique eloquence merged with his perfectionist self. John wielded the English language with such persuasive dexterity, the precise word ever at the service of a brilliant mind and a loving heart. Perfect English, never a wasted word.

The Houston Vanderbilt Club invited John to speak, and we had one of our biggest turnouts ever. It was in our home. He had a great typed speech in hand before he left Nashville. He polished his speech at the hotel. But John's standards were impeccable. He brought his portable typewriter and polished some more upstairs in our home while the overflow audience waited. I sent word to John I was starting his introduction, and he was still polishing!

And when he spoke, it was wondrous. He began with "Let us link arms with the giants of Vanderbilt past, with peerless Mims...." And with that, John roll-called the pantheon of Vanderbilt's most sublime professors. On and on. He invoked from his student days the memory of his beloved Miss Stella Vaughn whose parents taught mathematics for 40 years. He said Miss Stella "lived and breathed and exuded Vanderbilt." Every person present, I believe, has lived and breathed and exuded Vanderbilt ever since that magical evening, as has every alumnus of Vanderbilt who fell under his spell at all of John's countless "magical" speeches throughout the realm. They are legion throughout America and flow into Benton Chapel today.

John's intellect, breadth and depth of knowledge was surpassing. He was brilliant—Phi Beta Kappa and magna cum laude brilliant— on a vast array of subjects. One summer Judith, John, Susan, and I "barged through Burgundy." Among the two dozen passengers was a managing editor of the *New York Times* and other well-versed people. Daily along the way we were exposed to connoisseurs of finest wines, French food, European history, music, and literature. It quickly became evident that John was the master of every subject which arose. Never by upstaging and always by the penetrating intelligence and pertinence of his questions, John elicited the other person's expertise. It was as wondrous as watching John eat a lobster. John extracted every last tiny morsel of meat from a lobster. Knowledge and lobster were all thoroughly savored.

John had his idiosyncrasies. He was uniquely <u>beyond</u> proper. On the entire barge trip John was never seen without his tie and vest. After several days, a member of the crew was delegated to ask Susan and me, "Monsieur Poindexter, does he sleep in his tie?" We referred him to Judith. We do not know if he got an answer. The French had never seen anything like John!

I asked John one time if it were true, as I had heard, that while a student at Vanderbilt, he always carried an umbrella. He smiled and said, "As Oscar Wilde's character said, 'One can't be too careful about the enemies he chooses.' I can't be too careful about my health. I carried an umbrella and wore galoshes until May!"

The four of us spent wonderful days together in Paris, guided by the exquisite "Gourmet Poindexter." That was also how we learned about the uniquely "Thrifty Poindexter." I expect we are the only foursome ever to arrive at the splendid restaurant "La Tour D'Argent" <u>by</u> <u>subway</u>!

Our children, Margaret and Richard, adored John. When they were small, John would travel to Houston for Easter egg hunts.

When Margaret was getting her BA and MBA from Vanderbilt, John gave her a "PhD, in the aesthetics of the world!" When we emailed Margaret the news about John, she emailed back: "Oh, Mama and Daddy, this is such heartbreaking news. I have rushing through me so many memories of Mr. Poindexter. The world, Vanderbilt, and our family have lost a truly great being. I feel so privileged to have known him and to have had important touch points with him throughout my life. I am grieving with you and all so very much."

Yes, as with many here today, we loved this magnificent man with all our hearts. And when we would tell him so, this most eloquent of men, this paragon of precise articulation, would give his wonderful smile and delight in quoting his Mason boyhood nanny: "And it's mighty mutual on both sides!"

His wit was delicious. What delectable company he was. What gaiety and classy elegance he added to any gathering. His conversations flowed eloquently, and his interest in others was inexhaustible. Well, <u>almost</u>! After moving to Nashville as a bachelor vice chancellor, he was in such constant demand as an extra man that John teased Judith by saying he had to marry her because he "had run out of conversation."

John saw through people, but he was too kind to let it matter. He never demeaned. He ennobled us all. John was a man of utmost honor and Christianity—the Mason kind, of which there is no better.

John had another favorite saying, with which I will close: "In God's great plan of justice...." How many times have you heard him say it?

In God's great plan of justice, John, who was never without ailments—very severe ones in recent years—passed from us suddenly and without pain. He even died precisely. And he is with his beloved Mother, with his ethereal organ music soaring, and with his "Old Goat" and other cherished friends, like Gus Halliburton.

And in God's great plan of justice, John—the consummate arbiter of taste and goodness—knows his beloved niece Mary Louise O'Kelly has done her superlative best for him. John knows we love him as he loved us.

And in God's great plan, God knows—and all of us know—John Poindexter was one of Vanderbilt's most transcendent and noblest sons of all time.

Well done, John. We celebrate you. And we love you.

CHAPTER 18

Odyssey:
Discovering the Third Half of My Life

Traveler, there is no road;
You make your own path as you walk.
As you walk, you make your own road
And when you look back
You see the path
You will never travel again.

—Antonio Machado, *"Caminante, No Hay*
Camino / Traveler, There is no Road"
Favorite poem of Dr. Shoshana Zuboff,
Odyssey, Harvard Business School

Since 1993, when I turned sixty, I carefully had been preparing the firm (and myself) for the future. There were sound business reasons for this preparation but also personal ones that seemed to compound annually. We lost our dear friend and partner, Dick Nelson, in 1994. That same year Susan's sister, Janet Miller, died suddenly in Denver. On return from Janet's funeral, I was unloading the car when we received the call that Jerry Smith, my wonderful young friend and protégé at Vanderbilt, had died—again suddenly. Over the next few years, Susan and I were shocked and saddened by the sudden and too-soon deaths of several close friends and relatives. Each wake-up call about mortality gave reason to pause and think.

On the business front, in 1996 it was completely clear to Frank Scarborough and me that not only was the overall market and "growth" sector overpriced but money manager firms were selling at theretofore unheard of prices. To a specific key point, they were selling at five to eight times our internal trade agreement.

With comprehensive—and emotionally excruciating—planning, we set out to do a "strategic merger." It took over two years to overcome the emotional hurdles and find the right company and people. Because of my extensive service in the FAF, ICFA, and CFA Institute, I knew many people and firms. I narrowed prospects to a working list of approximately one hundred and hired an investment banking specialist in money management firms, Berkshire Capital, headed by a Georgia Tech friend of Frank's. Together we winnowed the list to seven and had exploratory visits with them. We then cut to two.

The emergence of New England Investment Companies, which was not on my original radar screen, seems wondrous even now. They paid us a full price and the highest price/earnings ratio (PER) they had ever paid to date, and they permitted us to operate completely independently with me as CEO. Moreover, it was a major strategic partnership because it gave us access to the tremendous resources of a multi-billion-dollar organization. Peter Voss, who was CEO, is one of the finest and brightest leaders I have known in the profession. Someone I trusted told me early on that if Peter Voss gives you his word on something, you can absolutely count on it. This was very important to me.

By the sale, we achieved financial security for our families to an extent I had never dreamed. I had sold my "baby," but it accomplished fulfillment of my entrepreneurial dream and paved the way for a fulfilling "third half" of my life. We had a marvelous, celebratory closing dinner at the Bayou Club. Two weeks later, I was taken to the emergency room and hospitalized with an E. coli infection so serious that our children were called home. I was out six weeks and at only a fraction of my normally very high energy level for six months. All this occurred in complete secrecy because Dick Nelson had died two years earlier from an infectious disease, and news of mine would have created immense anxiety among our staff and clients.

Dr. Jim Pool, who attended me in the hospital, had just months earlier become my internist after the consummate Dr. Tony Gotto (my Vanderbilt friend who was a star at Baylor College of Medicine and president of the American Heart Association) moved to New York to become the dean of Weill Cornell Medical College. Dr. Pool clearly saw the disease as a consequence of selling my "baby." Jim is the most meticulous person I ever have known. Nurses whisper to us that he is the best doctor in the Texas Medical Center. We believe it and know how incredibly lucky we are to have him looking after our family.

God blessed our family with matchless physicians who became steadfast friends. In addition to the peerless Drs. John Mendelsohn and Jim Pool, I expect I would have expired or have been severely enervated had it not been for the expertise of Dr. Tiana Schriver-Bonderer, who has devotedly treated my debilitating diabetes. We "discovered" each other when she was relatively new to the city. I introduced her to First Presbyterian Church and Dr. Vic Pentz, who led her to love, marriage, and her wondrous son, Will. In turn, she extended the effective lives of Ben Love, me, and many others. There was an admiration approaching love between us. Tiana and Jim Pool sat together in church most Sundays and "pressed my case" to God!

Because of the immense amount of ultraviolent rays I absorbed while cutting right-of-way for the TVA, Dr. John Wolf was entirely correct during our first appointment when he predicted, "We are going to become best friends!" John is chairman of the Dermatology Department at Baylor College of Medicine, a poet, a dedicated traveler (with wife Brandi), and a terrific friend. John introduced me to his gracious colleague, Dr. Ida Orengo, a relatively rare expert in Mohs surgery, which is essential in treating my TVA "sunbaked" body.

Jim Pool, who was the personal doctor of Dr. Michael DeBakey through his ninety-nine years, is the quarterback of our family's medical needs. He is immensely respected and connects us with the best in the Texas Medical Center, those whom he has deemed to be as meticulous as himself. Dr. James Key has expertly and faithfully cared for the eyes of Susan and me. And the nonpareil Dr. Ranjit Chacko, whose warm friendship and unerring grasp of not only pills but my innermost needs at times seems supernatural.

Dr. Pool had been monitoring my heart murmurs for some time, and when our family returned in 2011 from another superlative summer vacation in Sea Island, Georgia, he concluded his physical exam by simply stating: "It's time." Thus I soon underwent a seven-and-a-half-hour heart valve replacement by Dr. Joe Coselli, the Texas Heart Institute surgeon who had followed the world-famous Drs. Michael DeBakey and Denton Cooley. It was an unusually challenging operation requiring "some chiseling," and Joe was soaking wet. Importantly, I was even given "dispensation" by my friend Marc Shapiro to use a "porcine" valve!

When I went home, Joe would stop by just to visit. It turned out our political philosophies were perfectly aligned. Joe and Kelly are neighbors in both River Oaks and Washington County, and we cherish them.

So, Mam-maw, let your heart sing, because your hopes for my medical career have been realized by our being the beneficiaries of some of the best doctors in the world. And I have "done no harm!"

My health crisis after "selling my baby," in part, brought me to Odyssey. For several years, our great HBS friends Libby and Tom Broadus (Tom, my dear friend, was a director and top manager of T. Rowe Price) had urged Susan and me to attend the Odyssey course at Harvard Business School. It was advertised: "HBS is for Your Career. Odyssey is for the Rest of Your Life." In 1999, we made time to attend. Now we are evangelists for Odyssey.

Professor Shoshana Zuboff was brilliant! She was the second female to become a professor at HBS in its history. Odyssey was her "creation," her invention at HBS. Without any doubt, she is the best teacher I have had in my life, at any level. Opening night she told us to pick a partner—the terminology is "dyad" partner—and to choose carefully because by the end of this course, "You will know each other better than anyone on earth, with the possible exception of your spouses."

Among our twenty-six "couple" classmates were Mary and David Wolff from Houston. Susan knew Mary as they both served on the board of the Jung Center, and I was acquainted with her husband, David. David and I decided to team; it turned out to be an extremely fortunate choice. Dyad partners studied specially written, Odyssey-centered HBS cases at night but mainly concentrated on learning about the lives and "destinations" of each other. In the mornings the class dissected the cases in normal HBS style. Shoshana lectured—no, she dramatized—her philosophies on post-careers and life.

David and I really hit it off. The fact that we were both devotees of HBS greatly abetted our communication, confidence, and inherent trust. By the time Mary and Susan joined us two weeks later, thus completing our "quad" in Odyssey terms, David and I became very close and open friends. From that day forward, the dynamic effect of Odyssey compounded its influence on our lives. Neighbors in both River Oaks and Washington County, David and I stay in frequent communication about serious matters, such as his chairing METRO and my Center for Houston's Future, and maybe even more serious matters, such as his San Francisco Giants, of which he is a minority owner, and his yacht, *Halcyon*. Every Valentine evening for sixteen years, David and I have hosted a special Valentine Dinner for "JFK Profiles in Courage" recipient, former Houston Mayor Bill White, and his superlative wife, Andrea, who is a behind-the-scenes powerful vector for all things good in our region. Over the years, we were joined by guests with admirable kind hearts such as Ellen Simmons, Albert and Anne Chao, and John and Anne Mendelsohn, among others.

While at Odyssey, I was torn because I deeply loved the firm that I had fathered and to which I had devoted my career, yet my mind and heart were pulling me elsewhere. At age sixty-six, I needed to make decisions about Vaughan Nelson and the rest of my life. Swirling in my mind was Sir John Templeton, my professional role model for many years. He did not create Templeton Investments until he was 45 years old, but he ran his company hands on until he sold it at 82.

Also factoring into my thinking was the new breed of professionals on Wall Street in money management. They had made the classic mistake of confusing a bull market with brains. I realized, to my distress, that these same attitudes had crept into our firm. I knew well the lessons of investment history. I had a clear perspective that "Vestal Virgins" of 1972 were followed by the "73–74" decimation and that hard times came on the heels of sky-high markets. Our firm's "kids" did not doubt 1929 and 1973–74 had occurred. They just believed it had no relevance to them.

Odyssey led me to the understanding that I was in a whole new ball game. The crucial innings at sixty-six forward are neither played by the same rules nor scored in the same way as a young man's game. I

On this special November 1999 formal occasion, except for Peter Voss, no one but Susan and I knew I would announce I would pass the CEO baton at our firm on the afternoon of the first day of the New Year, New Century, and New Millennium.

grasped that you could succeed in this second adulthood, even reach mastery, only if you move from competition to connecting and aim for redirection rather than retirement. I reflected on my deep, all-encompassing love for my wife, daughter, and son, which is the core of my being. I thought about my decision to part with my "baby." I felt good about the decision to sell because it provided well for the families of principals and the future success of the firm. The decision was a matter of head over heart. But what next? Full retirement or redirection? Remove myself from the firm lest I crowd my successor? Status quo? If John Templeton remained at the helm until eight-two, could I settle for seventy-two? Or step up to chairman and pass the CEO baton to my successor in the near future?

Ed Mathias, my good friend from the Group of Nine in whom I had confided earlier in the year of Odyssey, wrote this message to me on a scrap of paper:

1) Set a time.
2) Leave from strength, under circumstances of your own choosing.
3) Have a platform.

I agreed with his wisdom, and Shoshana delivered the ultimate in internal interrogation and integration, but I still had no decision about continuing as CEO of Vaughan Nelson. Susan tells me there is a Jungian quote: "When the pupil is ready, the teacher will appear."

Talk about synchronicity; a member of our small Odyssey class was a key director of Peter Voss's New England Investment Companies. He gave me a terrific thought. A major part of my dilemma was that I pictured myself as the "father" of Vaughan Nelson. That made it very difficult for me to depart, like a father leaving his child. Outside the classroom my new friend counseled, "I have been listening hard to you and think I have your solution. Why not think of yourself as 'grandfather' of Vaughan Nelson?" Suddenly everything clarified. I would be "grandfather," with all the caring and restraint that relationship implied to the firm, and could focus on a new passion. It was so simple once I viewed it in this new light.

With that extraordinary Odyssey course, I accomplished a major step toward preparing for the future. No one but Peter Voss knew ahead of time that I would pass the CEO baton on January 1, 2000, to Lee Lahourcade. Everyone, most of all me, had assumed when I stepped down as CEO my successor would be Frank Scarborough. Frank was superb, the single, best all-around person with whom I worked anywhere in my entire career. He was smart (a slew of distinctions at HBS), totally honorable, great sense of humor, and he was nine years younger than I. Frank had earned it and was ideal, but he returned after a Christmas trip hiking with Judy at Jackson Hole to disclose to me he did not want to be CEO. This truly saddened me, but it was a good thing I had a "deep bench." After passing the baton to Lee, my official title would be founding chairman and my role "grandfather" until I "redirected" and moved to a new office.

The firm held an elegant party in my honor at the time of my "official" retirement. At the mid-point, Lee Lahourcade called for quiet and said some exceedingly nice words about me. He then presented me with a lovely box. Inside was—to me—the perfect gift. It was a gorgeous Mottahedeh porcelain bowl from Shreve, Crump & Low of Boston. It was approximately eighteen inches in diameter and six inches deep. On it was pictured the Boston Harbor, circa 1800, the birthplace of American commerce. It was a beautiful interpretation of a lithograph by DeRoy, after a drawing by R. J. Milbert from the early nineteenth century. On a plaque on one side of the base was inscribed:

Eugene H. Vaughan
Founder
Vaughan, Nelson, Scarborough & McConnell, L.P.
With Utmost Respect and Admiration
For Your Many Years of Inspired Leadership

On a plaque on the other side of the base was inscribed:

THE TIME AND THE DANCE WERE YOURS
YOU LIVED AND EMBRACED EVERY MOMENT
LEAVING NOTHING TO CHANCE

I was deeply touched. The Vaughan Nelson Bowl ever since has been in the place of honor as the first object anyone sees when they enter the front door of our home.

In the market, as in life, it is said timing is everything. Mine was, yes, miraculous. On January 10, 2000, nine days after I handed off the CEO baton, the Dow Jones crashed. On March 12, 2000, investors suddenly realized the high-flying dot-com stocks "had no clothes," and they plummeted. WorldCom and Enron lay just ahead. Enron would not have any impact on our firm. In fact, our firm and Fayez Sarofim were the only prominent investment management firms in Houston not to buy Enron. (I always have admired the Fayez Sarofim firm, twelve years our senior, and I admire it even more now because its outstanding young CEO, Gentry Lee, is a distinguished graduate of Vanderbilt and HBS. How did I let him miss my "academic nepotism?") When Enron's chairman, Ken Lay, had asked me point blank why we never bought any shares, I told him we didn't understand what Enron did. We sure got that one right!

As to everything it took to create and build the firm, with all the highs and lows, without a doubt, yes, I would do it again! And, yes, I believe <u>one</u> <u>half</u> of being an authentic entrepreneur is having the idea, then creating and building the enterprise; the <u>other</u> <u>half</u> is capitalizing on it. Without a doubt I would sell to Peter Voss all over again.

CHAPTER 19

"The Brode" Returns!
An Instructive Career Parallel

*In India, when an elephant comes to a rickety wood bridge, he tests it
with his trunk. Then he tests it with his front foot. Then he tests it with
both front feet. Then he sends another elephant across first.*

—Gerald Tsai, Founder, First Manhattan Fund
(I was in the audience when he spoke)

If I had devised an instructive parallel to my firm, I could not have done
better than Founders Group of Mutual Funds. It started in late 1970
when I received a highly welcome telephone call from my past: "This
is Lt. Brody, of the USS *Ross*." My instant response: "How are you,
Brode?" Then the familiar "Ter-rif-fic!!" A lot of catch-up, then he got
down to business. The Brode was president of Founders in Denver and
wanted me to be on his board. Ed Downe, who was married to a Ford
and owned a group of major women's magazines, including *Ladies
Home Journal*, had purchased the mutual fund management company
and entrusted it to Brody. My old friend and first female member of the
New York Stock Exchange, Muriel "Mickey" Siebert, and Donald Sto-
rey, editor of the prestigious *Bolton-Tremblay Money Credit Analysis*,
had already agreed to be directors. This married a couple of things I
liked the most: Gene Brody and mutual fund management. I also liked
that it took me four times a year to Colorado where Susan's sister, Janet,
and husband, Jim Miller, had a ski condo in Vail.

Founders offered insights into another investment management
organization, constant change, immense challenges, and an amazing
chairman. Unfortunately, the honeymoon period was short-lived.

Tragically, Ed Downe was sent to prison for insider trading. This was at a time when the SEC wanted to make an example of someone well known, much as they did to Martha Stewart some years later. Gene Brody left the board as CEO, but Ed Downe's other directors stayed on. They looked entirely to the professional investors to make the decisions. Offers to purchase the company poured in because Brody had really put Founders on the map. In the mutual fund industry, the board is all powerful on behalf of shareholders in deciding who owns a mutual fund management company. We decided on Bjorn "Erik" Borgen, an HBS graduate and brilliant analyst hired by Brody.

Timing was exquisite. 1973 and 1974 were dreadful for equities. In 1974, Erik put the funds into nearly all cash, and Founders Growth Fund was one of three best-performing mutual funds in America. It was phenomenal; money poured in. Erik stayed in cash in 1975 and missed the big rebound, but, nevertheless, the name was made and the funds prospered. It was a pleasure to serve on this board because everything was orderly and well considered. Very early on I thought the in-house legal counselor was weak. We engaged a splendid lawyer from another mutual fund organization, Ed O'Keefe, and I suggested we hire John Gillis, my foxhole buddy from FAF days, as counsel to the directors. After that, I knew everything would be done right.

Doing things right was very important to me. In the miserable solitude of the North Atlantic, I had set my course toward integrity and character as had been instilled by my family. Dick, Frank, and I wholly aligned on integrity in our firm. Even when I was asked to serve on the board of the prestigious New York–based Alliance Capital Reserve Fund, I made myself somewhat unpopular by insisting that as assets-under-management rose, the percent of fee should decline somewhat, a standard practice I believed was right. In a nice way I told management I would have to resign. A year or so later a fellow trustee wrote me that I was proven dramatically correct—the directors had been sued successfully on this issue and were forced to lower fees.

After Erik purchased Founders, we became close over the years. We had good chemistry although our views began to diverge as I believed the stock market, and growth stocks in particular, were getting fully priced. Erik had bought out his twenty-five percent equity partner during the 1987 plunge and now owned one hundred percent of Founders, except for phantom stock arrangements with the investment team. Over dinners when I came to Denver, we had endless discussions about whether to sell. We agreed that if one missed this opportunity to sell, it would be another decade or more before investment management valuations would reach these heights. But how close should he cut it?

When the bidding for Founders started in 1997, it was furious. Quickly this placed me in an intolerable spot. The two organizations most eager to acquire Founders, of the 9,000 or so mutual funds in America, were Dreyfus Corp., headed by my good Group of Nine friend Steve Canter, and New England Investment Companies, headed by Peter Voss who now owned Vaughan Nelson! How could this happen! The bids went higher and higher, beyond all reason in my opinion; all bidders dropped out except my friends. Each was determined to win because they had no entries in growth funds. Dreyfus won at $270 million! (I still recall Erik telling me over a private dinner a few months earlier that his highest offer was $12 million!) Erik had played his hand with ultimate guts, waiting until the last train was leaving. He undoubtedly was the biggest winner of anyone in the crazy market of the late 1990s. As always happens, markets get fully priced, then overpriced, then super-saturated, then a smash-up. Thus came the crash in January 2000.

I eventually became the reluctant chairman, not happily so, but Steve Canter asked me to serve in that role. I was mollified somewhat when Steve added to the board two people I knew and trusted: George Phillips, with whom I had negotiated so hard at The Boston Company, and Bob Mastrovita, who had followed me at Putnam and was a fellow admirer of Charles Werly. Trygve Myhren, a wise, world-class gentleman who founded several cable networks, including the Food Network, and was a member of the Cable Television Hall of Fame, joined the board; he was an invaluable asset.

"Growth stock" mutual funds now were totally passé. Meanwhile Mellon Bank bought Dreyfus and put pressure on Steve to consolidate the funds in New York. Steve had promised explicitly during the bidding process not to move Founders from Denver. Steve is a person of absolute personal integrity, and we worked every conceivable way to find a viable solution. Mellon also owned The Boston Company, and

Steve came up with a brilliant plan. The Dreyfus-Founders Fund managers in Denver would, more or less, co-manage the funds with the large, strong investment teams at The Boston Company.

Along in here in 2001, while Dr. Pool was away, a distracted neurosurgeon botched my lumbar surgery, and I had to endure the identical procedure a week later (as did the patient immediately behind me!). Then I contracted the dreaded MRSA infection in the hospital. I missed two board meetings and would have resigned, but Steve urged me to remain as chairman and did everything possible to facilitate it. I was so sick that Susan stood in for me on important conference calls. When I recovered somewhat, Steve flew to Houston, and we met over dinner to develop a strategic plan. Key to the plan was to hold a board meeting in Boston and have the portfolio managers and analysts fly from Denver to The Boston Company to discuss investment policy face to face. The board would meet the following day at The Boston Company. It worked. We still could not get "blood from a turnip," i.e., good performance from mutual funds which were mandated by law to growth during a period when "growth" was still wholly out of favor, but we accomplished a smooth, harmonious, two-city axis team.

In 2002, a new CEO, Robert Kelly, came to power at Mellon, and he agreed on a merger with Bank of New York, the oldest bank in America. Steve, who had honorably tried to please Mellon while honoring his pledge to the Founders board, chose to retire.

By 2008, I had been deeply involved in the Founders saga for thirty-eight years and chairman during the arduous final eight years of my tenure. I had reached the mandatory retirement age of seventy-five. I had led the board in insisting on that very retirement age mandate. Everyone went all out to hold a marvelous dinner in my honor at the Denver Country Club. Erik Borgen came from Norway. Movingly, John Gillis and wife, Marsha, flew from Richmond, Virginia, to give a "white hat" speech about me and to present me with, of course, a white hat! Bob Mastrovita wrote and recited an "Ode to Gene, Mr. CFA!" The climax was the presentation of a gorgeous painting, *The Rockies*, which hangs in our library at home. They claimed that for almost four decades they always had to save the seat with the best view of the mountains for me, and they wanted me to have the best view always. I look at that painting every night.

ODE TO GENE, MR. CFA!

Settle down and lend an ear my
  friends
For I'll now relate a tale
Of a legend of financial lore
No, not Baruch—or Buffett—or even
  Livermore,
Beside his their stories pale.
For the above are mere pretenders
Whose reputations yield
To the guy we call "Mr. CFA"
A veritable giant in his field.
For about 50 years in this biz it seems
He's done an awful lot
He's created firms, merged AIMR,
  chaired boards,
And beat markets, cold and hot!
He's inspired, taught and led us,
Prodded, beat and bled us....
But by God he's made us better
At whatever it is we do
With a heart the size of Texas
And an equally big IQ!
And to Gene's enduring credit
His career's had a hallmark obsession
To strive to see that this business of
  ours
Be considered a true profession.
He prepped at Vandy and at HBS
And prowled with IBM's young
  tigers,
No doubt this educational gauntlet
Propelled his zeal
To climb cerebral Eigers.
Along the way he was to find
The luckiest year of his life,

1963—The year he made
Incomparable Susan Westbrook
His dear wife.
His first investment job
Was at venerable old Putnam Funds,
It formed the cornerstone of his
  career.
It was there he learned to buy 'em low
And then to sell 'em dear.
But it was in his next endeavour
That his singular genius shone,
He could assemble and lead invest-
  ment talent
Like none other e'er has known.
He started up Vaughan Nelson
And built its staff from scratch
Putting together a team in Houston
That few on earth could match.
Selecting people was of course Gene's
  true calling,
As all gathered here must know,
Because picking us to join this board,
  this team,
Has certainly proved it's so.
You've regaled us with soaring
  rhetoric
That often made us weep,
But you never spared the gavel,
to inhibit boardroom sleep.
A silver tongued orator
Storyteller without peer
I'll never forget that giant pea fight
Where you took one in the ear!
You've oft quoted Shakespeare's
  sonnets

The profound wisdom of Mahatma
   Gandhi,
Exhorting us with Winston
   Churchill
Dazzling all with Tristram Shandy.
As you've cited great philosophers
And waxed on all their labors,
It occurred to us
You really knew these guys,
You grew up with them as neighbors!
No, Gene, we know you're not that
   old
Though even John McCain is
   younger;
Or so at least we're told.
Yes, your legend gathers luster,
As we turn o'er the pages of time
Enshrined as the CFA Institute's first
   Chair
Still seeking bigger mountains yet to
   climb.
In the world of community service
You're known as one in a million
Leading Center for Houston's Future
Sure to build their endowment to a
   trillion!
But with time comes senior
   statesmanship
Though much is taken, much will
   abide,
And you've left us with a legacy
That'd make John Gardner beam
   with pride.
Sadly, Gene indeed is stepping
   down,

Though no one here's denyin'
He may have slowed down just a tad,
But he's still got the heart of a lion!
In truth he's been a beacon to us all
Who worship down at Broad and
   Wall.
And now for us the curtains fall.
Yes, other financial seers, in other
   years
Will hold their sway,
But can they evoke the same far-
   lasting dreams
To span the sunset of an older day?
What master brush will paint for
   weary eyes
Without Gene to light up the
   boardroom's dullest skies?
Walter Lippmann, it is said,
Spoke of men who planted trees
   instead;
And thanks to them we'd get to sit
   under these
For generations to come with
   comparative ease.
The "trees" Gene Vaughan has
   planted—
His ideals, organizations, friendships,
Guiding principles and high ethics—
Each of these, and more,
Will endure well beyond this
   day;
And so all of us—with all our hearts
Thank you, and salute you,
Gene Vaughan............
MR. CFA!

CHAPTER 20

Center for Houston's Future: My Give-Back to Our Beloved Houston

If you make no commitments you're an unfinished person.

—Dr. John W. Gardner

My first week in Houston, in 1964, I received telephone calls from two of its foremost citizens: Gus Wortham, founder of American General Insurance Company, and Jim Elkins Jr., president and CEO of First City National Bank and son of the legendary Judge James Elkins. They both wanted to welcome me and urge me to get involved in making our—"now your"—great city greater. Both these august men were good friends of Putnam's chairman, Charlie Werly, another profound gift from him.

In 1972, Paul Howell, a tremendously impressive business and civic leader, spoke to the Harvard Business School Club. It was in this moment that I began to realize what true greatness Paul possessed. He spoke about Houston and urged us all to find a "purchase" and do for the future Houston what giants of the past did for us. "How do you think this mosquito-infested swamp became the fourth-largest city in America?" he thundered. Indeed, Paul and his wife, Evelyn, were the foremost couple in inspiring greatness in Houston. (By amazing synchronicity, Paul had been the captain of Chancellor Heard's ship. Chancellor Heard said the crew worshipped Captain Howell and called him "Dixie.")

Yet by 1988, I felt that I still had not done enough for the city that Susan and I had adopted and of which our children were natives. I had

I started the Bayless Lectures at The Houston Club, named for the incompara-
ble Jim Bayless. The purpose was to bring in the best investment minds in the
country to speak. I am blessed to call three of the very best minds my friends:
(left to right) Dave Williams, Walter Cabot, and Walter Stern.

been president of The Houston Club, Houston Forum, Vanderbilt Club, and Harvard Business School Club, had served on various local boards including Houston Grand Opera, Goodwill Industries, and St. John's School, and helped found Presbyterian School. I was extremely active on the national level in my profession but felt lacking in my service to Houston. When my foothold appeared, it came in an innocuous way, appropriately in The Houston Club.

My partner—and good friend—in arranging distinguished speakers at The Houston Club was Charles Foster, the head of the largest immigration law firm in our region and advisor to U.S. presidents on this vital topic. He is married to the beautiful and vivacious Lily, formerly a famous Chinese actress. Both Charles and I have been very actively involved civically purely out of love for our community. When Jesse H. Jones built his exceptional building, he so wanted <u>his</u> club, The Houston Club, located there that he gave it a highly generous sixty-year lease for 30.5 <u>cents per square foot</u>. Although Charles and I had not had leadership roles for many years, we grieved mightily when the lease expired several years ago. The building was demolished, and the Club was forced to downsize and become part of a club chain. Charles and I joined the Coronado Club, the new "Nerve Center."

In addition to being president and chairman of The Houston Club Lyceum Distinguished Speaker Committee for twenty years, I was chairman of the Centennial Celebration in 1984. I wrote the foreword to Dorothy Knox Houghton's splendid centennial history.

Foreword

On the evening of June 20, 1994, an elegant capacity crowd filled the storied Texas Room to celebrate the centennial birthday of The Houston Club. Symbolically the guests linked arms with previous generations of civic-spirited members who had gathered in the club over the decades in camaraderie to will, nurture, and thrust Houston forward from a muddy Main Street in 1894, to become one of the principal cities of the world. Permeating the celebration was the palpable sense of the presence of such legends as Captain James A. Baker, Jr., a charter member; Jesse H. Jones, nephew of a charter member and the club's foremost benefactor; John Henry Kirby; Dr. Edgar Odell Lovett; J. S. Cullinan; W. S. Farish; W. W. Fondren; Will and Mike Hogg; Ben Taub; Hugh Roy Cullen; Mayor Oscar F. Holcombe; Judge James A. Elkins; Herman and George Brown; M. D. Anderson; Will Clayton; Judge Roy Hofheinz; and many others. The club's membership has included mayors, governors, senators, cabinet members, and even a president, George H. W. Bush, a former director of the club. Keynote speaker Jack S. Blanton, a past president of the club and one of Houston's current leaders, observed that during most of its history The Houston Club "was in every way at the nerve center of the entire community and almost every decision critical to Houston was made here."

One of the largest and best-known private, member-owned clubs in the United States—in the number of its members, in the size of its facilities, and in the number of its reciprocal arrangements with quality clubs around the world—over the years The Houston Club has sought not to be elitist but has recognized people for their self-worth and contributions to Houston. The spirit and character that dwell in The Houston Club molded Houston, and, in turn, the inherent entrepreneurial spirit and hospitable graciousness of the City of Houston have suffused the club. The institutional impact of The Houston Club on our great city is of overriding importance because multitudes of civic, corporate, cultural, social, and educational enterprises were conceived there and sustained by its members. But essentially, like all relationships of the heart and mind, the club is personal, and each member sees it through his or her own prism.

To many of us, the club is the late Judge John R. Brown at his regular table in the Azalea Room, dispensing keen wit and wisdom to the daily stream of young and old who came by to pay their respects and to bask in the sunburst of his personality. It is the awe we felt in the barber shop and dining rooms as young businessmen in the presence of such Houston heroes as General Maurice Hirsch, Gus Wortham, and Eddy Scurlock. Their compelling inspiration, encouragement, and personal interest in the next generation is a club tradition continued today.

To many Houstonians, the club is the Gulf Coast Suite where the directors of the Greater Houston Partnership meet regularly and where over the past four decades more gatherings to foster the commerce and the common good of Houston have taken place than in any other single room in the city. It is the Rusk Room where the extraordinary David Adickes mural of Houston in 1894 covers an entire wall, filling one with quiet pride at how incredibly far our city has come since the year of the club's founding. The Houston Club is a place imbued with old-fashioned hospitality and politeness, where honor in business and love of one's city, state, and country are venerated qualities.

To the business community, the club is the enrichment of ideas presented at the Texas Room podium by a constant stream of such diverse leaders as Prime Minister Margaret Thatcher, Admiral Elmo Zumwalt, Supreme Court Justice Sandra Day O'Connor, Alistair Cooke, Leo Durocher, and Presidents Ford, Carter, Reagan, and Bush. For over three decades the club has had one of the largest and most comprehensive series of influential speakers of any private club in this country. The power of ideas is frequently accompanied by poignancy or wit. No one present will forget the pleasurable chuckle of Admiral Thomas H. Moorer, the chairman of the Joint Chiefs of Staff, as he related Admiral Nimitz's World War II retort to the Japanese when the latter proposed dividing the Pacific: "Good. You take the bottom half!"

To me, The Houston Club is the gracious, vital extension of my firm, where I go to engage in business-oriented camaraderie with people in whom I believe and in whose company I rejoice. My business and civic enterprise are inextricably intertwined with the life of the club and are much better for it. Over the years The Houston Club is where I have brought into union my family life and business life. The club is where our children visited Santa Claus, where a former dining room captain cared enough to come out to watch my son play football, and where the staff created an ice sculpture of a black-eyed pea in my honor for a private family gathering. Sustaining the warm, dignified, and hospitable atmosphere conducive to both worlds is the skilled and dedicated staff exemplified by such distinguished longtime staff members as Joyce McWashington and Rogers Jackson, who carries in his wallet and shows with pride laminated clippings about club members. The genius of The Houston Club is that for one hundred years it has met the individual needs of each member, as it has with me.

The Houston Club and Its City—One Hundred Years relates with facts, photographs, and anecdotes the extraordinary symbiotic relationship between our city and its oldest private club. The rich history of The Houston Club has been written by a singularly well-qualified person, Dorothy Knox Howe Houghton. The author is a respected historian who grew up in the club, her grandfather having joined in 1900. She has written this history in honor of her family, who have been members, past and present. It is her gift, not only to present and future generations of Houston Club members, but to the citizens of the City of Houston, because, as Dorothy Knox observes in the opening line, "the story of The Houston Club is, in many respects, the story of twentieth-century Houston."

Simply put, since its inception in 1894 The Houston Club has been the finest downtown and businesspersons club in the city. Jim Henry, my barber and longtime friend, always was interested in what was going on in my life and in Houston. One afternoon while I was getting a haircut, Leo Linbeck Jr. was sitting in the next chair and picked up on our conversation. Leo was a brilliant leader; a builder of buildings, organizations, and communities, locally and nationally; and the definition of gravitas. Several days later, Leo called and told me that Charles Duncan, who was past chairman of Coca-Cola and former U.S. Secretary of Energy, was the incoming chairman of the Greater Houston Partnership. Charles just had finished serving two years on the Ross Perot State Education Reform Task Force and wanted to make education in Houston the centerpiece of his chairmanship. There was just one herculean problem. The Greater Houston Partnership never had an education committee! Charles and Leo had been looking for the right person to be chairman of the first ad hoc education committee in Houston's history. Would I consider it? Yes, of course!

I tackled the task with pent-up enthusiasm. First, I created the "Houston Business Promise" in which Houston corporations and organizations made nine key promises to support schools, teachers, and students. Over 300 corporate CEOs signed. I asked Marc Shapiro, CEO of Chase Bank Texas, to be in charge, and he did a terrific job. Part of the problem in education, I realized, was a highly fractionalized and overlapping system. There were so many organizations trying to help students that they were stepping on each other's toes and exacerbating the problems. By coordinating, much improvement was accomplished; the inestimable Ernie H. Cockrell took on that vital role.

The upshot is that for the high-profile outcomes in education my leadership produced, I was asked to join the Greater Houston Partnership board. This was one of the most exciting days of my life. Now I was at the beating heart of Houston. It was like the curtain had risen on my beloved city. Suddenly I knew everything going on in Houston: its problems, potential, victories, and vulnerabilities—and who was doing what. I served on the Greater Houston Partnership board—and later the executive committee—for fifteen years. I loved almost every minute of it.

My first major assignment, of course, was to chair the fundraising committee. That is not a popular assignment, nor will it ever be, but I had done so much fundraising at Vanderbilt, First Presbyterian Church, and St. John's School under far more difficult circumstances that I broke the goals without a problem. Next came a truly mesmerizing request. Would I chair the "emerging issues" committee? This innocuous title, "emerging issues," masked trying to deal with some of the most difficult issues threatening Houston's future viability and livability. I recruited some of the best brains in Houston and matched them with important issues, including the possible integration of city and county into a "METRO" government, coordinating an intermodal transportation system, addressing race relations, and increasing abundant sources of venture capital locally.

The twenty-person committee made excellent progress during my two years of chairing, but it became clear to me that it was not practical to have businesspeople work all day on immediate problems and at 4 p.m. ask them to switch their minds and stretch their vision far into the future. I was strongly of the opinion the Greater Houston Partnership needed a related but entirely separate organization with a distinctly different time horizon. Every chance I had, I talked up my concept to Partnership leaders.

The hoped-for response was not too long in coming. In early 1999, the incoming chair of the Partnership, Ned Holmes, who was the epitome of a fine leader, called and said, "The Partnership has a great name lying around but completely unused: Center for Houston's Future. Would you take it to where it needs to be for Houston?" That was the entirety of his commission. Would I! The very name sent my mind racing with possibilities.

I long had believed the city is filled with people just like me who deeply believe in Houston and who long for a means to give back in a substantial way. Moreover, in 1999, it seemed evident Houston needed

Dr. John Mendelsohn even came to my "ringing of the bell" ceremony to celebrate the successful conclusion of my forty-two days of radiation.

many more effective civic leaders. Major national corporations rotated their top officers through Houston, so CEO turnover was rapid and discontinuity high. Term limitation meant a minimum of four mayors every twenty years. Additionally, civic leadership tended to be Anglo and male-dominated in a city with powerfully changing demographics. The powerful Lamar Suite 8-F gathering was all male except for Oveta Culp Hobby. Leadership that was reflective of Houston's increasingly diverse population would be a foremost need in the future, I reasoned.

Thus was born an embryonic plan for Center for Houston's Future (CHF). Throughout my business career I had observed how important it is to whom the bud of an idea is first exposed. It can be so easily quashed. Again, great luck! One evening Susan and I had dinner with Dr. John and Anne Mendelsohn. I consider John to be one of the truly great men of our times, and I believe he is the epitome of all that is fine and good in medicine. I know this from firsthand experience. When I was diagnosed with prostate cancer in 2002, filled with dread remembering my dear mother's cancer experience, I received a call from John assuring me that he and MD Anderson would take care of me—a promise kept. He is a superb physician and leader. Thus, everyone I encountered on staff at MD Anderson was more than remarkably skilled; they were kind, uplifting, and exuded love and caring in the image of John. John is also a superb friend. He and Anne are the essence of humans at their best. Susan and I cherish their friendship. When I sketched the idea for Center for Houston's Future, John exclaimed, "That is exactly what Houston needs! May I be your first director?" That thrilled me and encouraged me!

My concept included three keys to creating a great over-the-horizon future for Houston. First, there needed to be goals. We had to know what was most important to make our region a truly great place for families and businesses. Second, there needed to be solid strategic plans to reach these goals. Third, there needed to be stout-hearted, public-spirited civic leaders to create and carry out those plans, and these civic leaders needed to be more reflective of the population. It was simple in concept, not simple in execution. And it could not be created in that one-two-three order. Goals and strategic plans had to flow from the leaders.

A key part of the plan was for Center for Houston's Future to hold leadership retreats that would equip and motivate both proven and rising business leaders to become civic leaders. Again, great luck. Our daughter, Margaret, worked for a Boston-based consultancy, the Centre for Generative Leadership (CGL), chaired by Joseph Jaworski. Joe had begun his career as a celebrated trial lawyer at Bracewell and Patterson in Houston. In the mid-90s, with several partners he founded CGL. As a CGL consultant, Margaret was trained in the methodology of scenario planning and had participated on the facilitation team for scenario-planning initiatives around the world.

Margaret and I excitedly began fruitful brainstorming about the tremendous possibilities of using scenario planning as a way of identifying the central goals for Center for Houston's Future and galvanizing a group of committed business leaders around them. I shared our ideas with Jim Kollaer, CEO of the Greater Houston Partnership, and together we approached Joe Jaworski about CGL facilitating a scenario-planning process for Center for Houston's Future. To me, it was a natural. Joe was the son of Houston hero Leon Jaworski, and Houston was their native city. Joe said yes! The first major initiative of CHF became a possibility.

At its October 1999 board meeting, the CHF board approved the initiative, and we laid plans to launch the business/civic leadership workshops (later changed to Leadership Forum) in 2000. The scenario-planning process required a huge commitment of time. Houston Endowment became enthusiastic about CHF and donated $150,000 to cover expenses so participants could attend free the first year.

Next, Jim Kollaer and I set out to select participants for the inaugural class. We were advised thirty-six was an ideal number for scenario planning. We knew the future would rise or fall on this inaugural group. It was asking much of busy people to give up so much time for an untried experiment in a scenario-planning process about which few knew anything. Jim and I prepared our stellar list and started calling. Many said "Yes" immediately, and we were exhilarated. But almost as many, understandably, were dubious. Michael Jhin, the brilliant CEO of St. Luke's Hospital, told me in recent years he and several others agreed they would come the first weekend because I twisted their arms, but they would be "busy" the next sessions. Happily, no one has remained a greater stalwart over the years than Michael.

For weeks I worked with the incomparable Ben Love to arrange a highly motivational luncheon kick-off for our inaugural class, the "Seminal 36." Ben had terrific wit, and I enjoyed introducing him. Ben loved it, especially my spoof about the Lord's Prayer! President George H. W. Bush wrote me a personal note about how much he enjoyed my emceeing that day.

BEN F. LOVE

MILLENNIUM DISTINGUISHED SPEAKER

THE HOUSTON CLUB, MARCH 16, 2000

What today is all about—honoring Ben Love—comes straight from Emerson's ringing declaration: "There is no history. There is only biography."

Houston was loved and willed and built and thrust ever upward by devoutly caring, consummate businessmen—such as Ben Love. But the most extraordinary aspect of Ben Love's business astuteness is that he not only built Texas Commerce Bank into one of the great banks of the nation but when the energy crash loomed, he took prescient, decisive action to make a strong, favorable merger with Chemical Bank, while many other banks in the Southwest perished.

Like Hakeem Olajuwon in his prime, Ben was that rare combination—Most Valuable Player on offense and Most Valuable Player on defense. Dr. John Mendelsohn will aver to you that the Texas Medical Center, and certainly the world-renowned MD Anderson Cancer Center, has no better friend than Ben, who recently chaired a Capital Campaign that raised $151 million for the Cancer Center.

Still, Ben not only inspires admiration, his very long needle and fabled quick wit inspire a host of Ben Love stories—for example, several years ago Ben played a round of golf at River Oaks Country Club with Farah Fawcett. When asked what he had learned, he said, "I learned you can't hold your stomach in for 18 holes."

And, Ben, one of your long-time directors at Texas Commerce joyfully recalls telling you that when you dance, you "look like a snake falling out of a tree."

I see Dr. Vic Pentz, Pastor of First Presbyterian Church, is in the audience today. Ben and I go to Dr. Pentz's church. An extraordinary ecclesiastical experience is to sit behind Ben during the Lord's Prayer. This infinitely urbane, this articulate consummate banker, when he gets to the part about "and forgive them their debts," starts to mumble, stutter and cough. He just can't get the words out of his mouth!

Ben and Margaret, your beloved pastor, Dr. Pentz, is here today to tell you, Ben, that the Lord does not give a man a burden more than he can bear and gives you dispensation to just say "I can't forgive your debts but I'll let you have the money at prime plus 2%."

There is one other aspect to Ben Love, an ennobling aspect. He believes in people. And if he believes in you, there is no way you are going to let him down by failing. He has believed in countless young entrepreneurs, as myself thirty years ago, and backed his belief with precious loans.

A few years back, teachers had a wonderful slogan: "Teach and touch the future." Ben Love, by inspiring thousands of us, hundreds of whom are in the room, is teaching and touching and inspiring and literally shaping and elevating the future of our magnificent city.

Ben Love towered over me—as indeed "Mr. Houston" towered over all of our great city—but he uplifted me with his inscription: "Smiling with two of my most 'honorable' leaders and friends." How fortunate I was to share warm friendships with both Ben Love (center) and James Baker (right).

Please join me in honoring a small town boy from Paris, Texas, who became the head and heart and élan vital, the vital spirit, of the fourth largest—and the greatest—city in America, The Houston Club Millennium Distinguished Speaker, Ben F. Love.

Ben gave a magnificent luncheon address entitled "Seeds of Greatness in Houston's Past and Future" embodying, in his incomparable eloquence, his deep love of Houston and his beliefs about the responsibilities of civic involvement. He hit the mark exactly!

But the opening evening event was shaky at best. The speech delivered, which I had expected to instill fervor, was technical and dry. My heart sank. The reaction of the participants was subdued skepticism. I went to bed with the sick feeling the scenario-planning process had crashed on take-off.

However, in the morning session, Ron Lewis, a young, impressive partner with Baker Botts who had expressed much disappointment the evening before, stood and said, "What I have come to understand through yesterday and today is that we all have shared values. With that foundation, we can accomplish great things for our future together."

His words turned it around. He was Thomas Paine at Valley Forge! Almost everyone returned for the second session a month later. But at the very start of the second session, Jodie Jiles, a successful entrepreneur, rose to direct a question to me. "Gene, I have a wife and wonderful babies at home. I do not get this scenario stuff at all. Tell me why I should stay here instead of being with them." Jodie said it, but I knew others were thinking the same thing.

There are times when you know the next words you speak will send momentum careening in one clear direction or the other. I thought a moment and then said, "Jodie, none of us in this circle has experienced the scenario-planning process. But it has worked with dramatically positive results many places throughout the world. If it works here, we can help the unknown future of your babies—and mine. Let's trust the process." On such slim threads the scenario-planning process hung, and then the magic took hold.

The human potential of these thirty-six ardent Houstonians was released. Key driving forces impacting Houston's future were identified. Informed by our conversations, we explored what might happen if the region allowed our diversity to divide rather than unite us. Led by Jackie Martin, head of Houston's United Way, we articulated a memorable "Houston Burning" potential scenario. Willie Alexander, entrepreneur and former Houston Oilers defensive back, coined the phrase, "Deepen the bench and widen the circle," incandescent shorthand for the goal of creating an ever-expanding pool of active, informed civic leaders representative of Houston's rich diversity. Beth Robertson, businesswoman and philanthropist, put forward the idea of recurring "Regional Leadership Summits" to generate the ever-expanding pool.

It was fascinating to see passion emerge as participants lit up with possibilities. James Calaway, a genius with a masters from Oxford and a high-tech entrepreneur with a prodigious heart, came on fire about education. Out of the blue, God gifted me with James Calaway. His glorious friendship has made a critical difference in my life. Bob Eury, president of Central Houston, sent imaginations soaring with possibilities of revitalizing downtown and linking it with several "livable city centers" around Houston. Into the air and onto the walls went the increasingly creative thoughts of the "Seminal 36."

In the process of identifying what kinds and qualities of leaders would be needed, it was necessary to ask what kind of Houston we envision, what qualities we cherish for our families and businesses over the next twenty-five years and beyond. Thus, the team focused on what will be different in tomorrow's world, what do we want Houston to be, what are the obstacles and the trade-offs, and most of all, what strategic plans, resources, and leadership are necessary to get there?

Myriad ideas had been generated, but they had to be translated into an intelligently coherent plan to present recommendations at the all-important board meeting in October. After the close of the summer forum our family went on a wonderful, and badly needed, vacation at Jenny Lake, Wyoming. Two individuals had been assigned by the Greater Houston Partnership to organize everything in my absence and have recommendations on paper for me. They certainly did have one recommendation. They said the Centre for Generative Leadership team had not fulfilled their mission and that the Forum had failed; there was nothing worth writing down.

I was furious and frustrated. With little time before the crucial board meeting, I was inundated with all this invaluable information and no one to help me translate it into its potential for Houston. At exactly that moment James Calaway stepped forward, never to leave. James, out of love for his city, put his career in the private sector on hold and became the volunteer president de facto and, later, the first full-time president and CEO of CHF in 2002. At this moment CHF had no staff. The Partnership staff did some modest organizational work, but almost all of the effort was undertaken by James and me at night in my office conference room on the sixty-third floor of Texas Commerce Tower. Looking out across our beloved city, the two of us took the essence of the scenario ideas and, our minds working as one, painstakingly transformed them into a solid action plan on paper to present to the board. James holds—and always will—a very special place in my heart. I cherish James as a friend of brilliance and prodigious heart.

Almost all the graduates of the inaugural Leadership Forum gathered in the Partnership board room on October 12, 2000, to present four powerful potential scenarios for the future of Houston and the resulting plan for diverse civic leadership cultivation and long-range strategic planning through CHF. Following the dramatic hour-long presentation, the board met independently down the hall. The directors were already in possession of a sixty-one-page document James and I had written. The recommendations emphasized that the work of CHF was to be regional and focused on "points of maximum leverage," analogous to pushing on the "small rudder on the big rudder" of ships.

The decision was now up to the board. They understood the recommendations entailed a major, difficult undertaking involving large amounts of money. The concept and two years of hard work were hanging in the balance. No one knew how these tough-minded business leaders would vote. I chaired the meeting. Long, tense silence followed a concise reading of the recommendations. Right away, Bill Barnett, managing partner of Baker Botts and chairman of Rice University, stood up and headed for the door with an apology that he was late for a meeting he had called. Halfway out the door, he paused. Then came fateful words, "Let me just say I believe this is an outstanding plan to assure more and diversified civic leaders. That is badly needed."

Yet suspense remained heavy because no one knew how the recommendation for over-the-horizon regional strategic planning would be viewed. Houston has accomplished many monumental projects, but long-term planning had never quite jibed with the independent spirit of Houstonians. In fact, the word "planning" was anathema to many Houstonians.

Ben Love stood and put on his most serious face. I knew this was it—one way or the other. Ben stated, "I have often thought, and sometimes said, that an average man with a plan will be more successful than a much smarter man without a plan." He then smiled and said, "I support Center for Houston's Future taking the lead in strategic planning." Without a facial change, I felt élan vital rising in me! With each director speaking, the recommendations were approved unanimously. Most important was the pervasive atmosphere of excitement about the entire concept of CHF.

I was thrilled to go down the hall to tell the Seminal 36 that their hard work had paid off. Center for Houston's Future was going forward! There was pure exhilaration from this exceptional inaugural group, which produced four of CHF's first five chairmen, including the peerless George Martinez who gave unflagging wisdom and support in executive sessions, kitchen cabinets, and, as the foremost community banker, financial strength. A dozen members of the inaugural class served on the board of CHF in its first decade.

With the green light, we hired a full-time executive assistant, a staff of one. The Greater Houston Partnership graciously let us use space and provided equipment and furniture. By August 2001, we expanded the board to twenty-seven, formed key committees, and produced a detailed work plan. James Calaway, still a volunteer at this point, and I carried most of the load with help from board members and GHP staff.

And Stephen Klineberg! Houston "knows itself" better than any city in the world because, as chairman of the honored Sociology Department at Rice University, Steve since 1981 annually has sent carefully designed, sophisticated, longitudinal surveys to every segment of our population. He has been the lead-off, perspective-setting speaker at every Leadership Forum and a wise and provocative member of our board since the beginning. I always introduce Steve as "Houston's Treasure." He and I are extremely close friends. Through his research insights Steve sees the future of Houston—and of America—with clarity and tells it with panache!

The scenario-planning focus on "Quality of Life" at the inaugural Leadership Forum in 2000 led directly to the Greater Houston Partnership creating its first standing Quality of Life Committee in 2001. This, in turn, led to collaboration with the Quality of Life Coalition of sixty organizations, which accomplished fine works for Houston's park system, linking bayous, tree-planting, and landscaping throughout the city. Of crucial importance to our ever-growing car-obsessed city, light rail advocacy by CHF and the CHF board—informed by CHF research trips to Chicago, Washington, Atlanta, and Portland—persuaded the GHP board to support the 2003 vote, which, over the strenuous objections of developers, passed narrowly. The high-impact Indicator Reports, which serve as the region's report card on factors necessary to maintain a competitive and sustainable place in the twenty-first century, were deemed vital by Houston Endowment and stem from the scenario planning. On and upwardly on!

In 2001, CHF brought high technology into Houston Independent School District classrooms. In its first year, CHF was instrumental in the game-changing achievement of placing 13,000 COMPAQ high-end personal computers into HISD, one for each teacher. Working with future U.S. Secretary of Education Rod Paige, CHF took the strategic lead in equipping teachers in the Houston region with powerful new internet education resources.

Quality education has been a major strategic focus for CHF since its inception. In 2002, CHF launched a region-wide, two-year effort to forge a plan materially enhancing the tremendous power of early childhood learning. This effort, partnering with Carol Shattuck and the Collaborative for Children, led to "Pre-School for All." In addition to Presbyterian School, I was on the board of Collaborative for Children—a true believer! The plan allows all the region's children entering the K–12 system, regardless of family income or status, to be prepared both academically and psychologically to succeed. "Pre-School for All" has elevated greatly the caliber of early childhood education in the Houston region and state.

In 2003, CHF designed a highly consequential "Quality of Place" regional conference bringing together thirty leaders representing every county in the region. Once convened, the group realized that without a commitment to <u>regional</u> governance and <u>regional</u> thinking, it was very difficult to actually create the quality of place envisioned by both urban and suburban planners. A second revelation at the Washington County–area conference was the need for a means to ensure that the region's major political leaders—including Houston's mayor and the judge of every neighboring county—know one another, trust one another, and are able to think together about how their combined interests could be blended for the greater good. This was the impetus for the creation of the "Simonton 6," confidential meetings organized and facilitated by CHF. The meetings served a vital, but unheralded, role in forging important alliances for the region's good. Looking back, it is amazing these all-powerful political leaders from the region did not know or barely knew one another and had spent so little time discussing how to work together to improve quality of life. Now, years later, the leaders of our region, expanded to the "Regional 9," gather regularly under the aegis of CHF to help develop broad consensus on how to think and act regionally.

While strategic awareness and forward planning are cornerstones of CHF, the Leadership Forums are the very foundation of the future. Occasionally I am asked these days: "Where are the Jesse Joneses and Ben Loves?" Whereas civic leadership in the Houston region in 2000 consisted of a few "giant oaks," now there is a "growing forest of strong oaks." Moreover, the "forest" reflects the diversity of our region. As of early 2017, over 1,000 Forum graduates—one-third women and fifty percent from diverse minorities—have stepped forward to take their turn. These "civic leader champions" are reflective of Houston's present and future.

One of the greatest unforeseen gifts CHF yielded was bringing Margaret back to Houston from Boston. Having departed in 1984 for Vanderbilt, Margaret had told us she had no intention of returning to Houston. However, through her participation on the scenario facilitation team in 2000, Margaret saw Houston through a whole new lens, and to our elation, decided to return to her native city, "where the future of America is being worked out," according to Stephen Klineberg. After assurances from the incoming CHF chairman that she would receive no special treatment (and in fact would be vetted all the more strenuously) because of her relationship to me, Margaret submitted a proposal and was selected to design and facilitate the huge potentiality of the Center's Business/Civic Leadership Forums. She thus became the original Leadership Forum architect and long-standing facilitator.

Another person deserves overflowing gratitude for the enduring successes of the Leadership Forums. Susan and I are exceedingly fortunate in our friends, in large part because Susan is such a loyal, giving friend herself. A generation ago, Aaron Farfel was the wisest, kindest, most universally admired leader in both the Jewish community and the Houston community in general. Lois Farfel Stark, his daughter, inherited his sublime character, talent, intelligence, and kindness. She and Susan are close friends. Lois thinks deeply and writes lyrically. In the second CHF Leadership Forum in 2001, Lois quoted a Hopi Indian

Barbara Bush received the Eugene H. Vaughan Civic Leadership Award at the Center for Houston's Future Annual Luncheon in 2015. Our grandchildren were let out of school so they could hug President and Mrs. Bush.

elder: "We are the ones we have been waiting for." This hit the mark so profoundly it has been the informal theme of Center for Houston's Future ever since.

Building CHF was not easy. Entrepreneurship never is. In this case the journey from aspiration to realization was steepened by the hard fact that from early 2000, our beginning, through 2001, the S&P 500 plunged forty-seven percent. Funds and support for start-ups almost evaporated throughout the nation. With the Enron collapse in 2002, we lost major funding and moral support. (It was very tough when, as a result of the Enron debacle, I personally had to ask Ken Lay to resign from our board.) American General and Compaq, two strong Houston civic supporters, were merged into corporations with headquarters elsewhere. And the horrific Tropical Storm Allison flooded much of Houston, a harbinger of much worse to come.

At one crucial point, CHF had to borrow, and, against my wishes, it borrowed from the Partnership. I went before the GHP executive committee and personally pledged the loan would be repaid, and then James and I did not sleep until we raised the money to pay off the loan.

In 2010, during its ten-year anniversary, CHF undertook an ambitious regional scenario-planning effort called "Scenario 2040," the most profound and far-reaching undertaking to date. During a climactic meeting of the Scenario 2040 Oversight Committee on which I served, it hit me like a beautiful revelation that, while I will not be here in the year 2040, through Scenario 2040 I will be present in my grandchildren's world—and I am helping to make it better. I felt a rapturous exhilaration!

Catherine Mosbacher provided outstanding CEO leadership from 2008 to 2016. She built great strength across the board, city vitality-measuring "Early Indicators," and powerful "salons" in topics key to the region, all with high competence and grace.

People frequently ask from whence did the inspiration for Center for Houston's Future come. Actually Center for Houston's Future was simply an outcome of my growing up in a family that was unfailingly "neighborly" to everyone they knew. Part of this stemmed from the traditions of small town, agrarian America and part from the family values ingrained by Papa and Mama Vaughan. To me, Houston was merely a larger neighborhood.

My specific inspiration accumulated over time, mostly from Houston civic patriots. The foremost person, however, who ignited the fire in my heart was Dr. John W. Gardner. He spoke to an overflow Houston Forum audience in Houston in 1993. I presided at that event, and we remained friends until John died. He said, "[Houston] is never finished. You can't build it and then leave it standing as the Pharaohs did the pyramids. It has to be built and rebuilt, recreated in each generation by believing, caring men and women. It is now our turn...."

Dr. Gardner said "nation," but some of us heard "Houston."

The degree of prescience of Center for Houston's Future in looking over the horizon will be revealed to our children and grandchildren and their children. All of us who have taken "our turn" can be secure in the belief that our Houston region will become the best place in America and, just possibly, in the world in which to live and work. Center for Houston's Future *is* the steward of our grandchildren's future.

Tretower, Texas

You may all go to hell—I'm going to Texas.

—Davy Crockett

When "Double Sunrise," our beach home, was severely damaged in 1995 by a storm not even big enough to earn a hurricane name, we spent two years struggling through Galveston and state land office red tape to get repairs approved. The coup de grâce was that we hired an excellent Galveston lawyer to cut through the red tape, and after a year he sent our money back. Too formidable, he said of the red tape. It was with reluctance we recognized it was time to let go of this wondrous place that had been at the center of our family's heart since 1972.

Ah, so many memories! Two years after we purchased "Double Sunrise," I acquired one of the great loves of my life, a Hobie Cat—one of the first on Galveston Island. To me there was nothing like the thrill of zooming over the waves with one pontoon out of the water and hearing the incomparable hum of being at one with the wind and waves. Just as I loved my "Blue Beauty" car, I loved my breathtaking, light-blue Hobie Cat with a blue slash across its white sail. We traded up in length and sail as the children grew. But here we were, after striving to restore our damaged home, and me with my neurosurgeon prohibiting me from sailing my beloved Hobie because of the torque it exerted on the bone spur near a cervical nerve. We were at the end of a marvelous thirty-three year run. It was time to re-deploy our funds.

One great possibility after another appeared. Most of our friends retreated to the Rockies. It was nearby, wonderfully cool in summer and with great outdoor resorts in winter. The Smokies held allure. Susan spent fifteen summers at her beloved Camp Merri-Mac, and it was very accessible to Vanderbilt. We spent two weeks on Cape Cod checking out lovely places for sale, but the heavy traffic ruined much of the thrill Susan and I had once known at Nauset Beach and our "Magical Orleans," where our love had flourished in the summer of 1962. The beat went on. We spent time with friends in Jackson, Wyoming, and we could see why they loved it. But I said from the start that three places—Aspen, Jackson, and Nantucket—had soared so incredibly in the prolonged bull market of the 1990s that I knew they were vastly overpriced. That was indigestible for a "value" investor.

The most tantalizing dreamland of our search was Anguilla in the Caribbean. A relative of Vanderbilt's Buzz and Florence Davis was married to Reverend Will Jones, son of Sissy and Walk Jones. Sissy and Jack Caskey had divorced and each remarried. Jack and his wife moved to Aspen, and Sissy and Susan worked diligently to bring Walk Jones, a prominent architect in Memphis, into close friendship with me. It worked! Sissy and Walk became our close "couple" friends. Susan and I truly loved and enjoyed them. Walk and I were both only children and closer than brothers in a way. In addition to our twenty-three, yes, twenty-three "February two-week" vacations for the four of us very close friends, and several family Christmases together in Grand Cayman, it was perfect, but too filled with precious memories. Walk passed away tragically from brain cancer. During Sissy's and our marvelous week as guests of Florence and Buzz in Anguilla, Susan and I discussed purchasing one-half interest in their Anguilla paradise. We negotiated and ended up agreeing to buy it entirely. Then things got bizarre and fell apart—part lawyer, part hurricane, part strange smells from the canal. The combination of events killed the deal.

With all the looking across America and beyond, we had not once thought about Texas. In 2003, while at the Center for Houston's Future "Quality of Life" retreat in the Washington County area, I looked out the window while shaving and was startled to see mist rising from a lovely pond, and beautiful rolling land lay beyond. I remember coming home and telling Susan I had seen something unexpectedly beautiful near Houston.

In March 2007, Richard and his wife, Ann, invited Susan and me to join them for a weekend in Washington County. The plan was to go Texas antiquing. Then fate took over. Susan had brought a *Houston Chronicle* and it featured the Bluebonnet Trail map. We made the decision to follow it along FM 390. I looked to my left and the scenes were unlike any I had seen in Texas. The land was rolling gently, old live oaks abounded, and patches of bluebonnets were all around. Ann repeatedly was saying, "That's so beautiful!"

I called David Wolff, my Odyssey friend, who owned land in the area and told him of our possible interest. Within a few days David called and told Richard, in my absence, about some beautiful land going on sale, and no one yet knew about it. Susan and I were in a vise; we wanted the whole family to see the property, but what if the children and grandchildren fell in love with the place and either Susan or I did not care for it? This had happened every place we had looked! Susan and I arranged for just the two of us to see it. The house was nothing special, and maybe that is what we liked so much—one story, no balconies, plain brown with a red roof. But the land was truly breathtaking to us. The home was on one of the highest hills in Washington County and you could see great distances in several directions. We were hooked, and it was just over an hour's drive from our home in Houston.

The next day our children and grandchildren fell in love at first sight—and one thing that was highest on our list was that our place be a magnet for our grandchildren. In the purchase of every property, I had followed my investment principles with total discipline. I bought distressed (at least cosmetically) properties during depressed markets. This time I had zero leverage. David told me that prime properties like this rarely came to market and were snapped up immediately. Furthermore, the owner, a doctor, was retiring in two weeks and hosting his retirement party there for over 200 young doctors. It was easy to imagine any number of them would love to purchase that farm. We understood the doctor to be a motivated seller. I crafted an attractive offer that met everyone's needs (except mine!) and they accepted. In May 2007, Susan and I gathered the family and told them that the farm was ours! We all were truly exuberant. Washington County is the birthplace of Texas.

Richard has the same love of land possessed by my father and his great grandfathers, John Corbin Bolinger and Daniel Richard Vaughan, the admirable men for whom he is named. It was, and is, beautiful to see his depth of feeling about the land and all associated with it. I asked him to be the "manager" of the farm, and Susan fit perfectly into the role of "boss lady."

There was an animated discussion about the name. "Double Sunrise" was popular, and, indeed, we could see both sunrise and sunset. Skye, as the name of our beloved first Sheltie and our family's unforgettably wonderful stay on the Isle of Skye, was a favorite. However, as our minds turned to our fabulous family trip to the ancestral home of the Vaughans, it was unanimous that the one and only right name for our new land in Texas was Tretower Farm.

Margaret, as always, worked her magic. As we were leaving Tretower Castle and Court, Margaret observed a "T" and "F" in a circle. She converted those letters into our "brand." Since then she has given glasses, jackets, caps, and other items with the brand affixed. We even have a "branded" Tretower flag flying proudly near our forty-foot U.S. flag pole.

Running through our new property is a lovely stream that spills into two beautiful lakes. Our granddaughters got to pick the names for the lakes, which they aptly called Lake Avery and Lake Corbin. More recently—after selling my half of the "old home place" in Tennessee to my beloved cousin Danny Vaughn—we have added two tracts of land directly across FM 390, partly to prevent anyone else from putting something hideous on the land which is directly in our line of sight and partly because we believed it would be an excellent investment.

On one of the pieces of land we bought is a two-chimney home built in 1836, the historic year Texas became independent and the year Houston was founded. The acreage behind the "1836 House" runs to the top of another hill, almost as high as Tretower Farm, from which we can see miles and miles of beautiful rolling land. One has to be careful just how one praises the extraordinary beauty of Washington County. I told a neighbor: "This land is so beautiful it reminds me of Tennessee." He said, "I think I am going to throw up."

In fact, our view to the north looks like the Smokies, which Susan

Our July 4 Independence Day Texas Parade entry—driven by Margaret, with me riding shotgun and granddaughter Corbin (foreground) and her friend Sophie in back—is my fifty-four-year-old Mercedes 380SL. We keep the vintage car in our barn except when we are zooming over the exhilarating hills and curves of this wonderful "Tennessee-like" land.

Tretower Farm! From our "Smoky Mountain Stream" and Shu Shu Falls in the Heart of Texas, Johnny Steele and Susan finished what God started. Our family loves gathering here.

adores, with ridge after ridge as far as one can see. I believe a key reason Susan fell in love with our Texas farm is the little stream that traverses it. Susan began working with the brilliant Johnny Steele to convert the modest little stream into a "Smoky Mountain stream." It is stunning. They even created a rock-lined "pool in the stream" for the grandchildren. They found natural springs which poured into the pool and eventually created a waterfall christened "Shu Shu Falls" in honor of Susan. More trees were planted to shelter our Texas version of an "Old Smoky" rock-lined stream from the highway. Future majestic cypress trees have been planted by the stream and luminous Louisiana irises in it. Harvard ivy is growing on the bridge that crosses it.

Johnny Steele is our "hero" and dear friend. He converted our garden at Inwood into a swimming pool surrounded by such exquisite designs and floral colors it takes our breath away all these years later. He and Susan have been collaborators in designing both the interior and exterior of Tretower. They inspire each other. We call him "Capability" Steele after the superlative "Capability" Brown who landscaped

Family surrounds "Shu Shu" in her "Boss Lady Mobile," with Lake Corbin and Lake Avery in the distance.

Churchill's Blenheim Palace and other magnificent English estates "to the horizon."

Washington County is as friendly as a scoop of ice cream on a hot summer day. The beloved Blue Bell Creamery is only twelve miles—as the contented cows walk—from our Tretower Farm. People in the area adore Blue Bell. The Blue Bell slogan is "We eat all we can and sell the rest." We are proud to be neighbors of the "best little creamery in the country." Our freezer is always full of Blue Bell.

In June 2016, the family thrilled Susan with the presentation of a "Boss Lady Mobile," a beautiful red golf cart complete with the Tretower brand, for her to ride herd over every acre of the property. Later that year we celebrated my birthday at the new Richard-installed swimming pool immediately north of the farmhouse. It has a huge, elongated, natural boulder from which to jump, and a whirlpool. The pool looks directly into the gorgeous sunsets and afterglow. Two Pawley Island hammocks hung between trees make one drowsily relaxed just to look at them!

Our wonderful "home assistant," Ana Medrano, loves Tretower and specializes in helping Susan keep gorgeous roses flourishing everywhere one looks.

Birds abound! We are greeted by one or two snowy egrets in the lakes. From April to early August we are thrilled by the spirited swooping of a large family of purple martins that fly up varying routes from Brazil each year—sometimes 2,000 to 3,000 miles—to stay with us in their four special houses. We love these amazing birds and they love us. We have mockingbirds (the state bird of both Texas and Tennessee) perched on the highest limbs. Pairs of cardinals. Bluebirds. Hummingbirds sipping nectar just outside the master bedroom near the enchanting wind sculpture we purchased in Maine with our great friends, Dan and Dottie Blitch. Hawks soar over occasionally. Richard is an ardent fisher of the lakes and consistently pulls out large big-mouth bass; now Bo, a natural sportsman, and Lizzie get up asking to go fishing. Five-year-old Lizzie, over three weekends, recently caught twenty-six fish! Coyotes howl at night.

This grandchild magnet captivates the entire family. PERFECT!

We are deep in the heart of Texas, and we love it.

CHAPTER 22

My Family, You Are <u>My</u> <u>Very</u> <u>Heart</u>

I'm French born. In France, the moment it begins to get dark, we close the shutters. It is not a gesture meant to shut out the light. It is to enclose you inside the home. A house is a physical place. A home is where your sentiments are. A spiritual haven. It's where you and your wife shut out the disturbances of the outside world and concentrate on each other. A home is where love abides. It is a place of closeness and togetherness. You can see I believe in love.

Love is all about thankfulness, gratitude and appreciation. Love, if it is real, does not have a bottom line. The word, love, to me is divine. Love radiates from somewhere within, perhaps from a kind heart, and it is ethereal.

My wife was a remarkable woman. She left me [died] in 1978. She disappeared forever. I cannot touch her. I cannot kiss her. But, still, I hear her voice. I visualize her here with me. She was beautiful and smart. You have asked me questions about my life. There is no such thing as 'my life.' There is only 'our life.' I don't pass judgment on other couples. I was willing to make the total commitment. Love is what makes everything worthwhile.

People should love one another, even in competitive situations in business. The depth is not the same as loving someone. Love, in business, takes on the face of admiration or sympathy or respect. If people loved each other like that, we would get closer to the possibility of world peace. You have to be kind to people you don't like, that's a kind of love, too. I think God is love and that the manifestation of love is simple affection for each other.

—General Georges Doriot, tough-minded professor of Manufacturing, perennially the most popular course at Harvard Business School

Barging through Burgundy, 1989. One of our favorite trips and one of my all-time favorite pictures of Susan. Pure joy still when I look at it.

Of one truth I am absolutely certain. Love is the essential ingredient that empowers us, makes happiness possible, and is the ultimate reward. I was awakened every morning by a kiss on the cheek from Mother, and I always have felt self-worth because I was loved.

I fell in love instantly with Susan that Valentine's Day evening in Boston, February 14, 1961, the minute I saw her in her Chauncey Street apartment. Our love deepened the "magical summer of 1962" at Orleans and Nauset Beach on Cape Cod. Susan and I always have been each other's best friend. It has been deep love, to be sure, but it has been beyond that. We believe our friendship, closeness, and dependence on each other was annealed during our first fifteen months in Boston with no family on which to call for help. I can say right now, and I often do: Susan, I love you more today than ever in my life. I can also state we have not experienced <u>even</u> <u>one</u> <u>hour</u> <u>of</u> <u>ennui</u>!

Margaret and Richard have grown up knowing Susan and I believe in them and love them with all our hearts. We told them, but, far more important, we showed them. It is wonderful to see our children pass this disciplined but unconditional love to their children. I tell Margaret

Ireland is filled with Vaughan Pubs. The natural beauty captivated the Vaughan family.

and Richard I am glad you have children because now you know how much we love you. As Mama and Papa and Mother and Dad left me, I hope I am leaving Margaret and Richard the legacy of a good name. It cannot be said of me, as it was of Papa and Dad, that they lived for sixty years (over ninety for Dad!) in the same community and never was said a negative word about them. But I hope my family will take satisfaction from what the esteemed Larry Faulkner, CEO of the eminent Houston Endowment and past president of The University of Texas, wrote me:

> Dear Gene, You have my greatest appreciation and admiration for your ability to lift up a whole community. In all my days, I have seen no one else with your sense of community and your desire to help your neighbors to better their circumstances, while having a good time in the process. When I first came to Houston, people described you as a blessing to the city, and they indeed spoke the truth....

Thank you, Larry. Your words are a precious gift to me.

Susan, Margaret, and I celebrate Richard's twenty-first birthday in the Prohibition-era, secret "Bootleg Cellar" at the 21 Club in New York.

Margaret and Richard are certainly creating their own outstanding reputations, careers, and families. It means very much to me that two themes central to my life are being carried on so profoundly by Margaret and Richard: entrepreneurship and service to community. They devoutly believe in what I have so often advocated in words and practice: Nurture the institutions and communities that have nurtured you. Both they and their spouses very much live by that creed through volunteer efforts. Margaret and Ann and Richard are changing and shaping impactful organizations through their leadership, intellect, and hands-on support. And what an extraordinary example they are giving their children.

Margaret and Richard are genuine entrepreneurs. Margaret, for sixteen years, has headed MCV Consulting, a highly successful, Houston-based strategy consultancy serving institutions and multi-generational family enterprises internationally. Because of her talented service on the boards of the Salvation Army, Rice's Shepherd School of Music, the University of Texas Ransom Center for the Humanities, and others, she has been named to Houston's "Fifty Most Influential Women." Richard is president of Pinto America Growth Fund and Alloy Merchant Finance, two highly entrepreneurial enterprises with outstanding concepts and associates. He was invited to join the Young Presidents Organization (YPO) and is profoundly and joyfully involved. Ann is an outstanding research analyst with the prestigious Select Equity Group and an active director of the admired YES Prep Public Schools. Needless to say, Susan and I are exceedingly proud of their business abilities and moral commitments.

Susan, Margaret, Richard, and I always have been exceptionally close. There are numerous explanations, including the love we received from our own parents and our growing together at our beach home. Our extensive travel to all fifty states and every continent except Antarctica further annealed us. It may be my "distance running" extended, but both Margaret and Richard have run major marathons—Richard, the New York Marathon and South Africa's thirty-mile "Ocean-to-Ocean" run, and Margaret, the Music City Marathon in Nashville, Tennessee, and the Paris Marathon.

It may seem it was all work in the telling of my story, but concurrent with striving, Susan, Margaret, Richard, and I rejoiced in sports. We were there! For example, Richard and I were THERE for most of the greatest sports events in Houston history. We have had season tickets for the Rockets almost since they moved from San Diego in 1971—and still do. We were there together when the Rockets won the back-to-back NBA Championships in 1993–94 over the New York Knicks with the superb Hakeem Olajuwon and again in 1974–75 when fellow Phi Slamma Jamma teammate Clyde Drexler joined him. Margaret flew down from New York to rejoice in one of the playoff games. We were there when Coach Rudy Tomjanovich uttered his immortal (in Houston): "Never underestimate the heart of a champion." (Later Clyde Drexler and his fine family lived directly across from our Inwood home; with Jack Blanton we hosted a neighborhood welcome party in their honor.)

We rhapsodized in Luv ya Blue, Earl Campbell, and Bum Phillips. We were there when the Great Earl ran his pulsating eighty-three-yard TD which is still considered the single most thrilling play on Monday Night Football. We were also there when the Oilers were so bad I could not give away our tickets to orphanages. We praise our neighbor Bob

McNair for bringing pro football back to our football-crazy city after the "dastardly" Bud Adams took the Oilers away to Nashville, and we have had four seats for every game, starting with our Texans' heartening 19–10 triumph over the Dallas Cowboys in the opening game.

We were there to watch our Astros "Killer Bs" of Biggio, Bagwell (both in the Hall of Fame) and later Berkman. And we were there for the National League title games in Shea Stadium in New York—when METS fans dumped ice and vulgarity on us—to watch no-hitter pitchers Nolan Ryan and Mike Scott, a client of Vaughan Nelson, pitch to no avail. We were there and saw in 2005 Cardinal Albert Pujols power a massive moonshot to defer the Astros one game before going to their first World Series.

We were there for college Final Fours. We were there, with season tickets to River Oaks tennis tournaments and watched the best in amateur clay tennis. In the Astrodome we have thrilled to junk car races, prize fights, demolition derbies, the Ringling Bros. Barnum & Bailey circus, and all kinds of entertainment to which only a son whose boyhood grand passion was "Speed Racer" could entice me! We were THERE, and we loved every single minute of being together.

Susan and I had our special sports moments also. Astros owner Drayton McLane had front-row seats immediately behind home plate. He regularly invited President and Barbara Bush, but he liked my enthusiasm—or, as he once said, the fact that "You eat a lot of hot dogs and spill mustard on your shirt." Annually, Drayton invited Susan and me to sit with Elizabeth and him.

In Boston, Susan and I had season tickets on Sunday afternoon for the renowned Boston Symphony. Our cultural vein continues. We were present for the opening of the Jesse H. Jones Center for the Performing Arts, the Wortham Center, and the Alley Theatre—and regularly attended all. Of particular joy, I was invited to become a vice-president of the Houston Grand Opera when the renowned David Gockley—who discovered Renée Fleming—arrived as General Manager in 1971. Susan and I have had our lives enriched by season tickets over four decades of first-rate opera.

It is a profound tribute to the friendliness of Houston that we moved here in 1964, and in 1968 we were invited to join the Houston Country

London, I could never get enough. And what was the erudite Winston Churchill whispering in my ear? Wouldn't FDR like to know?

Club, with no connections, in the fourth-largest city in America. If you love Houston, it reaches out and pulls you in!

Our cultural proclivity encompassed art. I never have wished I was exceptionally wealthy except one time. During a soaring energy market years ago, a leading New York art gallery briefly opened a Houston branch and featured a large section of Monet's *Waterlilies* for $940,000 (around $2.8 million in current value). It was fabulous—and probably cheap—but we had to pass! Even so, Susan and I hold our breath often enough by gazing at the art on our walls at Inwood, Tretower, and the office, thanks primarily to the keen eye and taste of Meredith Long, Houston's premier art connoisseur and gallerist. We started collecting when the firm was new, and over the years we have acquired several pleasing works by Wolf Kahn, Dorothy Hood, Brian Cobble, Denny Pickett, Al Barnes, and others. They permit us to experience the ethereal. The exceptional taste of Meredith Long has abetted Susan and

Our family at our ancestral Tretower Castle on our first trip to Wales in 1981.

me in standing before beauty. We are gratified that Margaret, with a Masters in Connoisseurship from Sotheby's in New York (in addition to her MBA from Vanderbilt), carries this passion into the next generation as an avid collector of emerging contemporary art and trustee of the Contemporary Art Museum Houston. Her own fine paintings grace our home and lift our hearts.

Without a doubt, Susan, Margaret, Richard, and I were bonded with our four-legged family members. When Susan and I thought of getting a puppy for Margaret and Richard—no doubt still enchanted by "Lassie"—it was Shelties we thought of. It was a happy decision. We learned of Guy Mauldin Kennels, which specialized in Shelties. Out of dozens, Susan and I found a beautiful sweet little "piece of fur." It was instant love. I was looking through a travel book and came across the Isle of Skye and thought Skye was a lovely name. The children liked it and, without realizing it, set the precedent for British names. Skye was our first and all-time favorite. He was very gentle and intelligent as well as gorgeous. After Skye died tragically following Richard across the street to play first-grade football, the mourning period was very

Margaret and Richard with our beloved Shelties at "Double Sunrise."

long. Eventually we went back to Guy Mauldin and got Faire (of Faire Island). On the way home from a family trip to the East, we visited some stables in Kentucky. A cat had just given birth to a litter in a stable, and Margaret fell totally in love with one of the kittens. I could never say no to Margaret. She named her Little Blue (for Bluegrass), and the kitten rode all the way back to Houston lying on my neck. I must admit, having never liked cats, I fell in love with Little Blue. I can still picture Little Blue and Faire at home, lying in the back entrance sunshine together in a "T," with Little Blue's head across Faire's stomach, both asleep. That is my "Peaceable Kingdom." Over the years we were blessed with Fleet and Wick, for Piddlewick.

Duchess was Margaret and Richard's beautiful Siamese. She and I had an understanding about college basketball. Every Sweet Sixteen and Final Four—while the family was away—she and I sat in a chair intently watching the games and eating caviar.

Years later when we went to Guy, we returned with a beautiful, small-sized Sheltie we named Windrush for the small comely River Windrush in the Cotswolds. Our wonderful Windrush had a heart attack the week before our entire family left on our 2008 England-Wales trip. At a bridge crossing the River Windrush the family held a beautiful memorial service, watching flower petals float until out of sight.

Photographer and writer Roger Caras said, "Dogs are not our whole life, but they make our life whole." Our dogs and the cats were an integral part of the fabric of our family, woven into our hearts and memories. It's no surprise they populate the next generation of our family. Richard and Ann have given a gorgeous Sheltie named Sir Brody to their children: Avery, Bo, and Lizzie. Corbin has her sweet-tempered, lovely, and loyal Cecil, and her spirited Siamese cat.

Most of all, I believe our family trips have been the vital ingredient cementing our unique bond. Each trip was spectacular and memorable in its own way. The summer of 1988 was extra special. Susan and I were celebrating our twenty-fifth anniversary; Margaret was graduating from Vanderbilt and Richard from St. Andrew's. The previous year Walter Cabot spent a night with us and over dinner mentioned that his family's best trip had been a tented Safari in Kenya. BINGO! The Vaughans were on their way.

Batalor ("Eagle") Safaris was owned by an English family headed by a storied hunter with his wife and twenty-five-year old son, Michael. We lodged in tents that moved with us and set up different camps in the midst of the wilds. It was just us, the guide family, and Daniel, a young Maasai warrior, who stood guard all night with his spear and a fire to keep lions away. The only thing on earth a lion is afraid of is a young Maasai warrior who must kill a lion to earn his manhood. Daniel and Richard, about the same age, became great friends. We even got to meet Daniel's family; his father was a chief. At the end Daniel gave Richard his eight-foot long spear. Somehow we managed to bring it home with us. I remember lying in the tent after everyone had gone to sleep, reading *Out of Africa* by flashlight and listening to lions roar, seemingly right outside our tent. Incredible!

Our hunter took us walking through the high grass. There could be lions or cheetahs, any predator around us. He carried a high-powered rifle; we did not. Every night after dinner there were stories around the campfire. A chorus of wild animals roared in the background. The Serengeti was indescribably magnificent. At the entrance of the

Of numerous great family trips, I think we all agree our tented safari in Kenya was the best ever. Here Mt. Kilimanjaro "calls us."

park there is a sign that reads: "This is the way the world was in the beginning." While we had many memorable trips together, we agree that none has been more adventuresome and soul-satisfying than our Kenya safari.

Not surprisingly, the same depth of research that went into Vaughan Nelson investments also went into my preparation for family trips. I still get kidded unmercifully by Margaret and Richard that when Susan and I took them to England for a month, I created an itinerary with A, B, and C options for each day. Yes, I confess! After a week I learned to give everybody a "free" day every sixth day. Our trips were changed dramatically for the better by my adopting one new philosophy: We will come here again, so we do not have to see everything this time.

Susan and I celebrated our thirtieth anniversary in style. We went to England on the QEII and flew back on the Concorde! Margaret and Richard saw us off from the River Café in New York, looking at a gorgeous sunset through champagne bubbles. Aboard, we had been advised to request the Queen's Dining Room, and there we had the serendipity to be assigned to the "Lively Corner," which lived up to its name! During our two weeks in England we did "big-time" hunting,

With Susan in 2001 riding the rapids on Dart River, New Zealand, happy to be in all-cash instead of the "dot-coms!"

the proof of which resides in our gardens at Inwood: two large match-ing beautiful "staddle stones," a lion's head through which gushes a turbulent stream into the swimming pool, several large olive oil jars, and a very ancient stone sundial in our rose garden.

Susan and I adored traveling with Margaret and Richard, but we also cherished certain trips "à deux." Almost annually we spent a week, or at least a long weekend, in New York going to Broadway shows. All year long we looked forward to staying in a junior suite in the St. Regis, our favorite hotel in New York City. Its hospitality was unmatched. We were greeted warmly not only by the concierge but the doormen, "but-ler," and front desk. We dined at a variety of excellent restaurants, but we always savored the King Cole Bar, centered on its famous mural in the St. Regis; the Four Seasons Restaurant, again our personal favorite of the many outstanding restaurants we have experienced worldwide, where we had a special table poolside (and where I introduced Richard to a precious bottle of Petrus!); Sevilla Restaurant & Bar, 62 Charles at 4th Street, which served authentic Spanish cuisine and where I ordered "paella with clams" every time; and the Palm Court in the Plaza Hotel until the Plaza converted to a residential hotel. Susan and I went to the Four Seasons first with Audrey and John Poindexter the year before we married and returned many times through the years. On our first visit to Sevilla, in 1961 the night before Susan sailed for Europe, I bought her a small bunch of beautiful violets from "The Violet Lady." As the old saying goes, we would not want to live there, but we dearly treasure "our" New York City!

There is nothing in the world I cherish as much as being with my family—anywhere, anytime! Our family was enhanced mightily when it grew to include Richard's wife, Ann. A moment forever deep in my heart is when Richard and I were taking a walk around the neighborhood and talking. Suddenly Richard's voice became very soft. He said, "Dad, let me tell you about Ann." I knew instantly. Ann was a top writer for the *Wall Street Journal* (she had the "Wall Street Beat!") when they reconnected while both were working in New York. They had been classmates at Princeton. She also had a masters from the Columbia School of Journalism. I was delighted to hear she was not a New Yorker but from a lovely, multi-generational family in Asheville, North Carolina. Ann is very modest. I did not learn for over two years, and then only by accident, that she was Phi Beta Kappa and summa cum laude at Princeton. She joined Richard and me in earning her CFA Charter.

The rehearsal dinner for Ann and Richard was held at The Biltmore Estate, Asheville. With the wedding on November 1, 2003, the Biltmore House was ablaze for Christmas. The elegant, three-story home of George and Edith Vanderbilt, built in 1895, was augmented by exquisitely decorated Christmas trees, flickering candlelight, and cozy fireplaces. Everyone was offered a tour of the house, and as they stepped out of the library onto the Italian terrace, they were handed a glass of champagne just in time to see a gorgeous sunset through the bubbles! At the seated dinner for 140, Cat Stevens opened up full throttle with "Yellow Rose of Texas," and frivolity never slowed. Richard's groomsmen—including Princeton SAEs and the "Houston Rodeo Gang"—presented a hilarious video they had filmed starring Joe Buck, famed TV announcer, who interviewed sports stars about "Little Richie Vaughan." Ann's bridesmaids gave equally funny, loving toasts. I presided and felt very proud that everyone had such a great time, especially Ann and Richard.

Margaret married fellow Houstonian Clay Robinson, and while they eventually divorced, they remain good friends and active co-parents to our precious granddaughter.

If I thought God had granted me every blessing I could possibly want, He gave me more—grandchildren! Corbin is Margaret's daughter. Ann and Richard have three children: Avery; Richard Jr., who goes by Bo; and Elizabeth, who goes by Lizzie. Oh, how they tug at my heart!

I have been the recipient of professional and civic honors in life. However, the recognition that means the most to me is the kind I received on Father's Day 2012. The family gathered at the Houston Country Club, all together for the first time since my seven-and-a-half-hour open heart surgery. Being surrounded by my family was blissful enough, but then I received cards and gifts that flooded me with love. One card read:

> Pop Pop
> If you want to know how much
> You're loved,
> Count all the fish in the sea....
> Then multiply it by all the stars in the sky
> And that's billions and trillions!
> Thanks for being the best Pop Pop ever.
> Avery, Bo, Lizzie

Corbin, who had just returned from "Seafarer Sailing Camp" in North Carolina, loves my made-up "Howie and the Pirates" stories that I told to Margaret and Richard in the hammock at our beach house when they were children and now invent for my grandchildren. The Robinsons gave me a National Geographic CD of "Bluebeard—A Real Pirate" and a wonderful card saying:

> Daddy / Pop Pop
> Arghhh—
> Here's to lots of "keelhauling" and "Howie" stories this summer!
> We love you with all our hearts.

They fill me with love and send my spirit soaring.

In 2008 we leased a bus to take a monumental three-generation trip to Wales by way of England. The crowning finish was a celebration at Gravetye Manor. It is one of our two favorite hotels in the world, and Susan and I arranged to begin and end nearly every trip to England there.

I always promised myself I would not be the kind of grandparent who overshares his grandchildren's photos with unsuspecting company, and I have stayed true to that word. But how often I look at them myself! And Susan and I revel vicariously in watching our children travel with our grandchildren. How wonderful to see that we have passed on our curiosity and sense of adventure. Oh, the places they have already been and we know that they will go. That fills our hearts with wonder for the future.

At every stage of my life a line from Desiderata has brightened to have special meaning for that season. Now the line is: "Take kindly the counsel of the years, gracefully surrendering the things of youth." Age has taken its toll on the travels of Susan and me to our superb Harvard Business School and Vanderbilt reunions. But the one reunion we attended in 2016 was outstanding—the sixty-fifth reunion of Haywood High School in Brownsville, Tennessee. What better time to be there

My HHS class of '51 was loaded with smart and capable students who went on to distinguish themselves and our school. Taken at our 20th reunion in 1971 at the Brownsville Country Club, this photo reveals the zest embedded in us.

than in April; Brownsville was resplendent with dazzling white and pink dogwood and affirmed its reputation as the most beautiful small city in America. As president of my senior class (a position, as it turns out, you hold for life), I had the honor of addressing my classmates, many of whom have been friends since first grade: "Like an orchard planted decades ago, we have grown straight and true, and underneath our roots are entwined and closer than ever."

I am deservedly proud of my HHS Class of 1951. We have never missed a reunion, the only class in history for which this is true, and as our age has advanced, we have voted to hold them every three years instead of five. There are many high achievers. For example, Allen G. King, one of the region's most successful farmers, has been a County Commissioner for sixty-two years, the longest in the State of Tennessee,

Margaret and Jonathan's wedding. Over a hundred family and close friends came for the joyful occasion. © Jennifer Bowen Photography.

and his father was on the board of County Commissioners for twenty-six years before him, meaning a Gooch King has been a Commissioner of Haywood County for eighty-eight total years, a state record. The newly built Allen G. King Criminal Justice Center was named in Allen's honor. I dearly love Allen and Patsy King and cherish their invitations each time Susan and I are in Brownsville to have dinner in their home with them and their delightful, accomplished children. Bill and June Walker are also close and admired friends. Bill, an exemplary farmer and horticulturist who creates a gorgeous flower arrangement for our church every Mother's Day in honor of my Mother and Dad, has been Secretary of Agriculture which in the State of Tennessee is an utmost honor.

Tomcat Purple and White Football is big. Our class produced some of the most outstanding coaches and educators in the Mid-South.

Rockey Felker, son of the wonderful Mary Jane Felker, is the finest quarterback ever at Mississippi State and was SEC player of the year. He became the youngest head coach in America at his alma mater.

The visit to lifelong friends stirred many warm memories, but also wonderful was coming home to Houston, to look ahead. Life does not stand still at any age. In April 2017, Margaret married Jonathan Cox, a native of Westport, Connecticut, and very fine man, in a dazzling wedding at the Four Seasons in Scottsdale. Bollinger Champagne was served, of course, and the luminosity of their relationship inspired my "father of the bride" toast. Margaret was introduced to Jonathan by sister-in-law Ann.

Jonathan graduated from Columbia Business School with highest honors and is head of Energy Mergers and Acquisitions at Morgan Stanley. We're fortunate that this twenty-five-year New Yorker has now embraced Houston as his new home and are deeply gratified our daughter has found such fulfilling happiness and partnership with him. Jonathan joins Margaret in becoming engaged in Houston community service, with his having served in New York City in a leadership capacity with KIPP Star Charter School (Harlem). Jonathan has two lovely teenage children, Evelyn and Austin, which makes everyone happy because Corbin always has wanted siblings! The three children love being with each other, and we are enjoying getting to know our wonderful new step-grandchildren. Two months before their wedding, a party was held in honor of Margaret and Jonathan in the main dining room at the Bayou Club, the very place Susan and I dined our first evening in Houston. Once again, we sat under the watchful eyes of Baron Neuhaus, his portrait still hanging over the fireplace. Once again we were excited about new beginnings (and Susan, about the crème brûlée!).

Our days are not the fast pace they once were, and Susan and I are more than at peace with that. We treasure each moment. We love our time with our children and grandchildren, and we enjoy their comings and goings. Best of all, I have my sweetheart, partner, and best friend for over half a century, my Susan, at my side. One of the many things I adore about her is that she is deeply intelligent and, like Papa, stays universally informed and expresses world views. Susan and I love being together at home and Tretower, reading, exchanging opinions with wit, taking in the lush greenery of our Inwood garden and our wonderful farm vistas, savoring the stillness.

And still laughing! Our minds have the happy faculty, without preamble, to suddenly pull up funny events, even long-ago jokes, and laugh warmly and wonderfully together. Susan always has been beautiful and wonderful to experience; over time her inner beauty steals outward to compound her total loveliness.

CHAPTER 23

The Summing Up

Because we don't know when we will die, we get to think of life as an inexhaustible well. Yet everything happens only a certain number of times, and a very small number really. How many more times will you remember a certain afternoon of your childhood, some afternoon that's so deeply a part of your being that you can't even conceive of your life without it? Perhaps four or five times more, perhaps not even that. How many more times will you see the full moon rise? Perhaps twenty. And yet it all seems limitless.

—Paul Bowles, *The Sheltering Sky*

One enchanted evening at Tretower Farm, Susan and I once—and only once—after watching the sunset from across Lake Avery and Lake Corbin and driving home through a grove of live oaks in Bo's Meadow, beheld, as if by magic, a "billion" tiny lights. These were lightning bugs in such huge numbers we had never seen before nor seen since.

Thereafter, for several months during my recovery from open heart surgery, each night I experienced some magical, even mystical, moments. Nightly, several "lightning bugs" would illuminate positive events throughout my life. I have been blessed beyond all imagination. Even my Mother could not have wished as much for me, and that is saying a lot. My blessings have continued to flow beyond my dreams.

It is true, I believe, that one learns most from failures. I have had numerous "learning opportunities." For example, one time early on our firm was terminated on Christmas Eve—by a public relations firm, no less. Our beloved First Presbyterian Church, after dear Jack Lancaster died, eventually was taken over by a fundamentalist group that took our church, as with numerous "tall steeple" churches, out of the denomination. With heavy hearts, but with "invincible goodwill," our family left the church in which Susan and I had been so deeply and happily involved for over fifty years. (Our Presbyterian School is independent and flourishing.) We have found another profoundly uplifting church home. There have been other disappointments, of course, but few compared to the extraordinary blessings we have received.

Not a failure per se, but Hurricane Harvey was a monumental region-wide catastrophe in the final week of August 2017. Over fifty inches of rain fell, flooding throughout the area was devastating, the scale of destruction overwhelming, and multitudes of people—including our marvelous, "unsinkable" Ana Medrano—lost everything. Susan and I and our nearby immediate families were safe and dry. I have a quirky mind that remembers odd things. Will Rogers said, "Trying to stop the spirit of America is like trying to stop a locomotive by spitting on the track." This has two applications to me: one, Hurricane Harvey was utterly relentless. Two, trying to stop the resiliency of Texans helping Texans and the kindness of Americans is, inspiringly, like trying to stop Will Rogers's locomotive. In particular, the mission and astuteness of Center for Houston's Future in thinking and planning over the horizon is more needed than ever.

In October 2017 following the dreadful August floods of Hurricane Harvey that ravaged our beloved Houston, my blessings continued to flow beyond my dreams, this time for our entire region. The Houston Astros, having lost over 100 games in each of 2011, 2012, and 2013, started winning. As though magically putting our beleaguered populace on its back, in the post-season the Astros beat the storied Boston Red Sox and New York Yankees. In the World Series we faced the Los Angeles Dodgers, the "best team money can buy," whose massive $265 million payroll dwarfed the Astros' $149 million and included pitchers routinely described as best on the planet. The lesser-known Astros won the hearts of America. Famous sportscaster Joe Buck said it seemed to him, and other long-time observers, to be the best World Series ever played. Certainly everyone in Houston suspended disbelief. The seventh game was played in Los Angeles. Incredibly, our Astros won.

Christmas 2017! Our family celebrating joyously, in the home of Margaret and Jonathan, the Astros' superb Championship in the World Series. (Notice the trophy!) David Shutts Photography.

World Champions, the first time ever! It was like God, having tested Houston, like Job, with almost more than it could endure, had blessed us profoundly.

Richard got tickets for all post-season home games. This time eight-year-old Bo joined us. We all rejoiced. Margaret and Corbin were ecstatic and stood in line for an hour to get "Earned History" shirts and orange-and-blue World Series Champions caps for the entire family. They draped a beautifully gaudy World Series Champions pennant on our front door at Inwood. Schools, businesses, everything, closed for a parade downtown honoring our Astros. What a thrilling elevation of spirits for our still-sodden city! I awake every morning still with a bit of disbelief and then smile anew when I remember that yes, indeed—we did win the World Series!

Without question, Susan, Margaret, Richard, and their families are the center of my heart and being. They have said: "Daddy has a kind heart and a tough mind." That is exactly the kind of person I have strived to be.

Margaret and Richard also would say their father is a "Founder." That word has resonated with me throughout my career. Their recognition of me as a founder, and all that it implies, makes it all the more meaningful. Husband, father, grandfather, and founder are the roles I cherish most.

It's been quite a journey from Brownsville, Tennessee, to Vanderbilt, the Navy and ports of call, St. Louis, Harvard Business School and Boston, and then Houston. The decision at Putnam to switch from exciting, rewarding IBM to security analysis and investment management has afforded me a career of constant challenge and exceptional reward. I take pride in stepping up as a leader with the FAF and ICFA during their most difficult and contentious of times. This I can aver: I never shirked a commitment or responsibility to my profession, no matter how difficult.

A recent short journey, and one deeply meaningful to me, was when Richard, for a birthday present, gave me a trip for the two of us to Warren Buffett's annual meeting in Omaha. Unspoken, but it was a masterpiece, as a "changing of the guard."

I was honored immensely by a recent visit from Paul Smith, the new CEO of the CFA Institute. He is a very fine leader of ability and integrity. Paul had heard that I am now called the "George Washington of the CFA Institute." Not bad company! He asked me what message I would send to our members. I had two. First, the life-enhancing words I often quote of Sir John Templeton: "Investment management, properly done, is a ministry." Second, the Arabian proverb: "When you drink the water, remember who dug the well." I believe we all owe so much professionally, and personally, to those who did the hard pioneering work before us and made what we have possible.

Vaughan Nelson Investment Management is one of the two largest investment management firms in Houston—many dozens have come and gone since 1970—and has survived and thrived through all markets with honor intact. I am deeply grateful to the staunch leaders and team who have kept Vaughan Nelson Investment Management successful and admirable since my "re-direction." True to my 1961 HBS personal business strategy, I chose the "Small Ship Navy," headed my firm and capitalized. An aspect of the "Small Ship Navy" uniquely right for me is what in New Zealand is called "braided streams." While there is a primary purpose, other important—and beneficial to the community—streams weave throughout and around the mainstream. I always have had enough focus, energy, and perseverance to make certain the mainstream effort is successful but also enough wide-angle focus, energy, and perseverance to make certain the "braided streams," or "collateral duties," are also fruitful. Importantly, I would do it this way all over again!

I was surprised one time when someone chided me about my idealism in judging people, i.e., that I have too much faith in people. I disagree—strongly. During my long and demanding career of sizing up several hundred managements, I have been seriously tested and always—between deep fundamental analysis and my native shrewd instinct—have been able to ferret out the charlatans and schemers. Further, I have set exacting standards—life enhancers—at work and home, so I have been surrounded by the high American standards of probity and civility and by basically decent people.

Among all the professionals in investments there occasionally are persons of such greatness of mind and heart they transcend all others. I have been amazingly fortunate to know, and have as friends, people such as Sir John Templeton, Walter Stern, Walter Cabot, and my superb Group of Nine, all of whom practice investment management as a "ministry." Of course, there are some culprits, but the codes and stalwarts of the CFA Institute weed them out.

And there is a quality I think of as quintessentially Houstonian. Former President George H. W. Bush and his luminous wife, Barbara, are the very epitome of decent, world-respected leaders. Many people (including myself) for years have believed the Honorable James A. Baker III would have been one of the greatest U.S. presidents ever. Ben Love could easily rank as the best banker of modern times. There is no question that Dr. John Mendelsohn is the most superb leader in combatting cancer in our generation—and maybe any generation. I am a <u>tough-minded</u> <u>optimist</u>, and nowhere am I prouder to be so than in my judgment about people.

Without a doubt my best decision, other than asking Susan to be my wife, was moving to Houston. New York City sings about itself that, "If you can make it there, you can make it anywhere." Perhaps so, but Houston is the greatest entrepreneurial city in America. The truth is, "If you can't make it in Houston, you'd be <u>hopeless</u> anywhere else!" Houston welcomes you, as city fathers Mr. Wortham and Mr. Elkins did me my first week. My business and my family have thrived in Houston, and I have been highly motivated to give back.

I am an unabashed devotee of Houston. It gives me a quiet inner glow that for fifteen years a highlight of the Center for Houston's Future Annual Luncheon has been the presentation of the "Eugene H. Vaughan Civic Leadership Award." Although I have no voice in the selection, it has thrilled me that many of the people I admire most have been recipients.

I am a man at peace. In 1960, the inestimable HBS Professor Theodore Levitt implanted in me a career-long striving for "the visceral feel of entrepreneurial greatness." Now I happily possess the certain understanding that, whether or not I achieved greatness, my fulfillment is complete in my surging impulse to survive gallantly.

I am suffused with deep gratitude. I only have one other wish—to keep my zest for life as long as I live!

It's a <u>Vaughan</u>derful Life, indeed.

Acknowledgments

"Life Enhancer" has been a concept of overriding importance in our family and, later, in Vaughan Nelson. Happily, Ann Boor, imbued with expertise and graciousness, is a "Life Enhancer" to the highest power and reappeared in my life at precisely the best moment. She has "kept the grain and let the chaff blow away." I admired Ann immensely when she worked at JPMorgan Chase writing with Ben Love and Marc Shapiro and I was chairing The Houston Club Lyceum Distinguished Speaker Series. I wrote, more correctly, "overwrote" every aspect of *Building Beyond Thyself,* and it was Ann who deftly, gracefully, and ever tactfully guided it to more "effervescence" without an overabundance of the "fermentation process." She is singularly wonderful, and through this process we have become dear friends. Ann and I engaged at exactly the right moment, just as her beloved Cubs, of whom she is a lifelong fan, were winning the World Series for the first time in 108 years! And, astonishingly, we are completing the book as the Houston Astros are winning the World Series for the first time in its fifty-six-year history! The odds that both of our beloved but trophy-less teams would finally be victorious, and back-to-back, seem impossible to calculate. Some might have said it will never happen. I had the occasional same thought about completing this book. But indeed we got our World Series wins and finished the book. Thus, our collaboration has been not only productive, it has been thrilling!!

Deeply intelligent, comely, gracious, our estate planner, "ultimate Life Enhancer" and trusted friend—Terri Lacy! A partner at Andrews Kurth, with probably the most enviable clientele in Houston, she nevertheless always has taken time to give our family wise counsel ranging far beyond estate planning, including reading this manuscript because of her intimate knowledge of our lives. Terri has my utmost admiration and gratitude.

My deep appreciation goes to two indispensable mainstays: my assistant at the office and my assistant at home. For a quarter of a century, Carolyn Ross has managed to decipher my handwriting and turn into coherence nearly everything I have written, including the first draft of my manuscript and the sinewy research on which it is based. Ana Medrano, with high competence to equal her smile and happy disposition, completes a task and immediately looks around to see what else needs to be done. What an indomitable spirit!

I am profoundly grateful my life has brimmed over with inspiring, accomplished family, friends, and other uplifting personages. What makes me cringe about this memoir is that so many marvelous people who have enhanced the lives of Susan and me are not named. At every stage—Brownsville, Vanderbilt (as student and trustee), U.S. Navy, IBM, Putnam, Underwood Neuhaus, Vaughan Nelson Investment Management, Presbyterian School, Center for Houston's Future, UTHealth, and the numerous "braided streams"—I have been thrust upward by incandescent, deeply caring, Life Enhancers who became admired comrades and friends. Yet your names do not appear, simply for lack of space.

Just one example: fellow Vanderbilt trustee Ridley and Irene Wills frequently hosted us at their surpassingly beautiful "Gathering of the Waters" country home in Williamson County and sponsored us into Belle Meade Country Club. We honor and cherish them. Ridley is a foremost historian of Tennessee history—over twenty books, including a splendid biography of Sam Fleming, *Yours to Count On*. It is my fervent hope he will write the definitive history of Vanderbilt University. No one knows and feels it as fully as Ridley.

No one could read *Building Beyond Thyself* without knowing how very much I love and treasure my family. To all the other reasons should be added their reading and critiquing this manuscript, always bringing to mind my early church messages, "Speaking the truth in love!" Before we married and during our early marriage, Susan was an editor at the excellent Ginn & Company in Boston. Thus, once again, I am indebted to my wonderful life partner for handling superbly the photographs and publishing responsibilities.

At every stage of my life there have been outstanding, wholly committed, fellow knights-errant and friends. You are part of me, and I hope I always will remain a part of you.

Appendix

At the close of 1971 I was so deeply grateful to the clients who had entrusted funds to our neophyte firm I wrote them a heart-felt thank you letter. The mounting gratitude of our firm resulted in my writing an End of Year letter (EOY)—always mailed the day after Christmas—for most of the next thirty-one years until closing in 2002 with the death of my "philosophical beacon," John W. Gardner. Regrettably, the EOYs from 1971 through 1978, and some others, perished when a MENSA "temp" threw them out!

My final EOY was appropriate for several reasons. One, my "mainstream" was evolving to creation of Center for Houston's Future. Two, both Richard and Margaret would be getting married, and I was happily focused on my children and, a few years later, grandchildren! Last, writing the final EOY in 2002, focusing on the splendid John W. Gardner in the year "the sun went down and did not come up the next day," was ending on the highest note for me.

Year-end 1979

More than a decade ago, a client sent us a copy of a little book published in 1948 entitled *The Poems of Max Ehrmann*. Its prose-poems are notable for their beauty, spirituality, wisdom, and social vision. One in particular, called "Desiderata," has had special meaning to us. Clients with whom we shared it in 1971 have observed that over the years different lines have special pertinence at different "passages." At the start of a new and prime decade, we again want to share "Desiderata" with the friends of our firm.

DESIDERATA

Go placidly amid the noise and haste, and remember what peace there may be in silence. As far as possible, without surrender, be on good terms with all persons. Speak your truth quietly and clearly; and listen to others, even the dull and ignorant; they too have their story.

Avoid loud and aggressive persons; they are vexations to the spirit. If you compare yourself with others, you may become vain or bitter; for always there will be greater and lesser persons than yourself.

Enjoy your achievements as well as your plans. Keep interested in your own career, however humble; it is a real possession in the changing fortunes of time.

Exercise caution in your business affairs, for the world is full of trickery. But let this not blind you to what virtue there is; many persons strive for high ideals, and everywhere life is full of heroism.

Be yourself. Especially do not feign affection. Neither be cynical about love; for in the face of all aridity and disenchantment it is perennial as the grass.

Take kindly the counsel of the years, gracefully surrendering the things of youth.

Nurture strength of spirit to shield you in sudden misfortune. But do not distress yourself with dark imaginings. Many fears are born of fatigue and loneliness.

Beyond a wholesome discipline, be gentle with yourself. You are a child of the universe, no less than the trees and the stars; you have a right to be here.

And whether or not it is clear to you, no doubt the universe is unfolding as it should.

Therefore be at peace with God, whatever you conceive Him to be. And whatever your labors and aspirations, in the noisy confusion of life, keep peace in your soul.

With all its sham, drudgery and broken dreams, it is still a beautiful world. Be cheerful. Strive to be happy.

We are acutely aware and grateful that in the conduct of our business we are privileged to deal with people of competence, goodwill, and good humor—qualities which greatly enhance our lives. May the decade of the 1980s be a time of restoration of spirit and character for our nation, and may it bring joy and satisfaction to you and those you love.

Year-end 1980

On December 19th our firm celebrated its tenth anniversary. We were reminded of the line from "Good Company": "Today I have grown taller from walking with the trees," because, in that sense, our firm has grown taller, its members enhanced, from walking with fine people. We learned early that our clients and the industry professionals with whom we align do much to determine the character of our firm as well as the pleasure and satisfaction of its principals.

We feel extraordinarily fortunate to derive the satisfaction we experience from our associations. In *O Pioneer*, Willa Cather wrote, "The history of every country begins in the heart of a man or a woman." We believe the same is true of an enterprise. At our firm we have always believed that while certain head-based qualities—analytical judgment, tenacity, hard work, for example—are essential, over time the paramount point is whether the firm puts the integrity of its dealings with others in the first place or the second. In turn, we have nearly always been dealt with in this manner.

As we permit ourselves a brief glance backwards we are grateful that this was our tenth consecutive year of rising assets under management, a rarity in this profession, but most of all we are grateful for the opportunity to do business with people we respect and enjoy.

May 1981 begin to see the fulfillment of the hope of 1980 for our nation—and may it be a special year of happiness, success, and satisfaction for you and those you love.

Year-end 1982

At the recent funeral service of Leon Jaworski, a fitting occasion worthy of a magnificent man, Dr. John W. Lancaster pointed out that Mr. Jaworski was fond of quoting from Alexis de Tocqueville on the subject of his quest in 1835 to find what made America a great nation. Tocqueville, after observing he did not find the source of America's greatness in Washington, or in the Supreme Court, or even in its marvelous Constitution, said "America is great because America is good and if America ever ceases to be good, America will cease to be great."

This sent us searching for something attributed to Will Rogers years ago in a little book called *This I Believe* by Edward R. Murrow:

> I may have sometimes exaggerated a little. But, whatever I've said I tried to base on truth. I'd a whole lot rather have people nudge each other and say, "you know he is right about that," than get a big laugh.
>
> Now, everybody got a scheme to set the United States back right again. Although, come to think of it, I can't remember when it ever was right. There been times when it has been right for you and you and you, but never all of you at the same time. I believe this country's pretty much the same as it always was, and always will be, because it is founded on right, and even if everybody in public life tried to ruin it, they couldn't. Trying to stop this country now would be like trying to stop a train by spitting on a railroad track. No element, no party, not even Congress or the senate, can really hurt this country now. And we're not where we are on account of any one man. We're here on account of the real common sense of the big normal majority. This country's bigger than any man or any party. They couldn't ruin it even if they tried.
>
> But in believing this, I don't believe that you can just sit down and do nothing. There ain't no civilization where there ain't no satisfaction, and satisfaction don't come from just money and property and a bunch of bathtubs. I can be mighty rich, but if I ain't got friends, then I'm poorer than anybody.
>
> And if I fell out with people because of a difference of opinion, I wouldn't have many friends. Difference of opinion is what makes horse racing and missionaries.

Every man has an angle on living, or on life, or on something, and when you get it things are apt to look different. Every man's got something good or worth knowing in him.

Well, this is what I believe, and because I believe it, I can honestly say, I never met a man I didn't like.

This Christmas it seems to us that after a decade of accelerated shocks our nation is beginning a revival of its spirit. Our wish for next year is that each of us might have a little more of Will Rogers in us, especially his ingredients of sincerity, humor and spiritual balance. What a collective difference a bit more of this would make in our country.

A turbulent year such as 1982 can bring out the best or the worst in people. We feel so privileged at our firm to work closely with outstanding people such as you. We hope for you and those you hold dear that 1983 will be one of those special years that will be remembered fondly forever.

Year-end 1985

At Christmas this year, members of our firm read to our families from a speech Sir Winston Churchill broadcast to the world from the White House, Washington, at the lighting of The White House Christmas Tree, December 24, 1941. It is with gratitude for the sacrifice and resolve of another generation that we realize "these same children" to whom Churchill refers—are ourselves:

This is a strange Christmas Eve. Almost the whole world is locked in deadly struggle, and, with the most terrible weapons which science can devise, the nations advance upon each other. Ill would it be for us this Christmastide if we were not sure that no greed for the land or wealth of any other people, no vulgar ambition, no morbid lust for material gain at the expense of others, had led us to the field. Here, in the midst of war, raging and roaring over all the lands and seas, creeping nearer to the spirit in each cottage home and in every generous heart. Therefore we may cast aside for this night at least the cares and dangers which beset us and make for the children an evening of happiness in a world of storm. Here, then for one night only, each home throughout the English-speaking world should be a brightly-lighted island of happiness and peace.

Let the children have their night of fun and laughter. Let the gifts of Father Christmas delight their play. Let us grown-ups share to the full in their unstinted pleasures before we turn again to the stern task and the formidable years that lie before us, resolved that, by our sacrifice and daring, these same children shall not be robbed of their inheritance or denied their right to live in a free and decent world.

And so, in God's mercy, a happy Christmas to you all.

How blessedly different it is forty-four Christmases later. How good God has been to our generation to give us astonishing prosperity and relative peace. We are especially thankful because this year has been one of the finest ever for investors.

We are deeply grateful for our fine friends and wish for you and those you love a splendid 1986 filled with continued prosperity, happiness, and appreciation for what it means to live in a free and decent world.

Year-end 1986

In past years we have occasionally sent out little-known pieces which we thought carried special meaning, such as Prime Minister Churchill's moving Christmas Eve address from the White House in 1941, or the evergreen wisdom of the remarkable "Desiderata." This year, however, we are sending one of the best-known poems of all time. Always relevant, Rudyard Kipling's "IF—" contains certain passages which capture the spirit which is both needed and present in Texas these days.

> If you can keep your head when all about you
>   Are losing theirs and blaming it on you,
> If you can trust yourself when all men doubt you,
>   But make allowance for their doubting too;
> If you can wait and not be tired by waiting,
>   Or being lied about, don't deal in lies,
> Or being hated, don't give way to hating,
>   And yet don't look too good, nor talk too wise:

If you can dream—and not make dreams your master;
    If you can think—and not make thoughts your aim;
If you can meet with Triumph and Disaster
    And treat those two impostors just the same;
If you can bear to hear the truth you've spoken
    Twisted by knaves to make a trap for fools,
Or watch the things you gave your life to, broken,
    And stoop and build 'em up with worn-out tools;

If you can make one heap of all your winnings
    And risk it on one turn of pitch-and-toss,
And lose, and start again at your beginnings
    And never breathe a word about your loss;
If you can force your heart and nerve and sinew
    To serve your turn long after they are gone,
And so hold on when there is nothing in you
    Except the Will which says to them: "Hold on!"

If you can talk with crowds and keep your virtue,
    Or walk with Kings—nor lose the common touch,
If neither foes nor loving friends can hurt you,
    If all men count with you, but none too much;
If you can fill the unforgiving minute
    With sixty seconds' worth of distance run,
Yours is the Earth and everything that's in it,
    And—which is more—you'll be a Man, my son!

Memorized in childhood by many of us, different lines of "IF—" have a way of coming into focus during certain passages of our lives. At this time, the line about meeting Triumph and Disaster with circumspection has peculiar relevance because it has been a triumphant period in the financial markets while a disastrous time for many areas of traditional strength in our region.

The members of our firm are deeply grateful that our business permits us to have close association with fine and thoughtful people as you. We hope for you and your loved ones that 1987 will be a fulfilling, joyful, and peaceful year.

Year-end 1987

Some years, like some poets and politicians and some lovely women, are singled out for fame far beyond the common lot, and 1929 was clearly such a year. Like 1066, 1776, and 1914, it is a year that everyone remembers. One went to college before 1929, was married after 1929, or wasn't even born in 1929, which bespeaks total innocence.

These are the opening lines of *The Great Crash*, by John Kenneth Galbraith, a book we find useful to reread whenever the market soars as it did this past summer.

The year 1987 is a candidate to join 1929 as a year singled out for fame far beyond the common lot. It is an extraordinary year in which one can experience an historic 508-point, one-day drop in the market and still have a sense of well-being about the year. There is a sense of what the young Winston Churchill said when grazed by a bullet while fighting in South Africa: "Nothing is so exhilarating as having been shot at with no result." Along with the lifting of investment innocence from a generation of investors, in 1987 there is also a restoration of confidence taking place in Texas, the spirit of renewal of hope hard-won akin to that expressed in Alfred, Lord Tennyson's "Ulysses."

> Tho' much is taken, much abides; and tho'
> We are not now that strength which in old days
> Moved earth and heaven, that which we are, we are;
> One equal temper of heroic hearts,
> Made weak by time and fate, but strong in will
> To strive, to seek, to find, and not to yield.

The members of our firm feel a special gratefulness at this time, the kind of glow one feels when weathering an ordeal with comrades for whom one has respect and affection. This is because we realize that our firm is blessed with extraordinarily fine clients, friends and business associates. May 1988 be a year of excellent health, enhanced worth, good cheer, much laughter, and the presence of those you love.

Year-end 1988

At this year-end, as hearts throughout the world hurt for the families of Armenia, we are reminded of the eloquently simple words of Chief Seattle. Around 1852, the U.S. Government sought to buy Indian lands to accommodate immigrants to the United States. The following is excerpted from Chief Seattle's response:

> The President in Washington sends word that he wishes to buy our land. But how can you buy or sell the sky? The land? The idea is strange to us. If we do not own the freshness of the air and the sparkle of the water, how can you buy them?...
>
> We know the sap which courses through the trees as we know the blood that courses through our veins. The shining water that moves in the streams and rivers is not just water, but the blood of our ancestors. Each ghostly reflection in the clear waters of the lakes tells of events and memories in the life of my people. The water's murmur is the voice of my father's father... earth is our mother. Your destiny is a mystery to us. What will happen when the buffalo are all slaughtered? The wild horses tamed? Where will the eagle be? Gone! And what is it to say good-bye to the swift pony and the hunt? The end of living and the beginning of survival....
>
> As we are part of the land, you too are part of the land. This earth is precious to us. It is also precious to you. One thing we know: there is only one God. No man, be he Red Man or White Man, can be apart. We are brothers after all.

As 1988 closes, cosmic problems confront our nation, to be sure, but of overriding importance is the fact that in our lifetime there rarely has been as much peace in the world. And Houston! As we drove about the city last week, we realized that we had never seen the homes and businesses so beautifully decorated for Christmas. It recalled the sense of profound relief and gratitude evident in the brilliance of London at Christmas 1945.

A blessing for which we are most grateful is the privilege of having our lives influenced by extraordinarily fine people of competence, goodwill, and good humor—qualities which enhance our lives. May 1989 continue progress toward peace and "brothers after all" in our world, restoration of the spirit and enterprises of our region, and bring fulfillment, enhanced worth and much laughter for you and those you love.

Year-end 1989

In the past, our year-end messages have conveyed the exceptional wisdom and warmth of Chief Seattle, Winston Churchill (from the White House on Christmas Eve, 1941), and "Desiderata," among others. "Where have all the heroes gone?" is an oft-asked question today. So we are especially pleased to draw on the words of a contemporary, an educator whose own greatness of heart and strength of character is touching the future through his students. He is Jon O'Brien, the headmaster of St. Andrew's School, a superb coed boarding school in Delaware where, incidentally, this summer's splendid movie *Dead Poets Society* was filmed. His farewell remarks to the Class of 1989, below in almost their entirety, are applicable to all ages.

First. Recognize that life is quite short. The distance between your youth and beauty and my craggy old age is only 33 years. That is not a long time. So enjoy your lives. "Seize the day," as the Robin Williams character urges his students in *Dead Poets Society*. Don't waste your lives doing trivial things when there are so many magnificent and exciting ways to celebrate your lives.

Second. Don't spend your lives seeking happiness. I once heard William Bennett say that happiness is like a cat. It eludes those who seek it and jumps into your lap when you least expect it. He is right. Choose your goals wisely and, with luck, happiness will be a by-product of your quests.

Third. Listen to your hearts. Don't be followers. Inside each of you is a unique individual with a unique song to contribute to the world. The time has come for you to sing your song, not the songs of your parents or teachers or friends. Don't be afraid of hitting a few false notes. We all do. As to popularity, some of the most beautiful songs ever written have had small audiences.

Finally, and most important of all, love God and your neighbors. If we believe only in ourselves and live only for ourselves, we are doomed to live shallow and ultimately lonely lives. But if we dedicate our lives to the service of God and our neighbors, even the most simple tasks become meaningful, our songs become brilliant and clear, and we are constantly surprised by the number of cats which leap out of the shadows and onto our laps.

You leave with our love and affection. We will be listening for your songs.

This memorable year has had a miracle-like quality. Foremost, the global spread of freedom and capitalism is the unexpected cat leaping onto our lap. America, in the words of Houston's Jim Baker, "is reaping the harvest of long-held values." As this astonishing decade ends, we are deeply grateful for the privilege of having our lives influenced by extraordinarily fine people of accomplishment, graciousness, and abiding good will. May the decade ahead hold fulfillment and much laughter for you and those you love.

Year-end 1991

Since his remarkable *Self-Renewal* in 1963, through *On Leadership* in 1990, John Gardner, our choice this year to follow General Georges Doriot, Jon O'Brien, Chief Seattle, Sir Winston Churchill, et al. in bringing our year-end message of appreciation to friends of our firm, has been a wellspring of wisdom, common sense and down-to-earth inspiration. In a sense, he packed the "summing up" of a lifetime into his centennial commencement address at Stanford University this year, from which the following is greatly condensed:

> Learn all your life. Learn from your failures, from your successes, learn by taking risks, by suffering, by enjoying, by loving, by bearing life's indignities with dignity. You learn not to burn up energy in anxiety. You find that self-pity and resentment are the most toxic of drugs. You discover that no matter how hard you try to please, some people in the world are not going to love you, a lesson that is at first troubling and then really quite relaxing.
>
> Your identity is what you've committed yourself to. If you make no commitments, you're an unfinished person. Freedom and obligation, liberty and duty, that's the deal. Self-knowledge isn't enough. You

build meaning into your life through your commitments beyond the self, in your family and community life, in the way you treat any and all humans, in the goals and standards you set for yourself.

Life is an endless unfolding, and if we wish it to be, an endless process of self-discovery, an endless and unpredictable dialogue between our own potentialities for learning, sensing, wondering, understanding, loving, and aspiring...and life's challenges—and the challenges keep coming. And the challenges keep changing. It is my hope that you will keep on growing and that you will be the cause of growth in others.

Let me conclude by saying as plainly as I can that this nation is facing a test of character, all the more profound for being diffuse, all the more difficult for not being precipitated by enemy attack. The test is whether in all the confusion and clash of interest, all the distracting conflicts and cross purposes, all the temptations to self-indulgence and self-exoneration, we have the strength of purpose, the guts, the conviction, the spiritual staying power to build a future worthy of our past. You can help.

The remarkable events unfolding in the Soviet Union vividly underscore that nations must be recreated in each generation. It is now our generation's turn in America. It seems to us that John Gardner has it right. To be totally committed to developing one's full potentiality as a person, professional and citizen. To teach values by living them. To nurture our families, community, profession, institutions, and nation. Freedom and obligation, that's the deal. This has been one of the finest years ever in the twenty-one years of our firm, and a prime reason is that clients, associates and friends of our firm possess these qualities to an uncommon degree. May 1992 be a magnificent, happy and generous year for you and those you hold dear.

Year-end 1992

Theodore Roosevelt, twice President of the United States and leader of the Rough Riders, in 1910 spoke eloquently of the importance of commitment in a manifesto for all those who lay it on the line in their daily lives:

It is not the critic who counts; not the man who points out how the strong man stumbles, or where the doer of deeds could have done them better. The credit belongs to the man who is actually in the arena, whose face is marred by dust and sweat and blood; who strives valiantly; who errs, and comes short again and again, because there is no effort without error and shortcoming, but who does actually strive to do the deeds; who knows the great enthusiasms, the great devotions; who spends himself in a worthy cause; who at best knows in the end the triumph of high achievement, and who at the worst, if he fails, at least fails while daring greatly, so that his place shall never be with those poor spirits who neither enjoy much nor suffer much because they live in the gray twilight that knows not victory nor defeat.

These words stir the souls and tingle the spines of all those, young and old, who are "in the arena" in some aspect of their lives. They seem especially pertinent in an era in which negativism, cynicism, and criticism are prevalent. At year's end 1992, here's to the multitudes of fine people—both unsung and in the public crucible—who commit, who strive valiantly, and who spend themselves in some worthy cause.

The principals and staff of Vaughan, Nelson, Scarborough & McConnell are deeply grateful for the high quality and graciousness of clients, industry associates, and friends—the life enhancers—who uplift our lives. We wish for you and those you cherish a 1993 of mutual love, personal enrichment, good health, and much laughter with friends and family.

Year-end 1993

Ever since Moses brought down the Ten Commandments on a stone tablet from Mount Sinai, people have been placing important words in stone. On the gracefully arched entrance to the Carl Jung Educational Center in Houston are the words Jung had chiseled into stone over the door to his home in Kusnach, Switzerland: *"Vocatus atque non vocatus Deus aderit."* ("Called or not called, God is present.") Etched beautifully in glass in the lobby of Houston's Methodist Hospital are Tagore's moving words: "I slept and dreamt that life was all joy. I awoke and saw that life was but service. I served and understood that service was joy."

Embedded unobtrusively in the stone of an arched entrance at Princeton University are words which penetrate to the core of all whose lives have been made forever better by any institution: "You will always be a part of Princeton, and Princeton will always be a part of you." Superficial thoughts are seldom cast in stone.

Carved into granite at Rockefeller Center is the creed of John Rockefeller, Jr., principles which he believed point the way to usefulness and happiness in life:

I believe in the supreme worth of the individual and in his right to life, liberty and the pursuit of happiness.

I believe that every right implies a responsibility; every opportunity, an obligation; every possession, a duty.

I believe that the law was made for man and not man for the law; that government is the servant of the people and not their master.

I believe in the dignity of labor, whether with head or hand; that the world owes no man a living but that it owes every man an opportunity to make a living.

I believe that thrift is essential to well-ordered living and that economy is a prime requisite of a sound financial structure, whether in government, business or personal affairs.

I believe that truth and justice are fundamental to an enduring social order.

I believe in the sacredness of a promise, that a man's word should be as good as his bond, that character—not wealth or power or position—is of supreme worth.

I believe that the rendering of useful service is the common duty of mankind and that only in the purifying fire of sacrifice is the dross of selfishness consumed and the greatness of the human soul set free.

I believe in an all-wise and all-loving God, named by whatever name, and that the individual's highest fulfillment, greatest happiness, and widest usefulness are to be found in living in harmony with his will.

I believe that love is the greatest thing in the world; that it alone can overcome hate; that right can and will triumph over might.

These are principles, however formulated, for which all good men and women throughout the world, irrespective of race, creed, education, social position, or occupation, are standing, and for which many of them are suffering and dying.

These are the principles upon which alone a new world recognizing the brotherhood of man and the fatherhood of God can be established.

It strikes us that this credo is a useful compass when truth, common sense, and goodness at times seemed drowned out by a cacophony of lawsuits, strident demands for rights, and waterfalls of words equated to deeds. To look out for neighbors, broadly defined, and to place reliance upon one's personal word, upon character, and upon one's duty and obligation to serve would go a long way toward assuring that mankind will not just endure, but will prevail.

This has been a remarkably fine year in our firm, made possible by the quality and generosity of spirit of our clients and friends who influence our lives. May 1994 be a year filled with unconquerable good will for you and those you love.

Year-end 1994

The year 1994 has been an uncommon one in which the usual alloy of good, bad, tragic, bizarre, and soaringly uplifting occurrences have seemed even more pronounced. Recently we were asked: "If your physician told you today that you have twenty-four hours to live, whom would you call? What would you say?" Then came the dénouement: "What are you waiting for?"

This reminds us of the compelling lines spoken by Helen Keller: "Use your eyes as if tomorrow you would be stricken blind." Blind for most of her life, she went on to describe what she would want to see if she had only three days in which to see.

On the first day, she would want to see the people whose kindnesses and companionship had made her life worth living. She would call in all her friends and look long at their faces. She would also look into the face of a baby. She would like to see the many books that had been read to her and to look into the eyes of her faithful and loyal dogs. She would take a long walk in the woods.

On the second day, Miss Keller said she would get up early to see the dawn. She would visit museums to learn of man's progress upward. She would also visit an art museum to probe man's soul by studying his pictures and sculptures. Then, at night, she would visit the theatre to see the grace of the great ballerina Pavlova.

On the last day she would again be up to see the dawn, to discover new revelations of its beauty. Then she would visit the haunts of men, where they work, children at play. She would stand on the busy street corner, trying to understand something of the daily lives of people by looking into their faces and reading what is written there.

On the last evening she would like to see a funny play to appreciate comedy in the human spirit.

The importance of being "present in the moment" has particular meaning to members of our firm now because Dick Nelson, our colleague and friend for 27 years, died suddenly in January at age 54. The year just concluded had been the best in the history of our firm. In every aspect of his life Dick went out vibrantly at the top.

We feel profound gratitude and appreciation for our extraordinary clients, business associates and friends who by their generosity of spirit and graciousness lift our eyes to the splendor and blessings which fill our lives.

As this year ends and 1995 arrives, brimming with hope, the members of our firm wish that you and those you hold dear may savor the little joys, the small pleasures, the meaningful moments that come each of our ways each day.

Year-end 1995

In 1995 Vaughan, Nelson, Scarborough & McConnell celebrated the 25th anniversary of its founding. The journey from a blank sheet of paper in 1970 to our present firm is cause for celebration, humility, and immense gratitude. It has been observed that "Feeling gratitude and not expressing it is like wrapping a present and not giving it." Over the years we have tried periodically to express our deep gratitude to clients and a widening circle of friends of the firm by sharing thoughts from wise persons which we found insightful or uplifting. In honor of our Silver Anniversary, in this special edition letter we reprise excerpts from a few favorites from the past twenty-five years.

In 1992 Eric Sevareid died. We recalled in that year what for us was a transcending piece of simple wisdom which he stated in an eloquent TV essay years earlier on the death of Walt Disney: "There are three kinds of people in the world—well poisoners, lawn mowers and life enhancers." In our personal and professional lives we have sought to surround ourselves as much as possible with life enhancers and to avoid well poisoners. In this we have succeeded. We believe this single line of wisdom has made a profound difference. In that same sense, in 1980 as our firm celebrated its tenth anniversary, we were reminded of the line from *Good Company*: "Today I have grown taller from walking with the trees." Over twenty-five years, our firm has grown taller, its members enhanced, from walking with fine people. We learned early that our clients, the industry professionals with whom we align, and our friends do much to determine the character of our firm, as well as the pleasure and satisfaction.

At our firm's Silver Anniversary Celebration in October we recalled the ringing manifesto to being "in the arena," spoken by Theodore Roosevelt in 1910 and quoted in our 1992 letter:

> It is not the critic who counts; not the man who points out how the strong man stumbles, or where the doer of deeds could have done them better. The credit belongs to the man who is actually in the arena...who knows the great enthusiasms, the great devotions; who spends himself in a worthy cause; who at best knows in the end the triumph of high achievement, and who at the worst, if he fails, at least fails while daring greatly, so that his place shall never be with those poor spirits who neither enjoy much nor suffer much because they live in the gray twilight that knows not victory nor defeat.

These 25 years have been short. And fulfilling. In an early letter we recalled that in *O Pioneers!* Willa Cather wrote, "The history of every country begins in the heart of a man or a woman." The same is true of an enterprise. At Vaughan, Nelson, Scarborough & McConnell we have always believed that while certain head-based qualities—analytical judgment, tenacity, hard work, for example—are essential, over time the paramount ingredient is of the heart, whether the firm puts the integrity of its dealings with others in the first place or the second. Our goal has always been to conduct business with first-class people in a first-class manner, in the belief that profits, as happiness, will be a by-product. It has been a total team commitment. As a senior member of our excellent staff said on the occasion of our Silver Anniversary celebration, "No one can whistle a symphony; it takes an orchestra to play it."

As we permit ourselves this rare brief glance backwards, before focusing again eagerly on the future, we want to express our deep gratitude to our superb clients, business associates and friends of the firm who by your own wisdom and graciousness have permitted us to never miss the joy. We are indeed surrounded by life-enhancers.

May 1996 be an uncommonly happy, successful, prosperous and magnificent year for you and those you hold dear.

Year-end 1996

With most of the year-end letters sent to clients and friends of our firm over the past 26 years, we have experienced trepidation before the mailing. How would they be received by pragmatic businesspersons? After all, a wise counselor observed that men rarely share their fears, failures, feelings, and fantasies. Do not worry, we have no fears, failures, or fantasies either! But we have shared feelings freely over the years and thus have appreciation for this exultation of a trusting friendship expressed beautifully by Dinah Maria Mulock Craik:

> Oh, the comfort, the inexpressible comfort of feeling safe with a person. Having neither to weigh thoughts nor measure words but pouring them all out, just as they are—chaff and grain together. Certain that a faithful hand will take and sift them—keep what is worth keeping—and with the breath of kindness, blow the rest away.

It has been said that love may not make the world go round, but it sure makes the ride worthwhile, to which Lily Tomlin rejoined, "If love is the answer, will you please rephrase the question?"

The greatest of these is love, but can you also imagine the world exactly as it is with only one ingredient absent—sense of humor?

> Laughter need not be cut out of anything, since it improves everything.
> —*Selected Letters of James Thurber*

Laughter is like a diaper change. It's not a permanent solution—
just something that makes life tolerable.
—Anonymous

I cried until I laughed.
—Anonymous

I made the joyous discovery that ten minutes of genuine belly
laughter had an anaesthetic effect and would give me at least two
hours of pain-free sleep.
—Norman Cousins, *in Anatomy of An Illness*

With a fearful strain that is on me day and night, if I did not laugh,
I should die.
—Abraham Lincoln

Where there is no laughter, and where there are no tears, not
much is happening.
—Anonymous

Laughter is the hand of God on the shoulder of a troubled world.
—Grady Nutt

You don't stop laughing because you grow old; you grow old
because you stop laughing.
—Michael Prichard

We believe James Thurber and Grady Nutt got it right. We also believe
Richard C. Halverson, the admired chaplain of the U.S. Senate, had it
right when he wrote before his death:

You're going to meet an old man someday! Down the road ahead—10,
20, 30 years—you'll catch up with him, waiting for you there. What
kind of an old man are you going to meet? He may be a seasoned,
gracious fellow, surrounded by a host of friends who call him blessed
because of what his life has meant to them. He may be a bitter,
disillusioned, dried-up, cynical old buzzard—without a good word
for anybody—soured, friendless and alone. The kind of old man you'll

meet depends entirely on yourself. Because that old man will be you! He'll be a composite of everything you do, say and think. His mind will be set in the mold you've made by your attitudes. His heart will be turning out what you've been putting in. Every little thought and deed of yours goes into this old man. He'll be exactly what you make him—nothing more, nothing less. It's up to you. You'll have no one else to credit or blame.

Every day, in every way, you are becoming more and more like yourself...getting to look...think...sound...more like yourself. Live now only for what you can get out of life—the old man gets smaller, drier, harder, crabbier, more self-centered. Open your life to others, think in terms of what you can give—the old man grows softer, kindlier, greater. Fact is, the hidden, little things in life—attitudes, goals, ambitions, desires—may seem unimportant now. But they're adding up inside, where you can't see them...crystallizing in your heart and mind. They'll show up sooner than you think!

It's time to pay that old man a visit and care for him! Like a wise businessman taking inventory of his stock, examine his motives, attitudes, goals. The product of life is of more value than merchandise. Work him over while he's still in a formative stage...before it's too late. You'll be more likely to meet a splendid, old man—the man you'd like to be.

Every four years is special, but 1996 had it all—Olympics in America, Presidential election, stock market like a rocket—and for Houstonians, the Rockets with three Hall of Famers: Hakeem the Dream, Clyde the Glide, and Sir Charles. It was a watershed year for our firm as we culminated comprehensive planning for the future by creating a strong strategic partnership with the outstanding New England Investment Companies, providing the "best of both worlds" for our clients by remaining totally independent with all our traditional strengths while adding strength through the diverse and powerful resources of our partner.

We are deeply grateful for the clients and friends of our firm—life-enhancers whose quality, graciousness, good sense and good will make business a privilege for all members of Vaughan, Nelson, Scarborough & McConnell. May 1997 be filled with love, laughter, and friends offering "faithful hands" to you and all those you hold dear.

Year-end 1997

Recently a friend of the firm stated that he carries in his wallet a sentence from our 1995 letter and reads it whenever he has to wait. The line is the transcendent wisdom of Robert Louis Stevenson: "To miss the joy is to miss all."

On the back of the wallet memo he has written the admonition of Carl Sandburg: "Time (and personal energy) is the coin of your life. It is the only coin you have. Be careful lest someone else spend it for you."

A wonderful client and friend has a magnificent attitude about this "finiteness" of life. He can say with Albert Camus: "In the midst of winter, I found there was within me, an invincible summer." He loves the North Carolina mountains and lives the spirit of e. e. cummings's celebration of life:

> i thank you God for this most amazing day:
> For the leaping greenly spirits of trees
> and a blue true dream of sky;
> And for everything which is natural,
> which is infinite, which is yes.

"How, then, shall we live?" is one of the oldest questions of mankind. Mark Twain told us how not to live. "I have been through some terrible things in my life," he said, "some of which actually happened."

How, then, shall we live our lives? The answers are uniquely personal, but good advice is abundant from new readings, from rereading favorite books (like visiting with old friends), and from listening and taking thoughtful notes to be reviewed over time. Our sources for these letters are varied.

We discovered Anne Morrow Lindbergh's *Gift from the Sea* about twenty-five years ago and reread it every summer at the beach. It is like revisiting a wonderful and wise old friend. One year we visited her simple "writing shed" on Maui near her famous husband's burial place. Her small book is as perennial as the grass, to be passed along to children and grandchildren. Using the "gifts of the sea" she makes an eloquent case against our overly compacted lives, what she calls "too much scribbling in the margins":

One cannot collect all the beautiful shells on the beach.

One can collect only a few, and they are more beautiful if they are few...ringed around by space—like the island.

For it is only framed in space that beauty blooms. Only in space are events and objects and people unique and significant—and therefore beautiful. A tree has significance if one sees it against the empty face of sky. A note in music gains significance from the silences on either side. A candle flowers in the space of night. Even small and casual things take on significance if they are washed in space, like a few autumn grasses in one corner of an Oriental painting, the rest of the page bare.

For it is **not merely the trivial** which clutters our lives but the **important as well**. We can have a **surfeit of treasures**—an excess of shells, where one or two would be significant.

A surfeit of good things! The symphony of sound can become a cacophony without silence and space. William James saw the "clutter" and "selection" issue through a similar prism: "My experience is what I agree to attend to. Only those items I notice shape my mind."

How, then, shall we live? One of the nicest ideas, which was read at our firm's Christmas Celebration last year, came in a Christmas letter from a former governor of Tennessee:

> As Christmas approaches, our family remembers our late friend Alex Haley, the author of *Roots*. He lived his life by six words, "**Find the Good and Praise It.**" Alex would walk into our home and pick up Leslee or Kathryn's school essay and say, "My, this is good. With a little work it could win a Pulitzer Prize." Or, he would see Will playing with a video recorder and whisper to him, "I think I will tell Stephen Spielberg about you." He might tell Honey and me, making certain Drew could hear it, too, "You would have been proud of your son yesterday." Once he asked, "Do you know how lucky you all are to have each other?" **Find the Good and Praise It.**

How, then, shall we live? By fulfilling duty and responsibility? Wise counsel for business and the living of life sometimes comes from most unlikely sources! Recently into our offices via a computer "screen saver" transmission came Moliere's powerful message: "It is not what we do, but also what we do not do, for which we are accountable."

Author Gabriel García Márquez in *Love in the Time of Cholera* brings this charge down from the national and community level to the personal: "…human beings are not born once and for all on the day their mothers give birth to them, but life obliges them over and over again to give birth to themselves."

How, then, shall we live? With zest? Emile Zola proclaimed, "I am here to live life out loud." At the sad yet triumphant joint funeral service of Tracy Lane Ritchie, 41, and Joel Brian Enlow, 40, Houstonian civilians who were gunned down in Pakistan in November, Pastor Victor Pentz, First Presbyterian Church, said: "Tracy and Joel lived more in their 40-something lives than most people will in 100 years. These were men who got up in the morning and took a great big bite out of life and let it dribble down their chins."

We are blessed to work with and have clients and friends who are true life-enhancers. Our 1998 wish is that you have the unmatchable joy of the presence of ones you hold dear and that each day is recognized as the great gift it is.

Year-end 1998

It was a year for remembering heroes. In the Foreword to *War and Remembrance*, Herman Wouk wrote: "I have faith that the human spirit will prove equal to the long heavy task of ending war. Against the pessimistic mood of our time, I think that the human spirit is in essence heroic. The beginning of the end of War lies in Remembrance."

During 1998 remembrance was stirred by an unforgettable movie, *Saving Private Ryan*, and an extraordinary book, *Citizen Soldier*, by historian Stephen Ambrose. They recalled vividly the actual personal horrors and sacrifices of World War II, especially of the foot soldiers and junior officers on the front line fighting from hedgerow to hedgerow. The movie and the book should be studied and absorbed by every American: by those of us whose rising prosperity dims the memory of "ordinary" patriots who shed life and limb to prevent Nazis from ruling the world. And by those of us to whom the individual sacrifices of Citizen Soldiers fighting from foxhole to foxhole are mere romantic history like the bitter winter of the Valley Forge soldiers under General George Washington.

Fifty-seven years later the current character of Americans and its leadership has been the major theme in America. William J. Bennett in his superb book *The Death of Outrage* put it squarely on the line:

We—all of us, but especially the young—need around us individuals who possess a certain nobility, a largeness of soul, and qualities of human excellence worth imitating and striving for. Every parent knows this, which is why parents are concerned with both the company their children keep, and the role models they choose. Children watch what we do as well as what we say, and if we expect them to take morality seriously, they must see adults taking it seriously.

We need leaders with rock-solid character, the type of person who mothers can point to and say to their children, "There is a man who will fight for his country, honors his wife, loves his family. Be like that person."

The ancient wise counsel of Solon has a powerful, ironic modern message: "Put more trust in nobility of character than in an oath."

Somewhat related, as one visits around it is interesting and instructive to see what words hang in the offices of leaders. In our experience, "If—" by Rudyard Kipling, "Desiderata," the "Creed of John Rockefeller, Jr." and "The Man in the Arena," the entrepreneurial manifesto by Teddy Roosevelt, are favorites. Such triumphs of character as these reflect and possibly reinforce the character and modus operandi of leaders.

Prominently in the office of Charles B. Johnson, the wholly admirable CEO of the Franklin-Templeton Funds, are these words of Calvin Coolidge:

Press on: Nothing in the world can take the place of perseverance. Talent will not; nothing is more common than unsuccessful men with talent. Genius will not; unrewarded genius is almost a proverb. Education will not; the world is full of educated derelicts. Persistence and determination alone are omnipotent.

In a similar vein, another CEO is daily reminded of Napoleon's advice on the importance of resoluteness: "When you set out to take Vienna, take Vienna."

Sam Fleming, who at 90 inspires the world as he did for over fifty years as a stalwart leader in the banking industry, has lived and repeatedly invoked the words with which Jeb Stuart signed his letters to General Robert E. Lee: "Yours to count on."

Finally, there is a leader who starts each day by re-reading the stirring words of Thomas Paine, written during the retreat of General Washington across the Delaware River, read to the dispirited soldiers and said to have inspired much of the courage that later won independence for America:

> These are the times that try men's souls. The summer soldier and the sunshine patriot will, in the crisis, shrink from the services of their country; but I love the man that can smile in trouble, that can gather strength from disasters, and grow brave by reflections. 'Tis the business of little minds to shrink; but he whose heart is firm, and whose conscience approves his conduct, will pursue his principles unto death.

Of what use is it to have heroes and uplifting counsel? Helen Keller said it well: "I long to accomplish a great and noble task, but it is my chief duty to accomplish humble tasks as though they were great and noble. The world is moved along, not only by the mighty shoves of its heroes, but also by the aggregate of the tiny pushes of each honest worker." Yes, everywhere life is full of heroism.

And then, every once in a while there appears a person such as Winston Churchill, Abraham Lincoln, and George Washington, of whom it was said: "There are some men who lift the age they inhabit 'til all men walk on higher ground in that lifetime." Who shall be next?

This has been a fine year for Vaughan, Nelson, Scarborough & McConnell.

We wish for you, and those dear to you, that 1999, the last year of this century, be a time of celebration, of appreciation of the people meaningful to you, and recognition that every single day is the greatest gift possible.

Year-end 1999

Our toast to clients and friends at this end of year, end of century, was voiced perfectly by Dag Hammarskjöld, a revered statesman, in his 1964 *Markings*:

> For all that has been—Thanks!
> For all that shall be—Yes!

Ours is a mentally tough investment management firm which has been described as "serious minds for serious money." But tough-mindedness need not mean tough-heartedness. Every once in a while we come across written words so beautifully expressive that we return to them again and again. Such are the thoughts of Aldous Huxley:

> We apprehend Him in the alternate voids and fullness of a cathedral; in the space that separates the salient features of a picture; in the living geometry of a flower, a seashell, an animal; in the pauses and intervals between the notes of music, in their difference of tones and sonority; and finally, on the plane of conduct, in the love and gentleness, the confidence and humility, which give beauty to the relationships between human beings.

From Meister Eckhart, a complementary thought:

> The eye with which I see God
> Is the very same eye with which God sees me.

With our more familiar "serious minds," we find ourselves thinking, as we traverse from one millennium to another, about the historians' thesis that throughout the sweep of world history in every period about fifteen percent of the people accepted responsibility for the well-being of their communities, and, by doing so, advanced civilizations. Our clients and friends are clearly among the foremost of the "15 percent" in our generation. Imagine, at this exhilaratingly hopeful time of Millennium Resolutions, what an America—and world—we could have in the decades ahead if that 15 percent grew to 25 percent or even 50 percent or more.

Gandhi called maintaining neutrality in times of moral crisis, which are continuous these days, "the curse of timid decency." We stand in awe of the incredible rate at which technology and knowledge are compounding. Imagine a future in which mankind's noblest instincts and kindnesses to each other are compounding at a rate similar to technological advances.

Last year our letter featured several clippings and quotes that leaders keep near their person, on walls or in their wallets. Throughout 1999 we have received numerous examples of special thoughts which influence the daily actions of executives. Here are some:

John Woodhouse, founding president of the immensely successful Sysco Corp. whose admirable corporate values have always reflected those of founders John Baugh and John Woodhouse, carries the following in his wallet: "Remind the idealist in us that it is the realist who feeds and protects us; remind the realist that it is the idealist who makes the 'impossible' possible; and to the cynic in us remind us that though we do not match our ideals, like the stars, we navigate by them."

Ambassador Robert Strauss for years has carried in his wallet this powerful warning from Walter Lippmann, the most influential columnist of his time, given in a speech to his reunion classmates in the summer of 1940 to prepare them and himself for the storm to come: "You have lived the easy way; henceforth, you will live the hard way. You took the good things for granted. Now you must earn them again. For every right that you cherish, you have a duty which you must fulfill. For every hope that you entertain, you have a task that you must perform. For every good that you wish to preserve, you will have to sacrifice your comfort and your ease. There is nothing for nothing anymore."

One of the rewards of reading a lot is to happen across eclectic thoughts, old and new, that clarify or change our perspective. Here are several "new" or "old" friends we came across this year. We especially like the first one.

Money is like a sixth sense without which we cannot make a complete use of the other five.
—Somerset Maugham

The corrosive influence of unearned capital: we have no more right to consume happiness without producing it than to consume wealth without producing it.
—George Bernard Shaw

If you don't bring Paris with you, you won't find it there.
—John H. Shanahan

No pessimist ever discovered the secrets of the stars, or sailed to an uncharted land, or opened a new heaven to the human spirit.
—Helen Keller

I left the woods [Waldon Pond] for as good a reason as I went there. Perhaps it seemed to me that I had several more lives to live, and could not spare any more time for that one.... I learned this, at least, by my experiment, that if one advances confidently in the direction of his dreams, and endeavors to live the life he has imagined, he will meet with a success unexpected in common hours.
—Henry David Thoreau

An aspect of our firm which provides us the most satisfaction is that we have tried hard to live up to the commitment stated in the preamble to our founding Memo of Understanding in 1970: "Build Beyond Thyself." The nurturing done directly by our firm is magnified greatly by the extraordinary good done by our clients. We are particularly gratified that over 40 percent of our clients are foundations and university endowments. We have long vibrated to the statement by Dr. Virginia Gildersleeve, Dean Emeritus, Barnard College of Columbia University, in 1954 about the goals of education: "The ability to think straight, some knowledge of the past, some vision of the future, some skill to do useful service, some urge to fit that service into the well-being of the community—these are the most vital things education must try to produce."

In 1900, America chose Theodore Roosevelt, and America went on to its greatest century. Strong, wise leadership—with values of decency and personal honor—is paramount in every endeavor. This is what Tallyrand meant when he said: "I am more afraid of an army of sheep led by a lion than an army of lions led by a sheep."

What it comes down to as we select leaders at all levels and as we resolve to make an essential difference with our own lives is Emerson's transcendent wisdom: "There is no history. There is only biography."

It is apropos, because our letters over the years have featured quotations in perspective, that we close with a quote from Gene Vaughan:

> On the afternoon of January 1, 2000, at a vigorous 66 years of age, I will remain Chairman but will step down as CEO. There is a nice symmetry about thirty years as founder and CEO and particularly about the infusion of fresh energy and ideas from a new leader for a new millennium.
>
> I have always tingled a bit when I read John Steinbeck's summing up of life, and I believe it applies to a career as well: "A man, after he has brushed off the dust and chips of his life, will have left only the hard, clean question: Was it good or was it evil? Have I done well—or ill?"
>
> Whatever the answer, I, with Lou Gehrig, can say I am the luckiest man on the face of the earth. I am living my dream and doing it with the family, at home and office, and with clients and friends and community—spirited heroes who bring me joy and fulfillment.

May the New Year and New Century bring you and those close to your heart much laughter and time together.

Year-end 2000

At the inception of our firm in 1970, we began expressing our gratitude to our valued early clients by occasionally sharing such thoughts in year-end letters. Each year we have been gratified by heartwarming calls and letters from friends of the firm and radiation from people we had not met from all around the world, reflecting an intriguing aspect of ideas: "You can count the seeds in an apple but not the apples in a seed," as someone expressed the "circulation power" of an idea.

The Olympics are just everyday life and everyday heroism writ large. Each Olympics is inspiring and this year's in Sydney, with all its beauty and genuinely healing spirit, was especially soaring. The eloquence of

Ronald Reagan captured the essence of the Olympic Games in a stirring salute to the U.S. Olympics Team in 1984: "You will be competing against athletes from many nations. But most importantly, you are competing against yourself. All we expect is for you to do your very best, to push yourself just one second faster, one notch higher, one inch farther."

Everywhere, in all fields of endeavor, there are men and women who make the world better by their gift of kindness, courage, loyalty, or integrity, and who inspire us to higher levels of personal achievements. Houston's Mary Lou Retton, America's Olympics sweetheart, articulated it beautifully: "Every great achievement is the result of a heart on fire. I'm very determined and stubborn. There's a drive in me that makes me want to do more and more, and to do it right. Each of us has a fire in our heart for something. It's our goal in life to find it and to keep it lit."

Oliver Wendell Holmes Sr. expressed the loss of not searching for that which fires the heart: "Some people die with their great music still inside them." The exultation of finding in life and investing oneself in that about which one believes passionately has been compared to eagles in flight:

> Eagles: when they walk, they stumble.
> They are not what one would call graceful.
> They are not designed to walk. They fly.
> And when they fly, oh, how they fly, so free, so graceful.
> They see from the sky what we never see.

In past letters we frequently have included the words that remarkable executives choose to keep around themselves. Last year Bill Wise, CEO of El Paso Energy, sent pocket calendars bearing the compelling words of William James: "The great use of life is to spend it on something which outlives life." That is the ultimate soaring of an eagle.

Some of the finest messages at all Olympics take place off camera. An elevating message from Sydney was the courage and sacrifice of those who swam in the 8th lane, did not get past the first heat, finished far back in the pack—the hundreds who did not even come close to winning a medal but had worked as hard and sacrificed as much as those whom the world cheered.

The first year of the new decade, century and millennium has been a challenging one. In investing, it has not equaled the exceptional years of the 1990s, but it has been an important building and transitional year. It is said that Christopher Columbus kept a journal every day of his adult life. On his most historic voyage, many days he wrote only a single line: "Today we sailed on." This was that kind of year for the markets and for our nation. As investors and citizens, we all have had to bravely "sail on" with confidence and trust that just ahead, as for Columbus, there is some great purpose.

At our Thirtieth Anniversary Dinner, a founder recalled Victor Hugo's words: "There is nothing like a dream to create the future." This is the case at our firm. Since its inception, at the core of Vaughan, Nelson, Scarborough & McConnell has been a passion for investing and a deep-seated belief in surrounding oneself with life-enhancing persons—and, yes, hearts on fire to be whole professionals and good citizens who nurture our communities, broadly defined. Thirty years is a significant time in the investment management business. We feel deep gratitude to our superb clients and friends and for, as Wordsworth expressed it, "the glory and freshness of a dream."

While reading the life of Anne Morrow Lindbergh recently, we came upon the prayer of Socrates that Plato recorded in *The Phaedrus*. This quiet "apple in a seed" has been part of the "torchlight procession" for minds over nearly two and a half millennia:

> Give me beauty in the inward soul, and may the outward and
> inward man be at one. May I reckon the wise to be wealthy,
> and may I have such a quantity of gold as a temperate man,
> and he only, can bear and carry.

Our best wishes to you for a fulfilling 2001 and may each of those you love find that something for which the heart is on fire.

Year-end 2001

When it is dark enough, you can see the stars.

Darkness enveloped America this autumn, a terrible darkness accompanied by headlines as those in London's *The Economist*: "*The Day the World Changed.*" Yet almost immediately citizens began to perceive the stars. In the first week, a friend sent these relevant words of philosopher

Joseph Campbell: "In myth, only at the bottom of the abyss comes the voice of salvation. The darkest moment is the moment when the real message of transformation comes." The transformation in America started quickly and profoundly.

In an instant, the tragedy of September 11 pulled us all close to those we love. Throughout the day our hearts went out to the myriad families who remained incommunicado, not knowing the fate of their loved ones. Poignantly, about 11 p.m. Peter Jennings related that Ted Koppel had started the day in Italy, had worked his way to London and now was standing by to provide the perspective of his distinguished career as a reporter. Koppel simply said: "No, Peter, I have three sons in New York City. I spent all day trying to reach them. Today I am not a reporter. I am a father." He spoke for us all. From that terrible morning we have seen the stars of those we love more vividly.

The tragedy pulled our badly splintered nation together as never before, and provided us reason and time to heal our separateness. At the beginning of my career in the early 1960s as a research analyst with Putnam Management Company in Boston, Susan and I marveled during those blissful years how friendly and "connected" everyone in the streets became during tranquil snowfalls. Following September 11, this admirable "snowfall" quality of neighborliness quickly enfolded our nation. We Americans are a vast and querulous family, who have been on a binge of self-indulgence. But we have great residual goodness that has emerged as we have been brought together. When President Kennedy was assassinated, a tailor in Philadelphia hung a sign on his door which said: "Closed for a death in the family." The national family has grown closer.

Some of the stars which emerged from the darkness were everyday heroes. Several years ago a cover of *Newsweek* plaintively asked, "Where Have All the Heroes Gone?" Actually, real heroes never left but were in our midst all along. Firemen went into the Towers. Passengers on a plane rose up against the terrorists. All sacrificed their lives for others. Firefighters, policemen and emergency medical workers emerged as the heroes they always had been, except that not many noticed. When called great during World War II, Admiral William F. "Bull" Halsey responded, "There aren't any great men. There are just great challenges that ordinary men like you and me are forced by circumstances to meet."

Another star that shown brilliantly—and immediately—in the darkness was the friendship of Great Britain. One of the sad truisms of life is Benjamin Franklin's observation that "Most people return small favors, acknowledge medium ones, and repay great ones—with ingratitude." This seems especially true in international relations. Not so with England. The day after the bombings, Tony Blair declared, "We stand shoulder to shoulder with our American friends in this hour of tragedy, and we, like them, will not rest until this evil is driven from our world." Prime Minister Blair personally flew over to be present when President George W. Bush spoke to Congress, and he has stood foursquare by America with worldwide advocacy on its behalf. Old-fashioned virtues such as loyalty and staunchness are to be cherished.

Perhaps the most profound and enduring star which could emerge from the darkness of the September 11 tragedy is the transformation within ourselves. On September 13, a full house gathered in the storied Texas Room of the Houston Club to honor Jack S. Blanton as an exemplar of community service and to hear him speak on "My Lifelong Love Affair and Aspirations for Houston." Four words revealed the essence of the man and brought out the stars in that time of darkness. During the introduction it was told how Jack, when walking across town with a friend, had put a couple of dollars in a beggar's hat. The friend had gently reproved Jack by asking why did you do that, you know he will just spend it on liquor. Jack quietly replied, "But he may not." If eventually the headline can be read "The day the world changed for the better," it is because each of us has transformed to do such daily small acts of kindness and decency.

The terrorists have clarified hatred and evil. What is it in people's character that make some great and others grotesque? It seems so clear-cut, but Aleksandr Solzhenitsyn years ago raised a troubling thought:

> If only it were so simple! If only there were evil people
>> somewhere insidiously committing evil deeds,
> and it were necessary only to separate them from the rest of us
>> and destroy them
> But the line dividing good and evil
>> cuts through the heart of every human being.
> And who is willing to destroy a piece of his own heart?

After thirty years of writing an institutional letter, this is a personal letter. Theodore Roosevelt had a wonderful way of expressing what is basic and exuberant in life. In addition to his superb *"The Man in the Arena"* (quoted in our 1992 letter), he said:

> We are face to face with our destiny and we must meet it with a high and resolved courage. For us is the life of action of strenuous performance of duty; let us live in the harness, striving mightily; let us rather run the risk of wearing out than rusting out.

His words have much meaning for me personally. "Duty" is a sacred word. Inscribed beneath the bust of Robert E. Lee in the Hall of Fame is "Duty is the sublimest word in our language. Do your duty in all things. You cannot do more. You should never wish to do less."

Since founding Vaughan Nelson & Boston in 1970, it has been my duty and joy to lead and help build our firm, to ensure it always placed clients first and stood for what elevates our profession and our community. My heart shall always be with Vaughan, Nelson, Scarborough & McConnell as my "third child." I have lived my dream—and I am still doing so! However, after passing the CEO baton on the first day of the new century, my duty and passion have redirected, as growth demands in one's personal and professional life. As Founding Chairman, I occupy my same office at the firm, but it is my great fortune currently, as for the past two years, to serve as Chairman of Center for Houston's Future in its formative years, an opportunity, as John W. Gardner advised, to "nurture the institutions that nurtured [me], not uncritically, but lovingly, not to preserve them unchanged but to renew them as the times require."

This is a labor of love and passion on behalf of this city I love. Just as we Americans can hardly bear to see the Twin Towers collapsing into dust, it has been very hard for Houstonians to witness the collapse of Enron. However, the same civic and entrepreneurial spirit which propelled Houston from a town on an unnavigable bayou 165 years ago into the fourth largest city in America is still intact and will prevail. Tolstoy wrote his fiancée: "One can live magnificently in this world if he loves his work and works for his love." In that sense I live magnificently. And that same sense of fulfillment is my New Year wish for you and those you hold dear.

This year grieving became a new national pastime. The price of freedom has gone up. Values most admired have been recalibrated. The story of courage and resilience of Sir Ernest Shackleton, who saved the lives of his 27-man crew in 1915 in an ill-fated Antarctic expedition, has become an uplifting metaphor for our national recovery. From *Endurance*, the story of the expedition: "His was a proud and dauntless spirit.... He was loyal and patriotic. Endurance, courage, determination, imagination... self-abnegation, the power to command, presence of mind in facing danger, humor, optimism and kindliness—such were his characteristics." By such qualities will America prevail. As William Faulkner stated in his short but powerful address when receiving the Nobel Prize, "...man will not merely endure, he will prevail...by lifting his heart, by reminding him of the courage and hope and pride and compassion and pity and sacrifice which have been the glory of his past."

Yes, this year is dark. There is laughter but no gaiety. But there is compassion, resolve and the restoration of patriotism. And the stars are shining brightly with the sure knowledge that each time a man or woman stands up for an ideal or acts to improve the lot of others or strikes out against terrorism, tyranny or injustice the world changes for the better. May the new year bring greater peace for the world and keep those you love safe and close to you.

Year-end 2002

Freedom and responsibility, liberty and duty, that's the deal.
—John W. Gardner

Boy and man, I always yearned for a genuine mentor, someone outside my family who would take a deeply personal interest and counsel me out of his wisdom and experience. It never happened. In some inchoate way, from the beginning I felt a responsibility to nurture those causes and institutions which nurtured my family and neighbors. In the preamble to the founding memo of understanding of our firm in 1970, we wrote the commitment: "Build Beyond Thyself."

Then something wonderful happened. Thanks to my mother-in-law, I began to read John W. Gardner. He articulated elegantly what lay inside me and became my philosophical beacon. A highlight of my life came in 1993 when, while chairman of The Houston Forum, I invited Dr. Gardner to speak, introduced him to a capacity audience of 1,100, and spent an electrifying life-lifting day with him. We became friends, corresponded and talked periodically. In a personal visit in his office in 1996 he ignited and elevated our daughter Margaret as he had me.

This February John W. Gardner died at the age of 89. As a close friend wrote, "So the sun went down yesterday and didn't rise this morning. What a man! What a friend!" This letter, a sharing, is dedicated to this magnificent person who profoundly influenced my life and made striving to reach my potentialities and to fulfill my responsibility to community feel like a privilege. As chairman of Common Cause and the Carnegie Foundation; Secretary of Health, Education and Welfare (the only Republican in LBJ's cabinet); director of Shell Oil, Time, Inc. and Stanford University; and author of *Self Renewal*, *Excellence* and *On Leadership*, he touched and stretched multitudes similarly.

I will begin at the end. In a speech shortly before his death Dr. Gardner ended with a paragraph a grateful father had sent him that was found in the billfold his 20-year-old daughter was carrying when she was killed in an auto accident. The words were an excerpt from an earlier speech of Dr. Gardner's.

> Meaning is not something you stumble across, like the answer to a riddle or the prize in a treasure hunt. Meaning is something you build into your life. You build it out of your own past, out of your affections and loyalties, out of the experience of humankind as it is passed on to you, out of your own talent and understanding, out of the things you believe in, out of the things and people you love, out of the values for which you are willing to sacrifice something. The ingredients are there. You are the only one who can put them together into that unique pattern that will be your life. Let it be a life that has dignity and meaning for you. If it does, then the particular balance of success or failure—as the world measures success or failure—is of less account.

John was fond of saying that "Life is the art of drawing without an eraser. Don't be too hard on yourself." But he was very clear about the root ailments of executives, young and old, particularly in the easy-come last decade of the century: a confusion of self-worth with net worth, an overvaluing of intellect versus character—"The world loves talent but pays off on character," he said—of getting there first versus growing in mind and spirit, of food for the ego as against food for the hunger of the heart. Meaning in one's life is at the core, he believed. "Old or young, we're on our last cruise," he quoted Robert Louis Stevenson. "We want it to mean something."

> People run around searching for identity, but it isn't handed out free any more—not in this transient, rootless, pluralistic society. Your identity is what you've committed yourself to. If you make no commitments you're an unfinished person. Freedom and obligation, liberty and duty, that's the deal.... You build meaning into your life through your commitments—whether to your religion, to your conception of an ethical order, to your loved ones, to your life work, to your community, to the release of human possibilities. **Is there a flame that you would guard with your life?**
>
> The commitments that people make to values beyond the self are manifested in various ways—in their family and community life, in the way they treat any and all humans, in the goals and standards they set for themselves. There are people who make the world better just by being the kind of people they are. They have the gift of kindness or courage or loyalty or integrity.... They teach the truth by living it.

He understood people with a rare blend of knowledge, wisdom and common sense. With a chuckle he would say, "Most people are neither for you nor against you, they are thinking about themselves. You learn that no matter how hard you try to please, some people in this world are not going to like you, a lesson that is at first troubling and then really quite relaxing." In maturity, he reassured, you learn not to burn up energy with anxiety. You learn that self-pity and resentment are among the most toxic of drugs. You come to terms with yourself. You finally grasp what is meant by "At the end of every road you meet yourself." You learn the art of mutual dependence, meeting the needs of loved ones and letting yourself need them.

John had understanding and compassion for failure. <u>Everyone</u> fails, he said. The question isn't did you fail, but did you pick yourself up and move ahead. And did you collaborate in your own defeat. He had great respect for the blows and defeats that life can administer. But he believed profoundly in striving to fulfill one's potentialities.

The luckiest people are those who learn early, maybe in their twenties, that it's essential to take charge of your own life. That doesn't mean that you don't accept help, friendship, love and leadership—if it's good leadership—from others. But it does mean recognizing that ultimately you're the one who's responsible for you. No excuses. Don't blame others. Don't blame circumstances. You take charge. And one of the things you take charge of is your own learning. It calls for character and drive. You have to understand that the potentialities you develop to the full come as the result of an interplay between you and life's challenges—and the challenges keep coming, and they keep changing. . . .

Someone defined horse sense as the good judgment horses have that prevents them from betting on people. But we have to bet on people—and I place my bets more often on high motivation than on any other quality except judgment. There is no perfection of techniques that will substitute for the lift of spirit and heightened performance that comes from strong motivation. The world is moved by highly motivated people, by enthusiasts, by men and women who want something very much or believe very deeply. I'm not talking about anything as narrow as ambition. Ambition eventually wears out and probably should. But you can keep your zest until the day you die. . . . The vitalizing thing is to be interested. Keep a sense of curiosity. Discover new things. Care. Risk failure. Reach out. . . .

I'm not suggesting that you let high motivation lead you to kill yourself with work, or to neglect your families, or engage in behavior that is destructive of other values. . . . In life itself, there is a time to seek inner peace, a time to rid oneself of tension and anxiety. The moment comes when the striving must let up, when wisdom says "Be quiet."

John Gardner had an unconditional, unshakable conviction about the potential in others, the potential of America, and, after his visit in 1993, the potential in the vision of the future held by Houstonians. He loved the tough-minded optimism of Houstonians and the way we had taken charge of a flat, mosquito-plagued swamp and turned it into the dynamic, fourth-largest city in America. He believed in the continuous renewal of individuals—he was a vigorous 80 when he visited here—and of cities and nations.

Another significant ingredient in motivation is one's attitude toward the future.... Someone said "Pessimists got that way by financing optimists." But I am not pessimistic and I advise you not to be. For renewal, a tough-minded optimism is best. The future is not shaped by people who don't really believe in the future. But I did say tough-minded optimism.... We have to believe in ourselves, but we mustn't suppose that the path will be easy. It's tough. Life is painful, and rain falls on the just.... Life is tumultuous—an endless losing and regaining of balance, a continuous struggle, never an assured victory. Nothing is ever finally safe. Every important battle is fought and re-fought. You may wonder if such a struggle—endless and of uncertain outcome—isn't more than humans can bear. But all of history suggests that the human spirit is well fitted to cope with just that kind of world....

One notable example was Winston Churchill.... Elected to Parliament at 26, he performed brilliantly, held high cabinet posts with distinction and at 37 became First Lord of the Admiralty. Then he was discredited by the Dardanelles expedition—the defeat at Gallipoli—and lost his admiralty post. There followed 24 years of ups and downs. All too often the verdict of him was "Brilliant but erratic.... not steady, not dependable...." A friend described him as a man who jaywalked through life. He was 66 before his moment of flowering came. Someone said "It's all right to be a late bloomer if you don't miss the flower show." Churchill didn't miss it....

Churchill is famous but everywhere in life there are examples of irrepressible lifelong vitality. All of my feelings about the release of human possibilities, all of my convictions about renewal, are offended by the widely shared cultural assumption that life levels off in our forties or fifties and heads downhill, so that by 65 we are ready for the scrap heap.... I'm not blind to the physical problems of aging. At the age of 88, I know there are bumps in the road, some of them really bad. But what I want for those youngsters in their forties and fifties is several more decades of vital learning and growth.... What I want for them is a long **youthfulness of spirit**. It doesn't sound like much to ask, but **it's everything!**... People of every age need commitments beyond the self to draw on the deep springs of the human spirit and to accept the gifts of life with thanks and endure life's indignities with dignity....

We want to believe that there is a point at which we can feel that we have arrived. We want a scoring system that tells us when we've piled up enough points to count ourselves successful. So you scramble and sweat and climb to reach what you thought was the goal. When you get to the top you stand up and look around and chances are you feel a little empty. Maybe more than a little empty. You wonder whether you climbed the wrong mountain. But life isn't a mountain that has a summit. Nor a game that has a final score.

Life is an endless unfolding, and if we wish it to be, an endless process of self-discovery, an endless and unpredictable dialogue between our own potentialities and the life situations in which we find ourselves. By potentialities I mean not just intellectual gifts but the full range of one's capacities for learning, sensing, wondering, understanding, loving and aspiring. The purpose is to grow and develop in the dimensions that distinguish humankind at its best— the capacity for awe, wonder, reverence....

As Chairman and founder in 1999 of Center for Houston's Future, I have been asked frequently where the idea came from. I think John planted the seeds in me during his visit in 1993 and they germinated under his master gardening.

I count it as one of the marks of maturity that men and women nurture the institutions and communities that nurtured them, not uncritically but lovingly, not to preserve them unchanged but to renew them as the times require. Today our communities need us desperately. Need our loyalty, our understanding, our support.

In February throughout America citizens observed that John W. Gardner transcends death because he not only wrote about the values that mattered, he also embodied them, creating a compelling common sense of head and heart that could transform individuals and elevate institutions. He reminded us that America—and its cities—at their best are about aspiring, upholding our ideals, engaging, and never standing on the sidelines. For me, for many of us, he was True North. With gratitude I dedicate this letter to my wise counselor and friend.

For you and all those you hold dear, may 2003 be filled abundantly with the seven one-word maxims John believed are the essence of humans at their best: LIVE, LEARN, LOVE, THINK, GIVE, LAUGH, ASPIRE.

The Future...!

back row: Richard Bolinger (Bo) Vaughan, Avery Vaughan, Corbin Robinson;
foreground: Elizabeth (Lizzie) Vaughan

Index

Page locators in *italics* indicate photographs.

Putnam Management Company,
continued: E. L. Bruce Company
research, 64–65; full-time job
offer, 56; Gene's career at, 61–65,
71–72; Houston energy industry
conference, 75; internship, 52–53;
speaking engagements, 64

Quality of Life Coalition, 186

racial discrimination, 39
Ramseyer, Jeff, 123
Randolph-Macon Woman's College,
49, 54, 57–58
Rauscher Pierce Securities, 85
Reynolds, Debbie, 135
Reynolds, Jen, 135
Reynolds, Roger, 135
Reynolds, Zach, 135
Rice, Grantland, 27, 30
Rice University, 148, 150, 185, 186
Riley, Robert E. "Bob," 53, 70–71
Rinfret, Pierre, 56
River Oaks Tennis Tournament, 120
Riviana Foods, 150
Roach, Tad, 128, 129
Robertson, Beth, 183
Robinson, Clay, 212
Robinson, Corbin, 194, *195, 197,* 208,
212, *215,* 216, *220*
Robinson, Jim, 51
Roche, George, 144
Roff, Hugh, 100
Rogers, John, 117
Rogers, Will, 219
Rootes, Jamey, 43
Rosenblum, Richard, 50
Rosewall, Ken, 120
Ross, Carolyn, 102
Ross Perot State Education Reform
Task Force, 176
Roth, Collins, 123
Rothschild Family, 101

Rupp, George, 150
Russell, Fred, 30, 31
Russell, Kay, 30
Russia, 132
Ryan, Nolan, 204

San Antonio, Texas, 144
Sarratt, Madison, 31, 137, 138–39
Scarborough, Frank, 75, 77, 78, 80, 81,
83, 94, 97, 104, 107–8, 145, 156–57,
162, 166
Scarborough, Judy, 162
Schiavone, Joel, 57
Schriver-Bonderer, Tiana, 158
Schweitzer, Albert, 29
Scott, Mike, 204
Scurlock, Eddy, 174
Securities Analysts Association of
Japan (SAAJ), 122
Sevareid, Eric, 103
75 Beacon Street apartment, 66, *69,*
72
Shamrock Hotel, 70
Shanks, Gene, 134
Shanks, Susan, 134
Shapiro, Marc, 130, 159
Shattuck, Carol, 187
Shaw, Dottie, 123
Shaw, Run Run, 123
shellfish allergy, 18–19
ship-handling drills, 42
Shu Shu Falls, 196, *196*
Siebert, Muriel "Mickey," 165
Sigma Alpha Epsilon fraternity, 16–17,
29, 123
Simmons, Ellen, 147–48, *148,* 160
Simmons, Ginny, 148
Simmons, L. E., 148
Simmons, Matt, 147–48, *148*
Singapore, 122–23
Sit, Gene, 110, 115, 116, 117
Sit Associates, 110
Skye (family dog), 194, 206–7, *207*

Vaughan Nelson Investment Management: addition of new principals to, 145–46; end of the year (EOY) letters, 109–10, 146; growth of, 100–101; Gus Wortham Foundation account, 103; ongoing success of, 221–22; research and investment philosophy, 101–2, 104; retirement from, xi, 160–64, *161*; sale to New England Investment Companies, 156–57, 161–62; separation from The Boston Company, 98, 99; target clients and Life Enhancers, 103–11; Vaughan Nelson Bowl, 163
Vaughn, Danny, 194
Vaughn, Stella, 133, 153
Vaughn, William J., 133
Vaughn, William S. "Bill," 132–34, *133*
Vertin, Jim, 115–16, 117
"via nostra dura est!," 72
Victoria, Queen, 106
Vietor, Helen, 78
Vinson & Elkins, 149
Voltermann, Ila, 10
Voss, Peter, 157, 161, 162, 164, 167

Wales, 1–2, *206*, *213*
Walker, Bill, 215
Walker, June, 215
Wall Street Journal, 59
Warren, Robert Penn, 23
Washington University, 49
Watson, Alma, 10
Watson, Beverly, 10
Weill Cornell Medical College, 158
Werlein, Ewing, 149
Werlein, Kay, 149
Werly, Charles, 53, 55, 62, 63–64, 167, 171
Wertheim & Co, 108–9
Westbrook, Audrey Bolinger, 58, 59
Westbrook, Charles Howard, Jr., 58

Westec Corporation, 73
West Galveston Island, 87–88
Westminster Abbey, 19, 211
Wetzel, Gladys, 10
White, Andrea, 160
White, Bill, 160
"White Columns" (Templeton family home), 121, 144
Willerson, James, 129–30
William M. Mercer-Meidinger-Hansen, Inc., 100
Williams, Annie Laura, 9, 14
Williams, Dave, 92, *172*
Williams, Elliot, 116
Williams, James, 73
Wills, Irene, 226
Wills, Jesse, 23
Wills, Ridley, 151, 226
Wilson, Bowden, Jr., 17, 23–24
Windrush (family dog), 207–8
Winn, Randy, 123
Wolbach, Bill, 93–94
Wold, Bill, 24
Wolf, Brandi, 158
Wolf, John, 158
Wolfe, Betsy, 38
Wolff, David, 159–60, 193
Wolff, Mary, 159, 160
Wortham, Gus, 171, 174, 223
Wortham Center, 106
Wortham Foundation, 106
Wren, Christopher, 19

Yates, Jim, 21
Young Alumni Trustee (YAT), 31
Young Presidents Organization (YPO), 203
Yura, Gentaro, 122

Zapata Offshore, 75
Zeppos, Nick, 139–40
Zuboff, Shoshana, 159, 162
Zumwalt, Elmo, 175